A EUROPEAN PUBLIC
INVESTMENT OUTLOOK

A European Public Investment Outlook

*Edited by Floriana Cerniglia
and Francesco Saraceno*

OpenBook
Publishers

https://www.openbookpublishers.com

This is the ninth volume of our Open Reports Series
ISSN (print): 2399-6668
ISSN (digital): 2399-6676

ISBN Paperback: 978-1-80064-011-5
ISBN Hardback: 978-1-80064-012-2
ISBN Digital (PDF): 978-1-80064-013-9
ISBN Digital ebook (epub): 978-1-80064-014-6
ISBN Digital ebook (mobi): 978-1-80064-015-3
ISBN XML: 978-1-80064-016-0
DOI: 10.11647/OBP.0222

Cover image: Mural in Białystok, Poland. Photo by Dominik Bednarz on Unsplash, https://unsplash.com/photos/luzUMbVUVRo

Cover design: Anna Gatti.

Contents

Preface

Franco Bassanini, Alberto Quadrio Curzio, and Xavier Ragot

The major part of this outlook was written before or during the COVID-19 pandemic, which has spread all over the world, but has erupted with special virulence in Europe, although with different speed and strength. This dramatic event is producing an economic slump and a social crisis of dimensions not yet assessable but certainly unprecedented, at least for our century. It does not nullify nor decrease the importance of the topic which is the subject of this research. On the contrary, it emphasizes the role of public investment in shaping not only the economy, but also society as a whole.

In the short and medium term, a strong boost to public investment will be needed to cope with one of the worst legacies of the pandemic, the widespread public debt increase, caused by public policies aimed to mitigate the economic and social consequences of the shutdown of almost all production activities. The huge increase in public debt and even more in the debt-to-GDP ratio can in fact be addressed, as Mario Draghi recalled at the beginning of the pandemic outbreak in Europe, only by public policies capable of supporting the growth of the denominator or to reduce its fall; public investment and effective incentives for private investment are notoriously the most effective tools of these policies.

But this is only the quantitative side of the issue: as Floriana Cerniglia and Francesco Saraceno appropriately underline in their Introduction, the COVID crisis is moreover triggering "a healthy soul-searching process on our long-term development trajectory, questioning our way of life, our utilization of natural resources, the very social and environmental sustainability of our economies". Public investment is in fact one of the key tools, with regulation and structural policies, to embed in the economy long-term horizons goals — such as sustainable growth, social and environmental objectives.

Furthermore, the COVID-19 crisis reveals, if necessary, that public investment must be analysed and coordinated at the supranational level, to attain some prominent European objectives, such as the fight against climate change or promoting an efficient mobility, but also to reach independent national objectives.

The *Outlook* goes to the heart of the subject of public investment, using two complementary angles. The first is to identify public investment trends and needs in

     https://doi.org/10.11647/OBP.0222.12

Europe and in selected countries. The second is the analysis of key domains where European public investments are needed to build a more sustainable Europe, such as transportation, climate change, social investment, etc. These two approaches show the value of public capital both within European countries and as a European public good.

Public investment is a tool which is used to reach different goals: innovation, education, social cohesion across European regions and countries, the fight against climate change, growth and high-quality employment. There are in fact little trade-offs between these objectives, and they should be seen as complementary.

This is all the more true after the eruption of the COVID-19 crisis. In this respect too, we are entering a world in which nothing will be as before. We have to be more ambitious in the goals we assign to public investment. As we have already mentioned, public policy toward a massive programme of investments will be needed to boost growth and consequently to make the higher public debt inherited from the crisis manageable. However, the quality of growth will be even more crucial. The "old" accounting approach of public investment, mostly measuring physical capital, is inadequate to fully grasp the nature of public investment. This increases the stock of human and social capital, which is part of the foundation of our complex European societies. The European Union should have a leading role in the new thinking about the role of public investment as a tool to reach the UN Sustainable Development Goals.

One might notice with some bitterness that we needed a pandemic that ground the world economy to a halt, to raise the awareness of policy makers around the world about the need of public investment. We believe that this timely Report will contribute to the debate that will, hopefully, continue past the emergency phase.

The outlook was brilliantly and efficiently coordinated by Floriana Cerniglia (Cranec) and Francesco Saraceno (OFCE) in a complex environment. The editors of the *Outlook* started their effort in December 2017 at the Centre "Cranec" of Università Cattolica, where a first workshop on the relaunch of public and private investments took place. A second workshop was hosted by Astrid Foundation in Rome, a few months later. The authors of the different chapters of the *Outlook*, from various institutional backgrounds, collaborated in an admirable way, enriching their perspective from different countries. These "diversities" valuably contributed to the quality of the *Outlook* and made the message emerging from this volume even more significant.

Franco Bassanini, President of Astrid
Alberto Quadrio Curzio, President of Cranec
Xavier Ragot, President of OFCE

The *Outlook* is the result of a joint effort by several economists belonging to a wide range of academic institutions and policy institutes; they all wrote in their personal capacity.

The work was coordinated by Floriana Cerniglia and Francesco Saraceno, with logistical and financial support by CRANEC — Centro di Ricerche in Analisi Economica e Sviluppo Economico Internazionale, Università Cattolica del Sacro Cuore — Milano; Fondazione Astrid; and OFCE-SciencesPo Paris.

The authors are affiliated to the following institutions:

- Agenzia nazionale per le nuove tecnologie, l'energia e lo sviluppo economico sostenibile, ENEA (Italy)

- Bartlett School of Construction and Project Management, University College London (UK)

- Cassa Depositi e Prestiti, CDP (Italy)

- Consiglio Nazionale delle Ricerche, CNR (Italy)

- CRANEC, Centro di Ricerche in Analisi Economica e Sviluppo Economico Internazionale, Università Cattolica del Sacro Cuore, Milan (Italy)

- Dalian Maritime University (China)

- Directorate General for Economic and Financial Affairs, European Commission

- Erasmus Universiteit Rotterdam (Netherlands)

- European Investment Bank, EIB

- European University Institute, EUI (Italy)

- Fondazione Astrid, Rome (Italy)

- Green, Università Bocconi, Milan (Italy)

- Hochschule für Technik und Wirtschaft, HTW Berlin (Germany)

- Institut für Makroökonomie und Konjunkturforschung, IMK (Germany)

- Institute for Innovation & Public Purpose, IIPP, University College London (UK)

- Institute for Innovation & Public Purpose, University College London

- International University College, Turin (Italy)

- Luiss School of European Political Economy, Università Luiss Guido Carli, Rome (Italy)

- Observatoire français des conjonctures économiques, OFCE-SciencesPo, Paris (France)

- Texas A&M University (USA)

- Universidad de Cantabria (Spain)
- Universidad Loyola Andalucía, Seville (Spain)
- Università degli studi di Bari Aldo Moro (Italy)
- Università Ca' Foscari, Venice (Italy)
- Università Carlo Bo, Urbino (Italy)
- Università del Salento (Italy)
- Università Luiss Guido Carli, Rome (Italy)

Acknowledgements

As this Report goes to press, we want to express our gratitude to those who made our work possible. First, and foremost, to our respective institutions. Franco Bassanini, President of Fondazione Astrid, Alberto Quadrio Curzio, President of CRANEC and Xavier Ragot, President of OFCE-Sciences Po. Their support and encouragement are the reasons why this Report exists. They helped us in defining the scope and the form of the Report, in contacting some of the authors, and of course in guaranteeing financial and logistical support. But they did much more than this: they have put the issue of public investment at the centre of the respective institutions' scientific project, carrying the weight of our endeavour.

We also thank all the chapter authors, who in general respected the deadlines despite exogenous shocks, interacted with us and with the referees, and exchanged on the different chapters at an informal workshop. The result is a collective volume that, despite the heterogeneity of backgrounds, has a consistent message throughout. Organizing the different chapters into a whole was a relatively easy task, and we are deeply grateful to the authors for this.

We also thank Giovanni Barbieri from CRANEC for his efficient editing of the volume. Last, but not least, we thank Rupert Gatti and Alessandra Tosi, of Open Book Publishers, who smoothly managed the refereeing process of the Report, and adapted to the new constraints posed by the COVID crisis.

Floriana Cerniglia
Francesco Saraceno

Author Biographies

Philipp-Bastian Brutscher is Senior Economist in the Economics Department of the European Investment Bank (EIB) where he is principally responsible for the EIB Investment Survey, a large-scale survey of corporate investment activities. Philipp acts as the focal point for the Department's analytical work on business and infrastructure investment activities. He holds a Master's and PhD degree from the University of Cambridge.

Rocco Luigi Bubbico is Policy Advisor in the EIB Permanent Representative's Office in Brussels. His research interests are in public investment, regional and urban development and transition to a zero-carbon economy. Previously he worked in the Directorate-General for Regional and Urban Policy of the European Commission. He holds a PhD from the University of Manchester and a Master's degree from the University of Bologna.

Mauro Bux (MSc in Economics of Public Policy, Barcelona Graduate School of Economics; PhD in Economics, University of Salento) is a research fellow at the Regione Puglia and teaching assistant in public finance at the Department of Economics of the University of Salento (Italy). His scientific research experience, both theoretical and applied, has so far focused on issues related to the evaluation of public policies, optimal taxation and the impact of EU-funded public investments.

Roberto Cardinale is a Visiting Lecturer at the Bartlett School of Construction and Project Management where he recently completed his PhD with Professor D'Maris Coffman on the governance of transnational energy infrastructure projects, including the unbundling of transnational supply chains, the partial privatization of state-owned enterprises, energy market de-regulation under the European Union's competition policy. His research has been published in *Energy Policy* and *Structural Change and Economic Dynamics*. During his postgraduate study at Università Cattolica del Sacro Cuore, he visited Sungkyunkwan University (Korea) and Galatasary University (Turkey) to gain an international perspective on state-owned enterprise, which was deepened by a further visit to Renmin University China during his doctoral education.

Floriana Cerniglia is Full Professor of Economics at Università Cattolica del Sacro Cuore (Milan) and Director of CRANEC (Centro di Ricerche in Analisi economica e sviluppo economico internazionale) She is the Co-Editor-in-Chief of *Economia*

Politica, Journal of Analytical and Institutional Economics. She received her PhD from the University of Warwick (UK) and her research interests are in Public Economics, mainly tax and spending assignment across government levels. She has published in leading international journals and she has coordinated and participated in a number of peer-reviewed research projects.

D'Maris Coffman is the Head of Department at the Bartlett School of Construction and Project Management at University College London (UCL). Her interests span infrastructure, construction, real estate and climate change. She is the Managing Editor of *Structural Change and Economic Dynamics* and is on the advisory board of *Economia Politica.* Before joining UCL, she spent six years as a fellow of Newnham College, University of Cambridge, where she variously held a junior research fellowship (Mary Bateson Research Fellowship), a post as a college lecturer and teaching fellow, and a Leverhulme ECF. In July 2009, she started the Centre for Financial History, which she directed through December 2014. She did her undergraduate training at the Wharton School in managerial and financial economics and her PhD in the School of Arts & Sciences at the University of Pennsylvania.

Paolo Costa is Contract Professor of Transport and Logistic Economics at the Ca' Foscari University of Venice. He is also currently Chairman of the Board of Directors of SPEA Engineering s.p.a., Member of the Supervisory Board of Nice and Cote d'Azur Airport of Nice, Member of the General Council of Fondazione di Venezia, editorialist at *Corriere del Veneto* and Founding Partner of C+3C Systems & Strategies s.r.l. Between 1980 and 2003 he was Full Professor of Economics, Economic Planning, Transport and Regional Economics, Tourism Economics at the Universities of Venice (IUAV and Ca' Foscari); he also taught at the Universities of Padua, Reading and at New York University. Rector of the University of Venice Ca' Foscari (1992–1996). In his past career he was Vice President of the University of the United Nations in Tokyo (1995–1999). He served as Italian Minister of Public Works and Urban Areas (1996–1998), Mayor of Venice (2000–2005), Member of the European Parliament (1999–2009) and Chairman of the European Parliament Committee on Transport and Tourism (2003–2009). He had been President of the Venice Port Authority (2008–2017). As an International consultant, he served at the OECD, the International Transport Forum at OECD, the European Commission, Italian Ministry of Infrastructure and Transportation.

Sebastian Dullien is Research Director at the IMK — Macroeconomic Policy Institute and professor for international economics at HTW Berlin — University of Applied Sciences. He has worked extensively on macroeconomic imbalances in the euro area and especially Germany's contributions to these imbalances. Prior to being appointed at HTW Berlin in 2007, he has worked as an economics editor at the *Financial Times Deutschland*, the German language edition of the *FT*.

Hercules Haralambides is Professor in Maritime Economics and Logistics since 1992, having taught at eight universities (and in six different countries), the most prominent of which being Erasmus University Rotterdam and the National University of Singapore. Currently he is Distinguished Chair Professor at Dalian Maritime University in China and Adjunct Professor at Texas A&M University. Hercules is the founder of the Erasmus Center for Maritime Economics and Logistics (MEL, www.maritimeeconomics.com) and also the founding Editor-in-Chief of the quarterly journal *Maritime Economics & Logistics* (*MEL*), published by Palgrave-Macmillan (www.palgrave.com/41278). He has written and published over 300 scientific papers, books, reports and articles in the wider area of ports, maritime transport and logistics and has consulted governments, international organizations and private companies all over the world including, for a series of years, the European Commission. In the period 2011–2015, he was President of the Italian port of Brindisi and at the end of that period (2015) he established "Haralambides & Associates": a global maritime think-tank engaged in executive education and strategic policy analysis. In 2008, he was decorated with the Golden Cross of the Order of the Phoenix by the President of the Greek Republic.

Anton Hemerijck is Professor of Political Science and Sociology at the European University Institute (EUI) in Florence. Having trained as an economist and political scientist, he obtained his doctorate from the University of Oxford in 1993. Between 2001 and 2009, he directed the Scientific Council for Government Policy (WRR), the principle think tank in the Netherlands, while holding a professorship in Comparative European Social Policy at Erasmus University Rotterdam. Before that, he served as a senior researcher at the Max Planck Institute for the Study of Societies in Cologne. Over the past two decades he advised the European Commission and several EU Presidencies on European social policy developments. Important book publications include *A Dutch Miracle* with Jelle Visser (1997) and *Why We Need a New Welfare State* with Gosta Esping-Andersen, Duncan Gallie and John Myles (2002), and the monograph *Changing Welfare States* (2013). His most recent book publication is the edited volume *The Uses of Social Investment* (2017).

Ekaterina Jürgens studied International Business at the HTW Berlin and Economics at the University of Cologne, and currently works as a research assistant at the Macroeconomic Policy Institute (IMK).

Adolfo Maza is Associate Professor of Economics at the University of Cantabria. Adolfo received his PhD degree in Economics from the University of Cantabria in 2002. Later on, he completed a postdoctoral stay at the University of Berkeley. His main areas of research include regional economics, economic integration and globalization, labour market, migration and energy economics. He has published more than fifty papers in various international scientific journals included in the *Journal Citation*

Report (*JCR*) databases. He has also participated in numerous international congresses and meetings, was awarded the "Young Researchers Prize" by the Spanish Regional Science Association. He has also acted as a reviewer for numerous scientific journals, as well as a reviewer for international funding agencies such as the *National Science Foundation* (USA) and the *Austrian Science Fund*.

Marianna Mazzucato (PhD) is Professor in the Economics of Innovation and Public Value at University College London (UCL), where she is Founding Director of the UCL Institute for Innovation & Public Purpose (IIPP). IIPP is dedicated to rethinking the role of public policy in shaping both the rate of economic growth and its direction — and training the next generation of global leaders to build partnerships that can address mission-oriented societal goals. She is winner of the 2014 New Statesman SPERI Prize in Political Economy, the 2015 Hans-Matthöfer-Preis, the 2018 Leontief Prize for Advancing the Frontiers of Economic Thought and the 2019 All European Academies Madame de Staël Prize for Cultural Values. She was named as one of the "3 most important thinkers about innovation" by The New Republic, and is on The Bloomberg 50 list of "Ones to Watch" for 2019. Her highly-acclaimed book *The Entrepreneurial State: Debunking Public vs. Private Sector Myths* (2013) investigates the role of public organizations in playing the "investor of first resort" role in the history of technological change, and asks fundamental questions about how to share both risks and rewards. Her 2018 book *The Value of Everything: Making and Taking in the Global Economy* (2018) brings value theory back to the centre of economics in order to reward value creation over value extraction. It was a 2018 Strategy & Business Book of the Year and was shortlisted for the 2018 Financial Times and McKinsey Business Book of the Year prize. She advises policy makers around the world on innovation-led inclusive and sustainable growth. Her current roles include being a member of the Scottish Government's Council of Economic Advisors; the South African President's Economic Advisory Council; the OECD Secretary General's Advisory Group on a New Growth Narrative; the UN's Committee for Development Policy (CDP), SITRA's Advisory Panel in Finland, and Norway's Research Council. Through her role as Special Advisor for the EC Commissioner for Research, Science and Innovation, she authored the high impact report on Mission-Oriented Research & Innovation in the European Union, turning "missions" into a crucial new instrument in the European Commission's innovation programme (Horizon).

Jing Meng is a Lecturer in Economics and Finance at Bartlett School of Construction and Project Management at University College London. She works on the nexus of climate change and air pollution policies: environmental economics, energy innovation and sustainable consumption and trade policies. Jing's recent research focuses on the impact of international trade on the distribution, climate and health impacts of black carbon. Jing received her PhD degree in Environmental Geography from Peking University, and holds a BA degree in Building Environment and Energy Engineering from Huazhong University of Science and Technology. Jing is a Guest Editor of the *Journal of Environmental Management*, and an editorial board member of the *Journal of Cleaner Production* and *Global Transitions*. She is also a fellow of the Cambridge Centre for Environment, Energy and Natural Resource Governance at the University of Cambridge. She has published over sixty papers in peer-reviewed journals, such as *Nature Climate Change*, *Science Advances*, *Nature Geoscience*, *Nature Plants*, and *Nature Communications*. She was awarded the "2018 Top 50 Earth and Planetary Sciences Articles" in *Nature Communications* and "2017 Best Early Career Articles" in *Environmental Research Letters*.

Zhifu Mi is a Lecturer in Economics and Finance at the Bartlett School of Construction and Project Management at UCL. He has published over fifty papers in peer-reviewed journals, such as *Science Advances*, *Nature Energy*, *Nature Geoscience*, and *Nature Communications*. He is the Executive Editor of the *Journal of Cleaner Production*. He currently leads the project on Uncertainty Analysis of Carbon Capture, Utilization and Storage (CCUS) funded by The Royal Society (IEC\NSFC\181115), and co-leads the Finance & Economics Working Group for "The *Lancet* Countdown: Tracking Progress on Health and Climate Change". He was awarded the 2018 World Sustainability Award for his leading research in the methodological developments and applications of carbon footprint. He was also honoured on the *Forbes* 30 Under 30 Europe in recognition of his innovative research in the economics of climate change. His research was awarded the "2018 Top 50 Earth and Planetary Sciences Articles" in *Nature Communications*, "2017 Best Early Career Articles" in *Environmental Research Letters*, and "2016 Highly Cited Original Papers" in *Applied Energy*.

Daniela Palma is a Senior Researcher at ENEA (the Italian National Agency for New Technologies, Energy and Sustainable Economic Development) in the areas of Economy of Innovation and Sustainable Economic Development, including themes of Regional Analysis. She graduated with honours in Statistics and Economics on issues of International Economics at the Sapienza University of Rome, and holds a PhD in Applied Economic Analysis from the same university. She was Visiting Research Fellow at the National Center for Geographic Information and Analysis of the United States National Science Foundation at the University of California at Santa Barbara. Since 1999 she has been coordinating the activities of the ENEA Observatory on Italy in the International Technological Competition.

Mathieu Plane is Deputy Director of Analysis and Forecasting Department at OFCE, the Research Center in Economics of Sciences Po Paris. He is in charge of economic forecasts for the French economy and works on economic policy issues. He has written several articles in scientific journals and has participated in a number of reports for public institutions. He teaches at Sciences Po Paris and at the University of Paris Pantheon-Sorbonne. In 2013–2014 he was economic advisor to the Minister of Economy,

Industry and Digital sector. He contributes regularly to media and newspapers. He has recently published, in collaboration with other authors of OFCE, "Budget 2019: Purchasing Power but Deficit", "Saving(s) Growth. Economic Outlook for the French Economy 2019–2021 " and "French Economy 2020" by Editions La découverte, Reperes collection.

Francesco Prota (PhD in Agricultural and Environmental Economics, University of Naples "Parthenope"; MPhil in Environmental and Sustainable Development, University of Glasgow) is Associate Professor in Economics at the University of Bari "Aldo Moro" (Italy). His research interests include regional economics and international economic integration; development economics; public policy evaluation; innovation economics. Francesco is the author of several articles in economics journals, including *World Development, Regional Studies, Papers in Regional Science, Journal of International Development, Development Policy Review, Economics Letters, European Planning Studies* and *Economia Politica, Journal of Analytical and Institutional Economics*. Besides serving as referee for international journals, he is Associate Editor for *Regional Studies, Regional Science* and for *L'Industria, Review of Industrial Economics and Policy*.

Debora Revoltella is Director of the Economics Department of the European Investment Bank since April 2011. The department comprises thirty economists and provides economic analysis and studies to support the bank in defining its policies and strategies. Before joining the EIB, Debora worked for many years on CESEE, first in the research department in COMIT, later as Chief Economist for CESEE in UniCredit. Debora holds a PhD in Economics and worked as adjunct Professor at Bocconi University. She is member of the Steering Committees of the Vienna Initiative and the CompNet, an alternate member of the Board of the Joint Vienna Institute and a member of the Boards of the SUERF and the Euro 50 Group.

Edoardo Reviglio is Head of International and European Projects at "Cassa depositi e prestiti" (CDP), Rome. He is Adjunct Professor of Economics at LUISS Guido Carli in Rome and President and faculty member of International University College of Turin. He has been a member of the Council of Economic Advisers of the Italian Ministry of Economy and Finance. He is one of the co-authors and chairman of the Working Group on finance of the Prodi report on investing in social infrastructure. He has a considerable and recognized experience in academic and policy research and has been representing CDP in international institutions (UN, G20, G7, OECD, EU) and worked extensively with them. He is on the Board and Scientific Committee of several think tanks at national and international level. He received his BA, Summa Cum Laude, from Yale College; was Senior Fellow at Department of Mathematics of Yale University; and Research Associate at the Department of Mathematics of Imperial College, University of London. He is the author of many scientific and policy publications. His fields of interest include: public finance, banking and finance, law and economics, and economic history.

Roberto Roson is Associated Professor in Economic Policy at Ca'Foscari University Venice, Full Professor at Loyola Andalusia University and GREEN Senior Research Fellow, Bocconi University Milan. He is the author of several articles published in international scientific journals and books. He has coordinated several applied research projects, and acted as consultant for many organizations, such as European Commission (JRC), United Nations and FAO, the World Bank. He is Scientific Director of the "CF Applied Economics" Centre for applied research and analysis. His research interests deal primarily with environmental economics, computational models for simulation of economic policies, and industrial organization in the services.

Federica Rossi is currently post-doctoral research fellow in Economics at Politecnico di Milano and she collaborates with Università Cattolica del Sacro Cuore in Milan (Italy). Federica received her PhD in Economics from Università della Svizzera italiana (Lugano, Switzerland) in 2018. Her research interests include topics in the area of regional economics and public investment.

Francesco Saraceno is Deputy Department Director at OFCE, the Research Center in Economics of Sciences Po Paris. He holds PhDs in Economics from Columbia University and the Sapienza University of Rome. His research focuses on the relationship between inequality and macroeconomic performance and European macroeconomic policies. He has published in several international journals. In 2000–2002 he was member of the Council of Economic Advisors for the Italian Prime Minister's Office. He teaches international and European macroeconomics at Sciences Po, where he manages the Economics concentration of the Master of European Affairs and in Rome (Luiss). He is Academic Director of the SciencesPo-Northwestern European Affairs Program. He is member of Confindustria`s Scientific Committee, and of the Scientific Board for the LUISS School of European Political Economy. He is active in the institutional dialogue, and in the public debate, on the EU. He advises the International Labour Organization (ILO) on macroeconomic policies for employment.

Alberto Silvani is a science policy analyst in the field of innovation, technology transfer, assessment and evaluation. He spent his professional life mainly at the National Research Council of Italy (CNR), acting as research director, with both research and management responsibilities. His academic teaching career includes University of Cassino (Management of Innovation) and University of Milan (Technology Transfer and Evaluation). He was national expert at the European Commission in Brussels for four years. He is national delegate in the European Network of Research Evaluation (EvalNet) and a member of the scientific committee of CRANEC at the Catholic University of Milan. He works with the Monitoraggio Economia Territorio (MET), a consulting company providing studies and analyses on industrial policy.

Alessandra Maria Stilo has a degree in Business Economics and has worked for the National Research Council of Italy (CNR) since 2007. Her work focuses on research project management, technology transfer, research policies and science policies at the national, European and international levels. She is a PhD candidate at the University of Urbino Carlo Bo; for her research project on researcher's mobility and migration she spent ten months as visiting scientist at the European Commission — Joint Research Centre (JRC) in Seville (Spain).

Gianfranco Viesti is Full Professor of Applied Economics in the Department of Political Sciences of the University of Bari. His main research interests cover local and regional development and policies, industrial and innovation economics and policy, international trade, European economic policies. His latest book is *Verso la secessione dei ricchi? Autonomie regionali e unità nazionale* (2019).

José Villaverde is Full Professor of Economics at the University of Cantabria. He received his PhD degree in Economics from the University of País Vasco. He has been visiting Professor at many universities in Denmark, England, Taiwan, China, United States, Belgium, Chile, Poland, Czech Republic, Ecuador and Argentina. His current research interests revolve around international and regional economics, economic integration and globalization and labour market. He has authored several books and published more than 150 papers in refereed journals. He has also participated in many international congresses and meetings, has acted as a consultant of the World Bank and the European Commission and has served as a reviewer for numerous scientific journals in Economics.

Sebastian Watzka heads the unit "European Macroeconomic Developments" of the Macroeconomic Policy Institute (IMK — Institut für Makroökonomie und Konjunkturforschung) in the Hans-Böckler Foundation. He studied economics at the University of Cambridge and received his PhD in economics from the European University Institute (EUI) in 2007. Before joining the IMK he was working as Assistant Professor at the Seminar for Macroeconomics at Ludwig Maximilian University (LMU) Munich.

Introduction

Floriana Cerniglia[1] *and Francesco Saraceno*[2]

In a recent *Financial Times* article Mario Draghi (2020) highlighted, in the midst of the coronavirus (COVID-19) outbreak, the challenges ahead for advanced economies, and for the European Union in particular. As we write (April 2020), the extent of the economic damage from the pandemic is yet unknown. Even in the best-case scenario of a fast recovery, the world economy will experience an economic slump that will be far worse than the one that followed the Global Financial Crisis of 2008.

Draghi's *Financial Times* piece brilliantly states something on what most, if not all, policy makers and economists today agree on, namely that, facing a crisis of this extent, all macroeconomic policy tools need to be mobilized. In particular, the titanic effort of central banks to keep firms and governments afloat through massive liquidity injections is only one leg of the effort to support the economy. The other leg needs to be fiscal support, that in most countries is, for the time being, taking the shape of short-term support to the productive system (temporary work schemes, loan guarantees) and to households' incomes on the consumption side. In Europe this happens against the background of the suspension by the Commission of the Stability and Growth Pact (SGP), and of a somewhat softer interpretation of State Aid regulations. Governments' efforts are unhampered by EU rules. The wager is that the joint operation of fiscal and monetary policy will succeed in preserving the vast majority of the productive structure and of incomes during the freeze associated to the lockdown, so as to facilitate a quick rebound as things go back to "normal".

Now, the problem is that the new "normal" will not be as before. The legacy of the crisis will be a widespread increase of public debt, and a drop of both private and public investment, with most of the expenditure in the next few quarters focused on short-term support to the economy. Furthermore, the COVID crisis is triggering a healthy soul-searching process about our long-term development trajectory, questioning our way of life, our utilization of natural resources, and the very social and environmental sustainability of our economies.

---

1   CRANEC — Facoltà di Scienze Politiche e Sociali, Università Cattolica, Milano.
2   Observatoire français des conjonctures économiques — OFCE SciencesPo Paris; School of European Political Economy — Università Luiss Guido Carli Roma.

    https://doi.org/10.11647/OBP.0222.11

This Report goes to the heart of this question by attempting to give a state of the art of public capital and investment needs in European countries and focusing on several of what we believe to be key sectors. Because of high debt, resources will be scarce; and because of the need to rethink our economic model, investment needs will be massive. Therefore, a careful assessment of these needs becomes paramount. Most of the chapters that compose this Report were submitted in their final form in the days preceding the outbreak of the virus in Europe. But they all deal with the existential questions posed by the current situation; more importantly, they collectively foster a broad approach to public investment that goes beyond the purely accounting definition that dominated the debate on public investment in the recent past.

Dealing with the environmental transition; needing to redefine the scope and extent of public services such as health care; making sure that we have in place the resources (human and physical) to face global crises that in the future are likely to increase in frequency — in all these cases we will need to invest not only in material assets, but also in intangible ones such as Research and Development (R&D), territorial cohesion or social capital.

When the group of researchers gathered in this Report first met, one year ago, nobody would even remotely have imagined what the world economy is going through right now. But none of us doubted that the "old" accounting approach to physical capital was inadequate to fully grasp the role of the state in building the multifaceted capital that our complex economic system needs, to strive and to ensure social cohesion. One might notice with some bitterness that we needed a pandemic that ground to a halt the world economy, to make these very same issues a priority for policy makers around the world. We believe that this Report will contribute to the debate that will, hopefully, continue past the emergency phase.

In assessing the government role in building the stock of capital of the economy, we do not start from scratch. In fact, the renewed emphasis on the importance of fiscal policy as one of the tools for economic stabilization is the most visible outcome of the process of "rethinking macroeconomics" triggered by the 2008 Global Financial Crisis. The New Keynesian theoretical consensus that emerged in the mid-1980s from the turbulence of the 1970s had abandoned the "Old Keynesian" focus on the stabilizing role of the State. Instead, emphasis was placed on the importance of market adjustment in absorbing shocks, and therefore on the fact that predictability and credibility of economic policy were its most important contributions to growth: by following monetary and fiscal rules, governments would anchor the expectations of efficient markets, and enhance their capacity to stabilize shocks. For the same reason, monetary policy was the preferred tool of the consensus. Lags and biases seemed inevitably linked to fiscal policy and that made it a source of uncertainty for markets.

The Global Financial Crisis has come to shake this consensus. In 2008, faced with the severity of the crisis, monetary policy was not able to sustain aggregate demand. Liquidity injections were pivotal in stabilizing the financial sector and in cleaning up the balance sheets of private (financial and nonfinancial) corporations of bad loans. But the infinite appetite for liquidity and the excess savings of the private sector, typical of balance sheet recessions, made it clear that monetary policy was pushing on a string, and fiscal stimulus packages in the Old Keynesian tradition had to follow to restart the engine of the economy.

The hasty reversal of the fiscal stance, beginning in 2010, left the recovery without momentum in the United States; more significantly, it caused a second recession in the euro area. Monetary policy was left alone to struggle with the tendency of the economy towards secular stagnation. The flattening of the Phillips curve and the "missing inflation" following the gigantic liquidity injections on both sides of the Atlantic (not to mention the permanent quasi-deflation of Japan), led policy makers and academics to reassess the merits of fiscal policy as the primary tool to push the economy away from the liquidity trap and (more importantly) from the tendency towards secular stagnation.

The debate on the size of fiscal multipliers started by the mea culpa of the International Monetary Fund (IMF) on the impact of austerity (Blanchard and Leigh 2013), initially focused on short run countercyclical impact of fiscal policy at large. Jordà and Taylor (2016) recently confirmed in a more systematic framework Blanchard and Leigh's conclusions, pointing at estimation errors in previous works. Once corrected these errors multipliers estimates tend to be much larger than was previously found, particularly in the event of a crisis. The meta-analyses of Sebastian Gechert and Henner Will (2012) and Gechert (2015) manage to extract from the abundant literature a number of broad conclusions: First, taking the average of the many studies they analyse, public expenditure multipliers are close to 1; this value is significantly larger than the 0.5 value that was taken as a basis of fiscal consolidation programs in crisis euro area countries; it had therefore to be expected that austerity triggered a second recession in Europe in 2012–2013. Second, consistently with the standard Keynesian argument, the spending multipliers are larger than tax and transfer multipliers. Nevertheless, these average values hide a very strong variability; this is not really surprising, as the value of the multiplier crucially depends on a number of factors such as the degree of openness of the economy and the distance of the economy from the natural equilibrium, known as the "output gap" (Berg 2015; Creel et al. 2011; Glocker et al. 2017).

Within the broader reassessment of fiscal policy, attention — especially that of policy makers — quickly switched to public investment. The Juncker Plan, while criticized in many respects, and probably closer to a Public Private Partnership (PPP) program than to a standard public infrastructure push, was an important symbolic act in that it officially brought back fiscal policy, and most notably investment, to the centre of the policy arena.

Since the seminal work of David Aschauer (1989) the role of public investment has been assessed both as a short-term aggregate demand support, and as a production factor that contributes to long-run productivity and potential growth. And yet, it is in fact in a downwards trend since the early 1980s across advanced countries (IMF 2014, and chapter 1 below). This trend, which can be thought of as a Kuznets cycle, accelerated with the financial crisis, as most countries tried to curb deficits and debt mainly through cuts in public investment, politically less sensitive than other items of public expenditure such as, for example, wages or entitlements. Figure 1 shows that the bias against public investment dates from the 1980s at least, and accelerated in the last decade (for further details see European Fiscal Board 2019, p. 74).

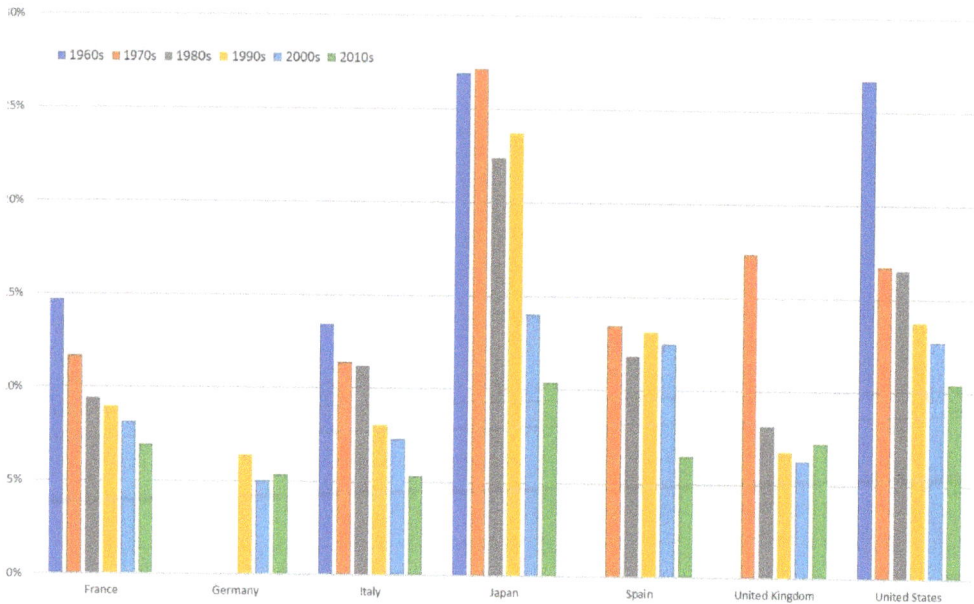

Fig. 1 Government Fixed Capital Formation as % of Primary Current Expenditure.

Source of data: OECD Economic Outlook. Figure created by the authors.

At times of persistently weak and fragile growth, and with interest rates at record low levels, the advantages of stimulus through public investment are even more evident: on one side, borrowing costs are low; on the other side, the depletion of public and private capital stocks during the crisis make investment particularly productive, and the multiplier large. This is why, based on a large sample of developing and advanced countries, the IMF recently made the headlines beyond the academic and policy-making community by speaking of "free lunch": public investment today is cheap and, boosting growth and fiscal revenues, it could pay for itself and ultimately reduce public debt (IMF 2014). Recent studies (e.g. Izquierdo et al. 2019) further show that this multiplier is higher when income per capita is low; in the European context this implies that investment would be particularly productive in the relatively poorer countries of the periphery.

The estimation of public investment multipliers crucially depends on two variables: the first is the *productivity* of public capital. This is a particularly difficult variable to assess, as measuring the public capital itself is rather complicated (see, e.g. Kamps 2006, and chapter 2 below). The second relevant variable is the time it takes for capital to evolve into productive capacity. Once the productive capacity is operational, public investment will influence productivity and supply. How this affects short-term multipliers, however, is more ambiguous, because the reaction of monetary policy and of private expenditure to an increase of public expenditure may be different depending on whether the latter is current or capital expenditure. For example, the central bank, can be less aggressive against current inflation, anticipating future deflationary impact of new productive capacity. The short-term investment multiplier therefore could also be larger than the multiplier of current expenditure.

The meta-analysis of Pedro Bom and Jenny Ligthart (2014) reports elasticities of private production to public capital. This elasticity is used in standard models to determine the multiplier of public investment; they exhibit the same degree of variability as the broader multiplier estimates. Consistent with this intuition, the multiplier (even the short-term one) increases in size when public capital is more productive, and when time to build is shorter (so that future increases in productivity are nearer in time). In these cases, the positive purely Keynesian short-term demand shock, is quickly associated with the positive supply-side impact on productivity.

The main takeaway of Bom and Ligthart's meta-analysis (confirmed by Gechert 2015) is that the multiplier associated with public investment is larger than the overall expenditure multiplier. This is particularly true in times of crisis (or when there is a tendency towards secular stagnation), when the economy is at the Zero Lower Bound.

The research on the impact of public investment triggered by the global financial crisis resonates with its recent surge in the public discourse. The centrality of public investment in addressing the issue of climate change, the debate on how to amend European fiscal rules so that governments have more incentives to adopt long-term strategies, the definition of public investment itself (is expenditure on human capital, for example in education or health care, less important than physical investment in ensuring long-term growth?): these are all questions of paramount importance, made yet more urgent by the events of recent weeks. Who would deny today that preparedness against pandemics is a crucial asset to protect not only lives but also the economy? An asset for which the current level of underinvestment is blatantly clear to the public! These are issues that will shape European policies (and politics) in the years to come. These are the reasons why we believe that our *European Public Investment Outlook* could constitute an important value added to the European debate. With this outlook — the first in a series of outlooks — we want to provide both an assessment of the state of public capital in (and of the needs of) the major European countries, and to identify areas where public investment could contribute more to a stable and sustainable growth. The scope of the outlook is not to advance the academic debate (although all the chapters present original material and data), but to provide a tool for the policy-making community in Europe to structure its discussion on the very notion of public investment. The *Outlook* does not want to be exhaustive either, as we selected some items (from transport to social capital, R&D and the environment) that we believe should constitute a priority in the policy debate. Other items are emerging in this very moment (such as specific investment in health care and biomedical research) that will certainly be treated in the next edition of the Report. It is worth stressing once more that our choice to broaden the definition of public investment beyond traditional measures is vindicated by the events of these weeks, and this makes the Report more relevant than ever in the current situation.

The *Outlook* is organized in two main parts. The first part sets the stage, providing trends on public investment in France, Germany, Italy and Spain. It is preceded by an initial chapter by Rocco Luigi Bubbico, Philipp-Bastian Brutscher and Debora Revoltella from the European Investment Bank (EIB) outlining the experience of Europe as a whole. The picture is as follows: between 2008 and 2016 public investment in the EU declined from 3.4% of GDP to 2.7%. Despite a slight rebound in 2017 and 2018, public investment still stands at only 2.9% of GDP, 15% below its pre-crisis levels. Fiscal consolidation pressure was at the core of such decline in public investment especially in countries that experienced a strong pressure to tighten their budgets. The negative effect of fiscal consolidation was in many cases amplified by a re-prioritization of public outlays away from investment towards current expenditures. Infrastructure investment was disproportionately affected by the decline in public investment. EIB estimates show that overall infrastructure investment declined by about 25% between 2008 and 2016, with the government sector accounting for the lion's share of this fall. From a sectorial perspective, investment in transport and education infrastructure experienced the strongest decline. The chapter clearly documents that the fall in government infrastructure investment does not reflect a saturation effect, the annual infrastructure investment gap is estimated to be about €155 bn and that construction of new infrastructure seems to continue to produce large positive economic spillover effects. This chapter advises, as a policy lesson, sound project selection: preparation and implementation are the keys to reversing the negative trend in investment activities in the EU, besides overcoming funding constraints. Obviously, to ensure the efficient use of available funds, sound infrastructure governance is also a key factor.

In chapter 2, Mathieu Plane and Francesco Saraceno take up the case of France, where public investment has seen contrasting trends in recent decades. Although it was rather dynamic until the 2000s, a real inflection took place at the turn of 2010 when the government turned to austerity, and a large part of fiscal adjustment was achieved by reducing capital expenditure. Their chapter starts by looking at the evolution of general government net wealth from the late 1970s. While still positive, the consolidated net wealth is today at an all-time low. Indeed, after reaching a record level in 2007 (58.1% of GDP) it has lost 45 points of GDP in the space of eleven years. Plane and Saraceno then focus on the evolution of the stock of non-financial assets held by the general government. Most of this is non-produced (land), and it has fluctuated greatly because of changes in prices. The stock of fixed assets, which represents the accumulation of public productive capital, has been much more stable, and it is owned mostly by local governments. The authors then focus on flows (investment), to conclude that, with the exception of intellectual property rights, all components of public investment are today at historic lows and it is "civil engineering works" that have experienced the greatest decline. For the last three years, public net investment was negative, meaning that France does not accumulate public capital anymore. In fact, since 2009 the increase of debt has not been used to finance new investment but mostly current expenditure. Finally, the chapter analyses, by means of a multi-sector macroeconomic model, the impact on growth in different macro sectors, of a permanent increase of public investment. Based on this analysis, the chapter concludes with an assessment of the public investment needs of the French economy, and, like other chapters of the Report, pleads for the introduction of a Golden Rule of public finances aimed at preserving capital expenditure.

Chapter 3, by Sebastian Dullien, Ekaterina Jürgens and Sebastian Watzka, reports on German debates about public investment. As with France, underinvestment by the public sector over the past two decades has led to a severe deterioration of the public capital stock. Moreover, demographic change, decarbonization and digitalization pose significant challenges for the German economy which imply additional public investment needs. A detailed sector-by-sector overview of investment requirements concludes that investment requirements add up to at least €450 bn over the next decade. Through a macroeconomic simulation, it is shown that a debt-financed increase of public expenditure of this magnitude would be compatible with keeping the debt-to-GDP-ratio below 60% and would have a positive impact on potential growth.

Chapter 4, by Floriana Cerniglia and Federica Rossi, addresses the case of Italy. They start from the premise that this country, over the last decade, has experienced the worst economic crisis, which has had a huge impact on the already weak public finance conditions. Italy had to implement extraordinary actions to contain and reduce its public debt. Public investments have been curtailed the most, with respect to other functional areas of expenditure. The chapter provides an overview of major trends in public capital expenditure, including local and national public companies, which in Italy are significant contributors to public investment. The chapter considers also the breakdown of public investment by levels of government. Since the reform of the Italian Constitution in 2001, the interactions between levels of government in Italy have become increasingly challenging. Coordination issues between the central government and sub-national governments in running current and capital expenditures as well as the financing of local expenditures (both current and capital) remain unsolved problems, which most obviously impact the time required to make an investment. Moreover, Italy's regional divide remains large, and sadly, it continues to grow. The issue of having shares of public investments in North-Central Italy and the Mezzogiorno, that proportionally reflect the population in those areas, has been a serious political concern these last years. Finally, the chapter discusses some legislative and bureaucratic factors that keep investments in Italy from taking off and hinder the transformation of resources into actual construction sites. The authors conclude by an assessment of some policy prescriptions for the relaunch of Italian public investment.

In chapter 5, José Villaverde and Adolfo Maza discuss the case of Spain, which, like Italy, has experienced the most acute economic crisis since the end of the Second World War. Because of that, the country had to face some important constraints in its public finances and public investment experienced a severe blow after the outbreak of the crisis. Before the 2008 Global Financial Crisis — namely during the period 2000–2007 — Spain was the country that registered the second highest increase in public gross fixed capital formation among the five biggest European countries (France, Germany, Spain, Italy and the UK), a rate (6.8% per year) that was also much higher than that of the EU (2.3%) and the euro area (2.6%). However, over the next period, 2008–2013, the situation changed completely: public investment dropped on an annual basis at a rate close to 11%; thus, Spain suffered the most acute decline in public investment by far among the among the big five. It also emerges that public investment in Spain has been very volatile and pro-cyclical over time (with large increase periods during boom times and huge falls during recessions); investment in infrastructures always represents the main component of public investment. This implies a policy agenda towards a more anti-cyclical stance and a rebalancing of types of investments, for instance the necessity to increase the share devoted to information and communications technology (ICT).

A common theme that emerges from the first part is that in Europe, and specifically in its largest economies, the legacy of the Global Financial Crisis is one of insufficient public investment. The chapters were written before the COVID outbreak, and the reader can easily imagine how current events will make the need for public capital, broadly defined, even more stringent. The second part of the Report investigates some possible areas into which resources could be channelled to reverse the recent trend and provide the European economies with an adequate public capital stock. Recently, economic literature has not only focused its attentions on the growth of physical infrastructures, as such. Economic analysis has sought to analyse more carefully types of investments which are very favourable to economic growth (OECD 2015). For instance: public R&D research investments, social investments, public infrastructure targeted to support private spending and business investments that may take advantage of location, and investments that may be necessary to respond to global climate emergencies. Understanding the challenges and opportunities of these types of investment could lead to improved infrastructural policy in Europe. In this respect, it is strongly recommended to have an assessment also on types of investments in the EU Cohesion Policy, to date the main investment policy in EU. The second part of the *Outlook* offers some ideas for the policy debate on these themes.

Chapter 6, by Daniela Palma, Alberto Silvani and Alessandra Maria Stilo, analyses the role of research and innovation as key drivers of economic growth, and as an object of renewed concern in the European policy agenda. In this regard, however, special attention has been paid to the role played by public funding with respect to the now more than ever complex evolution of technological innovation and the need for the productive structure to be supported to continuously capture the potential of new technologies. Starting from a well-established ground of most recent analyses carried out on main R&D indicators by major institutional organizations, the authors present a work aimed at bringing out the nature of "system infrastructure" of European research activity, calling for the need to assess to what extent the resources dedicated to R&D and the relative spending modes are able to turn into an effective development lever, starting from the structural characteristics of the entire research and innovation system. They claim that, in order to overcome the existing differential between EU countries in research and innovation performances, rebalancing public funding, while orienting intervention towards common initiatives, is not enough. The implementation of a new course of public investment research policies should instead envisage a renewed orientation of the strategies consistent with the new course of missions/objectives formulated at the European level and, at the same time, point to a coordination with policies aimed at increasing the innovative potential of the economic system, in relation to the characteristics of the productive specialization of each country.

Anton Hemerijck, Mariana Mazzucato and Edoardo Reviglio, in chapter 7, offer an original perspective: the most competitive economies in the EU spend more on social policy and public services than the less successful ones. However, the twenty-first century knowledge economies are ageing societies and require European welfare states to focus as much — if not more — on ex-ante social investment capacitation than on ex-post social security compensation. The growing needs for social services will require new and updated social infrastructure. According to a report on social infrastructure in Europe coordinated by former President of the European Commission Romano Prodi in 2018, the minimal gap is estimated at €100–150 bn per annum and represents a total gap of over 1.5 tn in 2018–2030. Long-term, flexible and efficient investment in education, health and affordable housing is considered essential for the economic growth of the EU, the well-being of its people and a successful move towards upward convergence in the EU. But how do we finance the great new needs with such a pressure on public finances? The chapter suggests innovative financial solutions using institutional and community resources to lower to cost of funding of social infrastructure. One such solution is the creation of a large European Fund for Social Infrastructure, owned by State Investment Banks (SIBs) and institutional long-term investors, which would fund its operations by issuing a European Social Bond. In this endeavour, a central role must be played by the EIB and by State Investment Banks. The authors discuss the potential role of these "mission-oriented" SIBs in social innovation by changing their mission. They should not simply "compensate market failures" but also become institutions that "shape the market" and become major providers of sustainable long-term and patient finance to deliver public value.

Paolo Costa, Hercules Haralambides and Roberto Roson, in chapter 8, look back at the genesis — in Europe — of the transnational transport infrastructure which has long coincided with the Ten-T network, developed — sometimes as a weak Keynesian stimulus — as a tool for strengthening the cohesiveness and economic efficiency of the internal market. Following the enlargement of the EU, Ten-T has been evolving from 1996 to 2013, and has been encouraging modal shifts from road and air to rail, inland navigation and short-sea shipping, in order to achieve higher environmental sustainability and combat climate change. However, during these notable efforts, little attention has been paid to the external dimension of European connectivity. Along with addressing a number of technical disruptions affecting transport and its infrastructure, the new wave of Ten-T revision — due by December 2023 — must depart from what has thus far been an introverted view of Europe as a single market (something that has often penalized European competitiveness) to an extroverted orientation of the Union as a key player in a global market. The growing economic centrality of Asia since China's accession to the World Trade Organization (WTO); China's strong interest in the Mediterranean Basin as the "super-hub" that connects four continents; and the eastward shift of the European economic barycentre: all of these developments indicate possible solutions for addressing the "geographical obsolescence" of the current Ten-T. In parallel, innovation-driven disruption of the worldwide maritime freight transport network and its infrastructure necessitates the streamlining of port nodes and rail networks around the world, in a way that at the same time addresses efficiently the current "technological obsolescence" of big parts of European infrastructure, predominantly of ports. The authors argue that new Ten-T network evolving into a Twn-T (Trans-Global) one ought to no longer be the product solely of European decisions: dovetailing Ten-T with China's "Belt and Road Initiative — BRI" will not only be unavoidable but also, rather, a most welcome development.

The global climate emergency is the main concern of chapter 9, by D'Maris Coffman, Roberto Cardinale, Jing Meng and Zhifu Mi. Anthropogenic climate change is widely understood to be the greatest existential threat to human societies in the coming centuries. The Intergovernmental Panel on Climate Change (IPCC) was established in 1988 to coordinate a global response to the coming crisis. The IPCC's publication of the *Special Report on Global Warming of 1.5 °C (SR15)* in October 2018 has helped to galvanize public opinion and has given rise to unprecedented climate activism. State actors now recognise a need for immediate action. Broadly speaking, possible responses to climate change fall into three categories: mitigation, adaptation and remediation. Mitigation means measures to reduce carbon and methane emissions or to enhance carbon sinks; adaptation means measures that ameliorate the effects of climate change on human populations; and remediation means intentional measures to counteract the effects of greenhouse gas (GHG) emissions, including global warming and ocean acidification. There are inevitable trade-offs between the costs of mitigation and those of adaptation over decadal time horizons. Nevertheless, with all three responses, large-scale infrastructure investment is required, with varying degrees of involvement by state actors, multilateral organizations, other non-governmental organizations (including religious groups) and, most significantly, private capital markets. In the current climate, multilateral development banks (MDBs) have taken a leading role. The EIB particularly is in the process of rebranding itself as a Climate Bank for Europe following Emmanuel Macron's call. The authors then explore the investment opportunities that arise as a result of the growing urgency of the low carbon transition.

As mentioned, the Cohesion Policy is the EU's main investment policy and — in the wake of the 2008 Global Financial Crisis — the European Regional Development Fund and the Cohesion Fund became the major sources of finance for investment in many countries. Francesco Prota, Gianfranco Viesti and Mauro Bux, in chapter 10, review how this policy has evolved over time in terms of financial size and geographical coverage. Firstly, in the programming period 2000–2006, the centre of gravity in Structural Funds allocation shifted from the Southern regions too the Eastern regions of Europe. What is interesting is that, looking at the expenditure composition by types, 'transport infrastructure' and 'environmental infrastructure' are the main expenditure items. The investments in transport infrastructure financed by the Cohesion Policy have changed the accessibility of EU regions. In particular, many regions in Eastern Europe have significantly benefitted from the Cohesion Policy financed transport infrastructure investments in terms of improved accessibility. Also, as result of the 2008 crisis, the Cohesion Policy has been the major source of finance for public investment for many Member States of the European Union. In 2015–2017 it represents around 14% of the total; this figure is larger than 50% in some small Central and Eastern European countries, in Portugal and Croatia; larger than 40% in Poland; larger than 30% in most of the other Central and Eastern European countries. In the EU-15, the figure is lower in most Member States (7% for Spain, 4.4% for Italy and 2.5 % for Germany). However, it has reached 20% of total capital expenditures in Convergence regions in Spain, 15% in Italy and 10% in Germany.

The authors of the different chapters of this *Outlook* come from different countries, and from different intellectual and professional backgrounds. The diversity of the topics they tackle and of their approaches, nevertheless, does not prevent a strong message from emerging throughout the volume; a message that in the current health and economic crisis is more relevant than ever: Without an increased role for public investment, without a less myopic approach to costs and benefits of fiscal policy, without embedding a long-term horizon into the trade-offs that inevitably characterize public policy, none of the challenges facing European economies will be properly dealt with.

While the policy prescriptions of the Report are varied and sector-specific, many of the chapters share the idea that European fiscal rules should be revised to eliminate the bias against investment. This is an idea that is now consensual even among European policy makers. We already cited the assessment by the European Fiscal Board (2019), highlighting the existence of the bias especially during the 2010–2015 fiscal consolidation phase. The same diagnosis motivates the consultation process recently (February 2020) launched by the Commission on the reform of the Stability and Growth Pact. While that consultation has been put on hold during the COVID emergency, it is likely that it will resume sometime in the future, and that the emergency itself will have pushed towards a rewriting of the rules with the aim of preserving public investment.

The old idea of a Golden Rule is now making headway again in policy circles; such a rule would allow debt financing of investment expenditure, requiring countries to balance current expenditure and revenues. In light of the discussions of the Report, the challenge would be to abandon a mere accounting approach, and to define investment in a functional way, so as to encompass all the sectors discussed here (Dervis and Saraceno 2014). But this is only part of the solution. The discussions on the 2021–2027 European Union budget stalled until very recently: held hostage by countries' defence of their positions around decimals of a point of GDP. The COVID-19 crisis is reshuffling the cards: a substantial increase of the EU budget, together with a more pervasive role to be played by the EIB, is one of the options on the table to end the stalemate on debt mutualization.

It is a *vaste programme*[3] indeed, that we face. The management of the emergency cannot be disentangled from a long-term rethinking of our growth model, of the role of the welfare state, of the best policies to preserve the social capital of the economy. As if this were not enough, in Europe this also forces us to ask the question of the appropriate institutions for macroeconomic governance. This Report provides a state of the art of these issues and starts by investigating some of the answers.

References

Aschauer, D. A. (1989) "Is Public Expenditure Productive?", *Journal of Monetary Economics* 23(2): 177–200, https://doi.org/10.1016/0304-3932(89)90047-0

Berg, T. O. (2015) "Time Varying Fiscal Multipliers in Germany", *Review of Economics* 66(1): 13–46.

Blanchard, O. J. and D. Leigh (2013) "Growth Forecast Errors and Fiscal Multipliers", *American Economic Review* 103(3): 117–20, https://doi.org/10.1257/aer.103.3.117

Bom, P. R. D. and J. E. Ligthart (2014) "What Have We Learned from Three Decades of Research on the Productivity of Public Capital?", *Journal of Economic Surveys* 28(5): 889–916, https://doi.org/10.1111/joes.12037

---

3   To borrow the phrase used by General De Gaulle, which translates as "wide-ranging agenda", in his famous response to a Minister who asserted that it was time for the government to start dealing with problems posed by idiots.

Creel, J., E. Heyer, and M. Plane (2011) "Petit Précis de Politique Budgétaire Par Tous Les Temps: Les Multiplicateurs Budgétaires Au Cours Du Cycle", *Revue de l'OFCE* 116: 61–88, https://doi.org/10.3917/reof.116.0061

Dervis, K. and F. Saraceno (2014) "An Investment New Deal for Europe", *Brookings Blogs — Up Front*, September 3, https://www.brookings.edu/blog/up-front/2014/09/03/an-investment-new-deal-for-europe/

Draghi, M. (2020) "We Face a War against Coronavirus and Must Mobilise Accordingly", *The Financial Times*, March 25, https://www.ft.com/content/c6d2de3a-6ec5-11ea-89df-41bea055720b

European Fiscal Board (2019) "Assessment of EU Fiscal Rules", August, https://ec.europa.eu/info/sites/info/files/2019-09-10-assessment-of-eu-fiscal-rules_en.pdf

Gechert, S. (2015) "What Fiscal Policy is Most Effective? A Meta-Regression Analysis", *Oxford Economic Papers* 67(3): 553–80, https://doi.org/10.1093/oep/gpv027

Gechert, S. and H. Will (2012) "Fiscal Multipliers: A Meta Regression Analysis", *IMK Working Paper* 97.

Glocker, C., G. Sestieri and P. Towbin (2017) "Time-Varying Fiscal Spending Multipliers in the UK", *Banque de France Working Paper* 643, https://doi.org/10.2139/ssrn.3046453

IMF (2014) "Legacies, Clouds, Uncertainties", *World Economic Outlook*, October, https://www.imf.org/en/Publications/WEO/Issues/2016/12/31/Legacies-Clouds-Uncertainties

Izquierdo, A., R. Lama, J. Medina, J. Puig, D. Riera-Crichton, C. Vegh, et al. (2019) "Is the Public Investment Multiplier Higher in Developing Countries? An Empirical Exploration", *IMF Working Papers* 19(289), https://doi.org/10.5089/9781513521114.001

Jordà, Ò. and A. M. Taylor (2016) "The Time for Austerity: Estimating the Average Treatment Effect of Fiscal Policy", *Economic Journal* 126(590): 219–55, https://doi.org/10.1111/ecoj.12332

Kamps, C. (2006) "New Estimates of Government Net Capital Stocks for 22 OECD Countries 1960–2001", *IMF Staff Papers* 53(1): 120–50.

PART I

—

OUTLOOK

1. Europe Needs More Public Investment

Rocco Luigi Bubbico,[1] Philipp-Bastian Brutscher[2] and Debora Revoltella[3]

Public investment went through a prolonged contractionary phase over the past decade. Between 2008 and 2016 public investment in the European Union declined from 3.4% of GDP to 2.7%. Despite a slight rebound in 2017 and 2018, public investment still stands at only 2.9% of GDP, 15% below its pre-crisis levels.

Fiscal consolidation pressure was at the core of the decline in public investment. This is witnessed by particularly strong falls in public investment in countries that experienced a strong pressure to tighten their budgets. The negative effect of fiscal consolidation was in many cases amplified by a re-prioritization of public outlays away from investment towards current expenditures.

Infrastructure investment was disproportionately affected by the decline in public investment. The European Investment Bank (EIB) estimates show that overall infrastructure investment declined by about 25% between 2008 and 2016; with the government sector accounting for the lion's share of this fall. From a sectorial perspective, investment in transport and education infrastructure experienced the strongest decline.

The fall in government infrastructure investment does not reflect a saturation effect. About one in three municipalities in the EU report that infrastructure investment activities in the last five years were below needs. In addition, the fall in infrastructure investment activities was particularly pronounced in regions with a poor infrastructure quality to start with. Moreover, construction of new infrastructure seems to continue producing large positive economic spillover effects (EIB 2018). Overall, using a bottom-up approach, the annual infrastructure investment gap is estimated to be about €155 bn.

Sound project selection, preparation and implementation are key to reversing the negative trend in investment activities in the EU, in addition to overcoming funding constraints. To ensure the efficient use of available funds, sound infrastructure

---

1   Policy Advisor, European Investment Bank's Permanent Representative Office — Brussels.
2   Economics Department — European Investment Bank.
3   Director of the Economics Department — European Investment Bank.

       https://doi.org/10.11647/OBP.0222.01

governance is key. This requires a comprehensive analysis of all economic and social costs and benefits. However, often such technical capacity is particularly weak in areas that invest little and face a range of other socio-economic challenges (EIB 2018). Addressing investment gaps, thus, calls for a series of complementary policies to increased spending, including lending, blending and technical advisory activities.

1.1. Recent Public Investment Trends in Europe

After a strong decline in public investment activities following the global financial crisis and subsequent sovereign debt crisis, public investment has started to gradually recover in recent years (Figure 1). After hitting its lowest level in two decades in 2016 (at 2.7% of GDP), government investment increased slightly in 2017 (to 2.8%) and 2018 (2.9%). Despite the reversal of the negative trend, public investment remains well below its long-term average of 3.1% of GDP between 1995 and 2017.

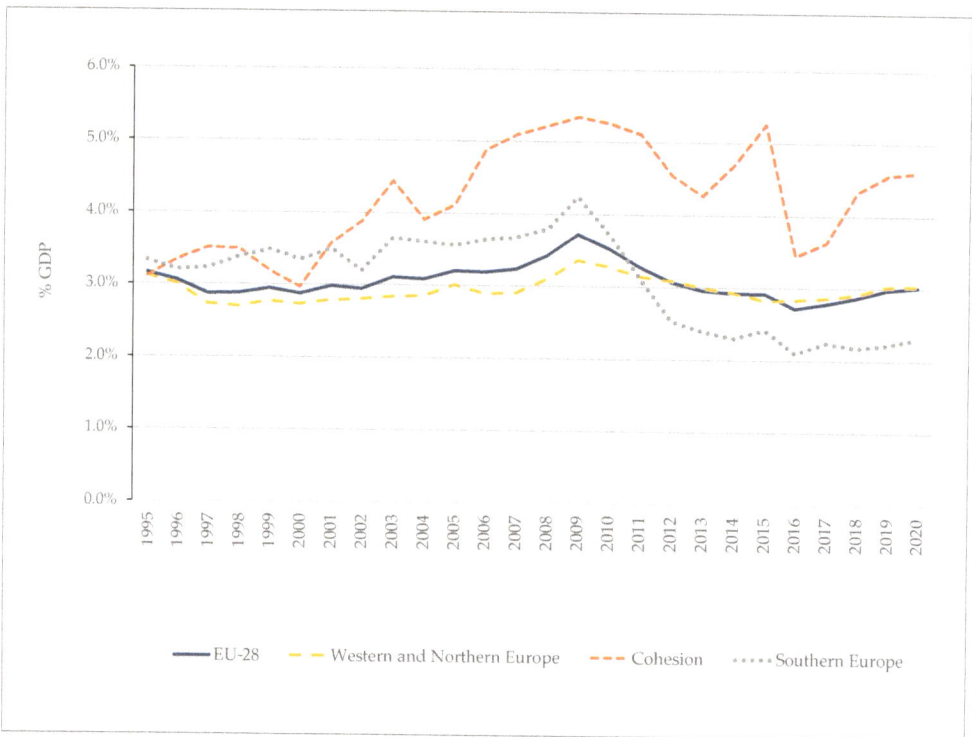

Fig. 1 Public Investment by country group (1995–2020)

Note: this chart reports Gross Fixed Capital Formation of the General Government as % of GDP. Forecast for 2019 and 2020. Data are missing for Croatia in 1995–2000. *Source of data*: Eurostat, AMECO. Figure created by the authors.

The recent increase in public investment was driven by investment activities in the Cohesion countries. In this group, gross fixed capital formation of the public sector increased from 3.6% of GDP to 4.3%. While positive, at least part of the increase reflects a mere rebound effect after a strong decline in investment activities in 2016 due to the start of a new programming period of European Structural and Investment Funds. Public investment in other parts of Europe remained broadly unchanged from their 2016 levels and well below their long-term averages.

From a cross-country perspective, investment increased markedly in Cyprus, Hungary, Latvia, Poland, Croatia and Bulgaria. The increase in Cyprus was, however, largely due to one-off accounting measures.[4] In Greece public investment continued to decline. Italy and the Netherlands also recorded declines in public investment, albeit more modest ones than in Greece, putting their investment levels at their lowest in twenty-five years, relative to GDP.

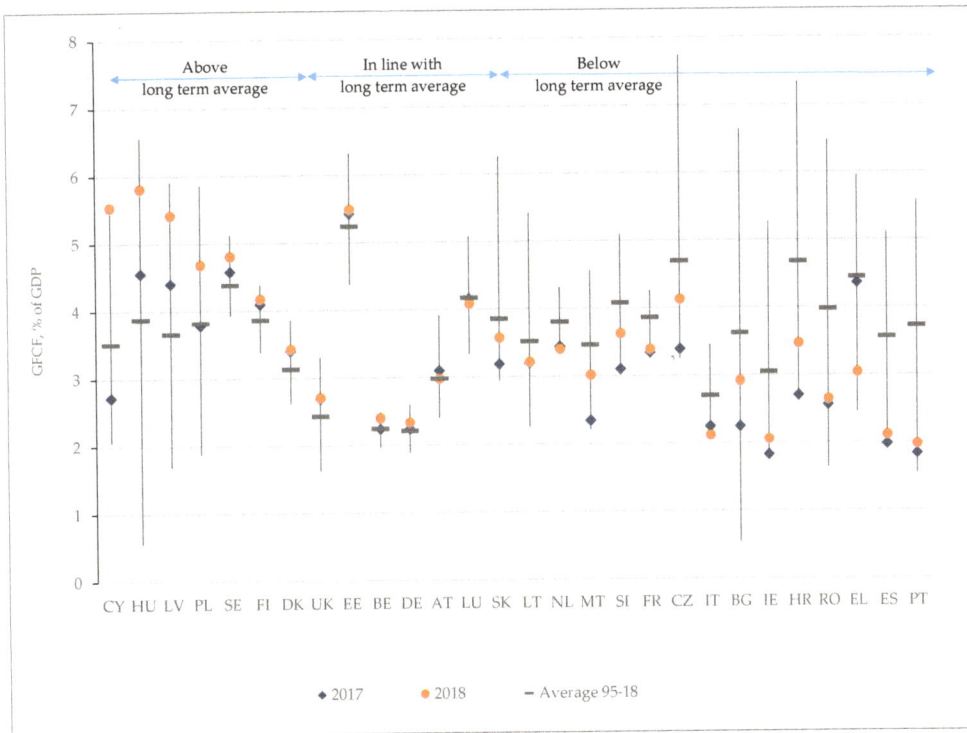

Fig. 2 Public Investment in 2018 by Member States (1995–2018)

Note: this chart reports Gross Fixed Capital Formation of the General Government as % of GDP. Vertical black lines report the range of values observed in 1995–2018. Thresholds for 'in line' with long-term average: +/- 0.25% from average. Data are missing for Croatia in 1995–2000. *Source of data*: AMECO. Figure created by authors.

---

4   Cyprus registered the strongest increase in public investment in Europe. However, the strong increase was largely due to one-off accounting measures.

Tight fiscal budgets and a change in spending priorities are at the core of the decline in public investment in recent years. Public investment has fallen most in countries that experienced strong pressure to tighten their budgets. The negative effect of fiscal consolidation was in many cases amplified by a re-prioritization of public outlays away from investment towards current expenditures. The budget share of current expenditures increased, for example, from 84.4% on average between 1995 and 2017 to 87.7% in 2018 (Figure 3). Instead, the budget share of capital spending dropped from 9.3% to 8.4%.

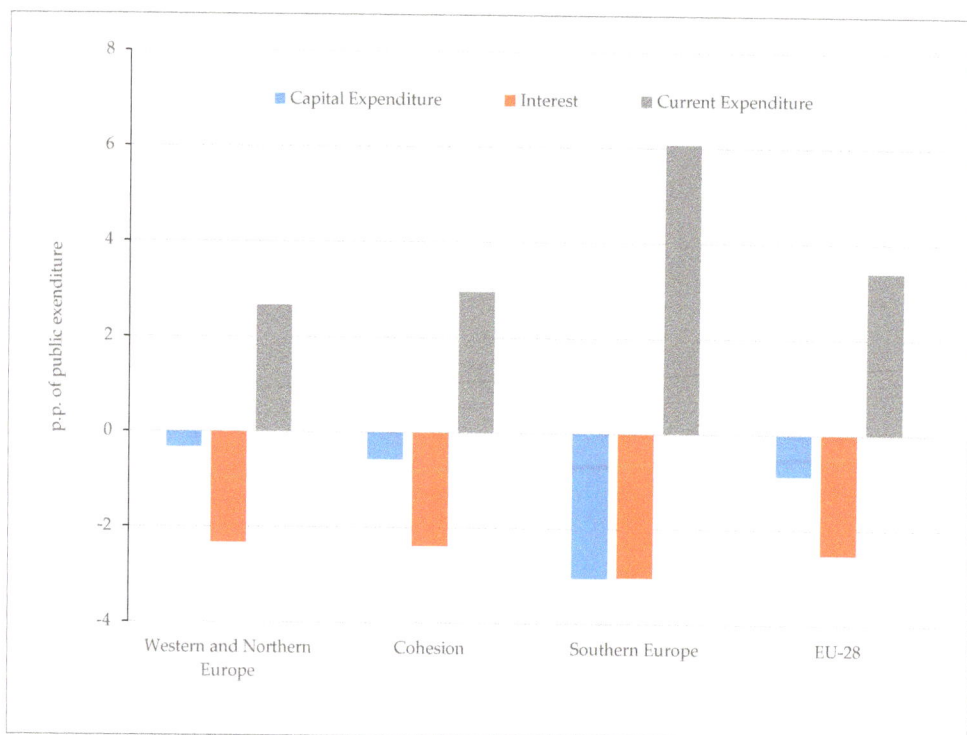

Fig. 3 Change in public expenditure composition (2018 versus 1995–2017 average)

Note: this chart reports the changes in public expenditure composition from a long-term average (1995–2017) to 2018 by expenditure category. The sum of the components equals zero. Capital expenditure includes Gross Fixed Capital Formation, capital transfers paid and other capital expenditures. *Source of data*: AMECO. Figure created by the authors.

After the considerable fiscal contraction of 2011–2013, the fiscal stance of the EU has started to improve (Figure 4). There are no signals, however, that this will translate into a strong pick-up in public investment any time soon. The fiscal forecasts of the European Commission suggest that, despite the positive fiscal outlook, public investment will increase only slightly in 2019 and 2020, to 3.0% of GDP.

What is more, there is no sign of a reversal of the deprioritization of public investment (so far): public investment as a percentage of total expenditure is expected to remain stable in 2019 and even decline slightly as a percentage of current expenditure; suggesting no change in expenditure prioritization between current outlays and gross fixed capital formation (Figure 5).

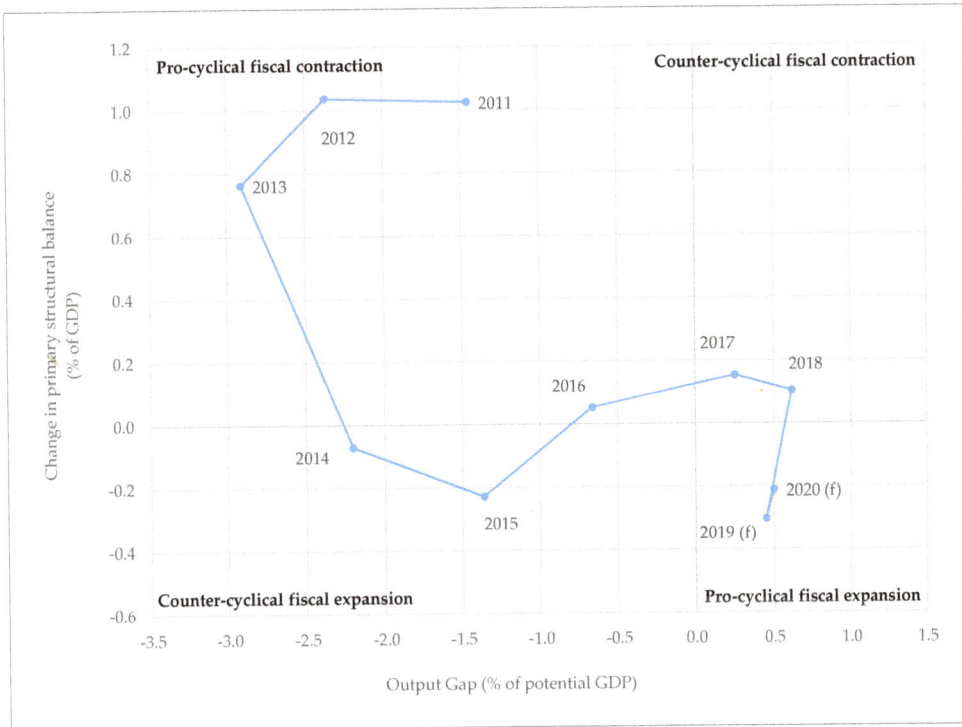

Fig. 4 Fiscal stance in the European Union

Note: output gap as difference between actual and potential gross domestic product. 2019 and 2020: forecast. *Source of data*: AMECO. Figure created by the authors.

Taking a medium-term perspective, public investment is projected to remain below its long-term average. The Stability and Convergence Programmes submitted during the 2019 European Semester show a steady outlook for public investment in the medium term. Budgetary plans report an aggregate public investment equal to around 2.9%–3.0% of GDP in Europe in 2019–2022 budget plans, which is below its long-term average of 3.2%.

The 2019 European Semester shows awareness of the issue. Compared to previous exercises, it has a stronger focus on investment. One of the general recommendations is to continue steps towards a 'growth-enhancing' composition of public spending. Member States with adequate scope, notably Germany and the Netherlands, are recommended to use fiscal and structural policies to increase public investment. The Commission also singles out, in each Member State, investment priorities. The Commission recommends most Member States to focus spending more on R&D and innovation, sustainable transport and energy (network infrastructure, low-carbon transition and/or energy efficiency).

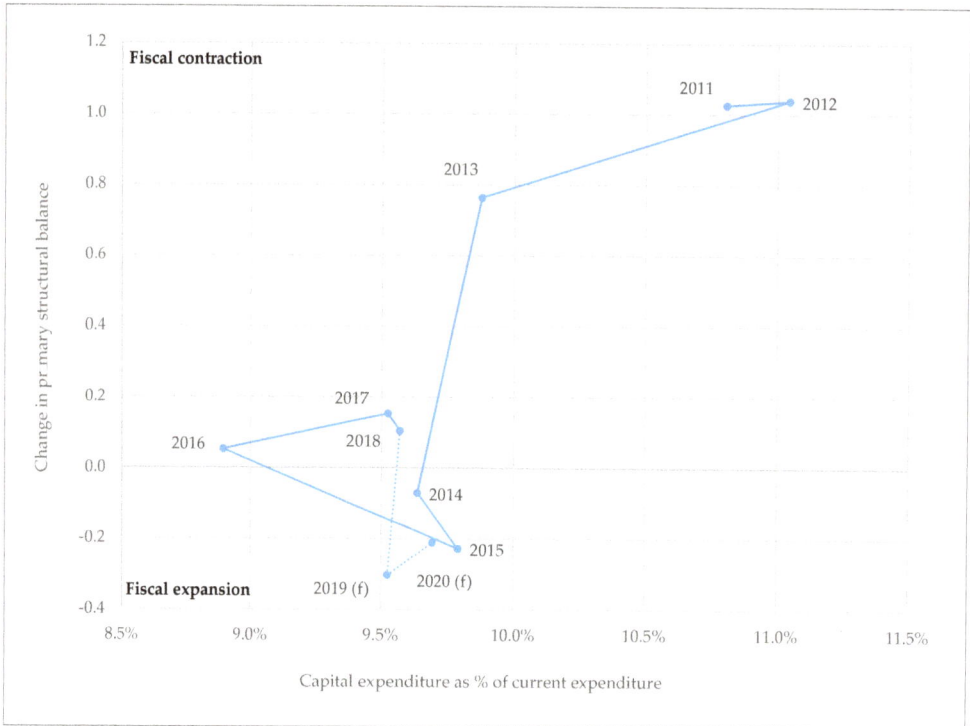

Fig. 5 Fiscal stance and capital expenditure in the European Union

Note: forecast for 2019 and 2020. *Source of data*: AMECO. Figure created by the authors.

1.2. Infrastructure Has Declined Substantially

An area that suffered disproportionately from the fall in public investment is infrastructure investment. Applying the EIB methodology to proxy infrastructure investment,[5] we find that infrastructure investment continuously declined since 2009. At 1.7% of GDP, overall infrastructure investment now stands at about 75% of its pre-crisis level (Figure 6).

The government sector is the main driving force behind the decline. Government infrastructure investment declined between 2009 and 2017 by 0.5% of GDP. Over the same time horizon corporate infrastructure investment increased by 0.1% of GDP while infrastructure investment activities by Special Purpose Vehicles declined by 0.1% of GDP. The decline in government infrastructure investment (as a share of GDP) corresponds to a fall of 37%; which is more than the fall in public investment reported earlier, suggesting that the latter affected infrastructure investment activities disproportionately.

---

5   We define proxy infrastructure investment as gross fixed capital formation in other buildings and structures in the infrastructure sectors (Revoltella et al. 2015).

a. Infrastructure investment (% of GDP) — by institutional sector

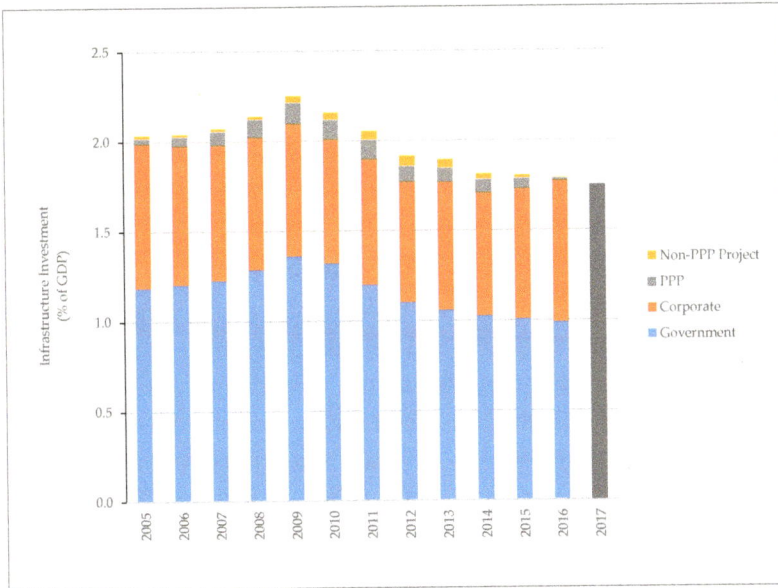

b. Infrastructure investment (% of GDP) — by sector of economic activity

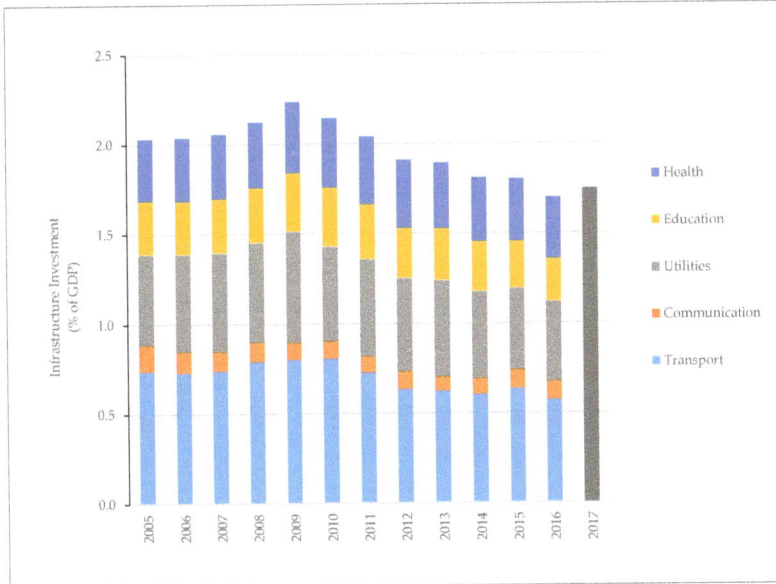

Fig. 6 Infrastructure investment by sector and promoter

Note: based on EIB Infrastructure Database. Data are missing for Belgium, Croatia, Lithuania, Poland, Romania and the UK. PPP: public-private partnership. *Source of data*: Eurostat, Projectware, EPEC. Figure created by the authors.

Government infrastructure investment includes fewer sectors and asset types than overall public investment. While public investment spans all sectors of economic activities including, for example, defence, security and recreational activities, infrastructure investment is limited to a narrower set of activities. Notably, for this paper it includes transport, energy, water, ICT, health and education. In addition, whereas public investment does not differentiate between investments in different asset classes, infrastructure investment activities are limited to gross fixed capital formation in 'other buildings and structures'; therefore excluding investments in machinery, equipment, vehicles and intellectual property. To the extent that infrastructure investment activities are often much more bulky than non-infrastructure public investment, they lend themselves more easily to delays and/or cuts (EIB 2017).

The decline in government infrastructure investment has affected primarily the transport sector and educational sector. Government infrastructure investment accounts for the biggest share of total infrastructure investment in the transport and education sector (with 80% and 90% of total infrastructure investment, respectively). The share of government investment is lower in other sectors (55% in health; 30% in the utilities sector; and 10% in ICT). If we compare the evolution of infrastructure investment across the various economic sectors, it is, therefore, not surprising to find that — on the back of the strong contraction of government investment in these sectors — it is in particular transport and education that saw the strongest declines in overall investment activities.

Sub-national governments reduced their infrastructure investment activities disproportionately. Subnational investment accounts for more than half of overall government infrastructure investment (Figure 7). If we compare the fall in overall government infrastructure investment and the change in sub-national infrastructure investment, we find that changes in overall government infrastructure investment often came with disproportionate changes at the subnational level in the same direction. This is true in particular in regions with little fiscal autonomy (EIB 2017).

The fall in government infrastructure investment does not reflect a saturation effect. The fall in infrastructure investment activities was particularly pronounced in regions which had a poor infrastructure quality to start with (EIB 2018). However, were the drop infrastructure investment driven by diminishing returns to the construction of new infrastructure, the opposite would be the case. In addition, the EIB Municipalities Survey shows that about one in three municipalities report that infrastructure investment activities in the last five years were below needs (Figure 8). Finally, and again in contrast with the view of a saturation-driven decline in infrastructure investment activities, there is evidence that the construction of new infrastructure continues to produce large positive economic spillover effects (EIB 2018).

a. Change in subnational investment share

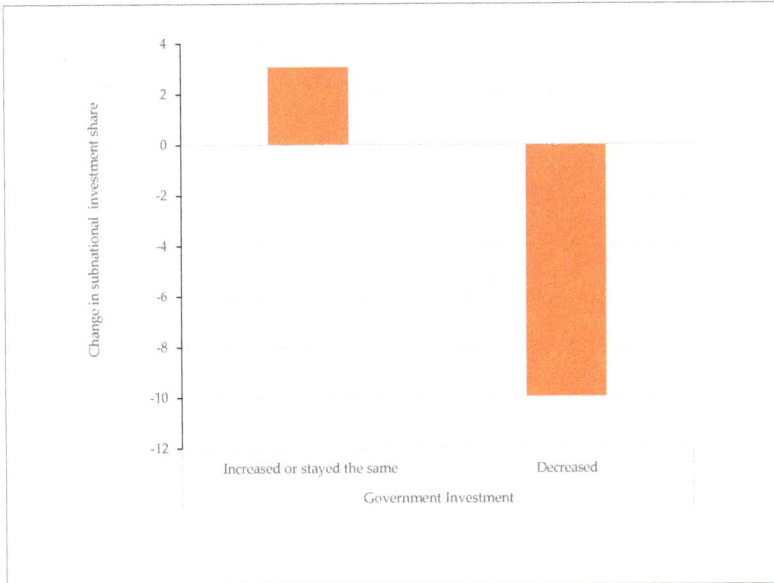

b. Change in subnational investment share by fiscal autonomy

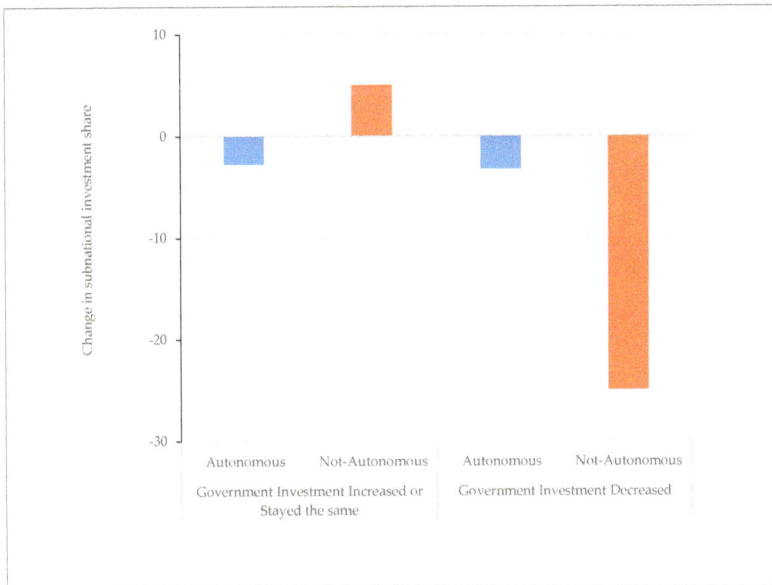

Fig. 7 Change in subnational investment share by overall government investment trend

Note: blue bars in Panel b refer to countries in which regions have relatively high fiscal autonomy, red bars to countries in which fiscal autonomy is relatively low. The change in subnational investment share by fiscal autonomy is based on a relatively small number of observations and should therefore be taken as indicative.

Source of data: Eurostat, Projectware, EPEC (for infrastructure investment) and Eurostat for subnational government investment in infrastructure sectors. Fiscal autonomy data comes from Hooghe et al. (2018). Figure created by the authors.

Weak infrastructure investment has led to substantial investment gaps. A bottom-up estimation suggests an annual "investment gap" of roughly €155 bn for the EU27 (i.e. all Member States except the United Kingdom) until 2030. This corresponds to 1.2% of the current EU27 GDP and 5.8% of Gross Fixed Capital Formation (Table 1). The investment gap is defined as the difference between investment needs and current investment levels. The infrastructure investment gap of €155 bn per year is only one part of the estimated overall investment gap of €403 bn, as investment needs in innovation and energy efficiency are also substantial. If dynamics in infrastructure investment do not reverse, this gap is likely to increase.

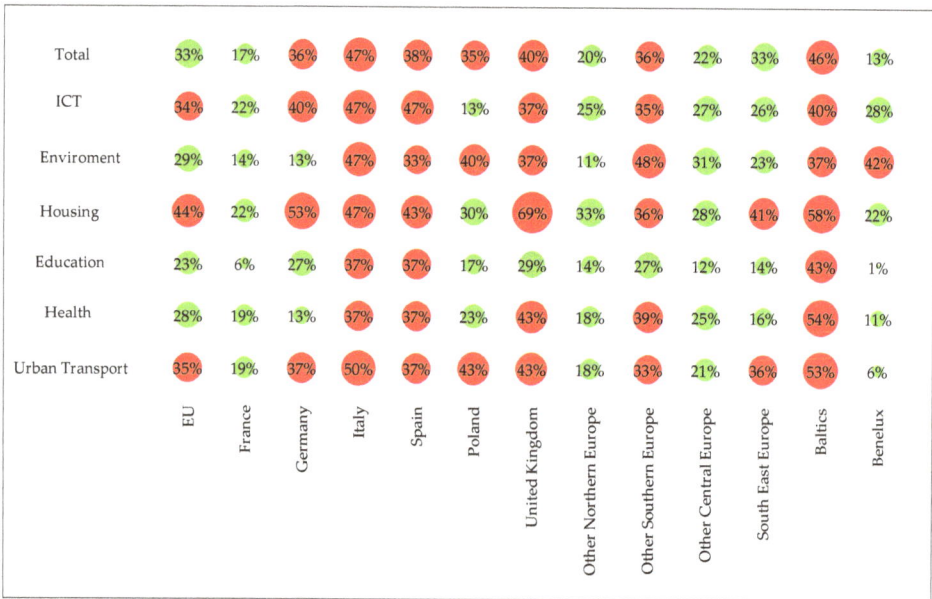

Fig. 8 Underprovision of infrastructure by Country and Sector

Note: the Figure plots the net balance of municipalities that report underinvestment by country/ region and sector. A green circle signifies a share of mentions below the median; a red circle above the median. The number inside each circle states the net balance of municipalities that report underinvestment vis-à-vis over-investment for a particular area in a country/country grouping. *Source of data*: EIB Municipality Survey. Figure created by the authors.

Question: for each of the following, would you say that, overall, past investment in your municipality has ensured the right amount of infrastructure, or led to an underprovision or overprovision of infrastructure capacity?

Table 1 Annual infrastructure investment gaps for EU 27

	EUR bn	% of GDP	% of GFCF
ICT (broadband and digitalisation)	50	0.38	1.86
Energy generation and grids	17	0.13	0.63
Water and Waste	7	0.05	0.26
Social and affordable housing	6	0.05	0.22
Education	8	0.06	0.30
Health	17	0.13	0.63
Mobility	50	0.38	1.86
Total	**155**	**1.19**	**5.77**

Note: GDP and Gross Fixed Capital Formation (GFCF) refer to 2017. All numbers refer to EU27, i.e. all Member States except the UK. Estimates of infrastructure investment gaps are based on EU policy targets and EIB expert judgements. Notably, EU policy targets for broadband (European Gigabit Society targets), energy (EU 2030 climate and energy targets) and water and sanitation (compliance with EU Directives) are considered. For mobility and social infrastructure, investment needs reflect past investment backlogs combined with higher future needs to accommodate demographic trends, migration and other megatrends. *Source of data*: estimates by the EIB Projects Department.

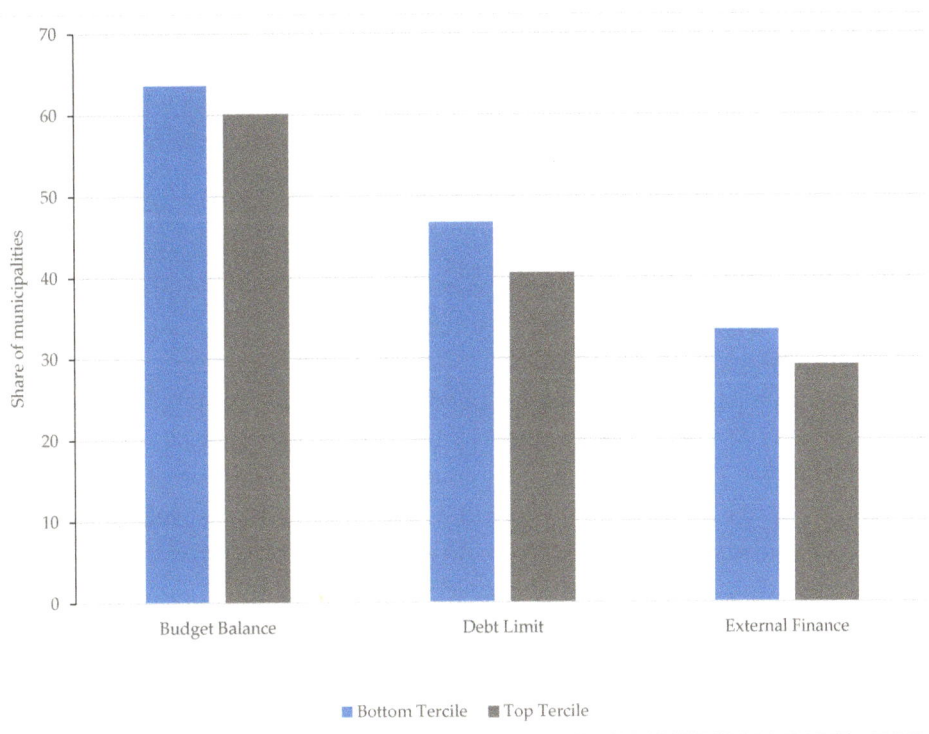

Fig. 9 Infrastructure financing and infrastructure quality

Note: bottom (top) tercile refers to the third of municipalities reporting the lowest (highest) average infrastructure quality relative to country mean. *Source of data*: EIB Municipalities Survey 2017. *Figure created by the authors.*

Questions: can you tell me approximately what proportion of your infrastructure investment activities were financed by each of the following? Thinking about all of the external finance you used for your infrastructure investment activities, how satisfied or dissatisfied are you with: the number of available external funding sources; amount of external funding available; interest rates offered; maturities available (i.e. the length of time over which the external finance has to be repaid); administration/documentation requirements associated with the external finance?

1.3. How to Support More Infrastructure Investment

Tight funding conditions are a key bottleneck to more infrastructure investment. This is true in particular for regions with low infrastructure quality. Cities with a low infrastructure quality (relative to the country average) perceive external finance, the budget balance and debt limits more often as major obstacles than municipalities with high infrastructure quality, according to the EIB Municipalities Survey 2017 (Figure 9). The Survey also shows that municipalities with low infrastructure quality fund their infrastructure more often through transfers and external financing. This may reflect that those municipalities more often face fiscal constraints.

Besides overcoming funding constraints, careful project selection and implementation are key to ensure that the funding goes to where it is needed the most. Cities that report infrastructure gaps seem to suffer more often from technical deficiencies in selecting and implementing complex infrastructure projects. 43% of municipalities that report their infrastructure quality to be lower than their within-country peers also report the technical capacity to implement infrastructure projects as being major obstacle, compared to 30% for within-country peers with high quality infrastructure. Moreover, municipalities with low infrastructure quality conduct independent assessments along different dimensions less often before going ahead with an infrastructure project. They also consider this kind of information to be important or highly important less often when taking decisions on individual projects (Figure 10). This is problematic as it suggests that, even if the necessary funding were available, municipalities may have difficulties in using it effectively to address gaps due to limited infrastructure governance.

The need to increase infrastructure spending and building up technical capacity must be assessed in the context of other challenges (EIB 2018). Notably, geographical and socioeconomic obstacles can create spending pressures and hamper governments' ability to invest more and better. The EIB Municipalities Survey suggests that low infrastructure quality is often associated with geographical challenges constraining the ability to upgrade infrastructure. For example, municipalities with low infrastructure quality tend to be more often characterised by a small population, a lower population density and are situated in border areas. Moreover, municipalities that assess the quality of their infrastructure to be low also face a number of socioeconomic challenges more often. They suffer more often from weaker safety conditions, lower income per capita, a lower share of fast-growing firms and employment ratios.

1.4. Policy Implications

Public investment and government infrastructure investment activities have been exceptionally weak in recent years. Despite increased fiscal space in most parts of Europe, thus far we see, at best, a modest reversal in the negative trend in public investment.

a. Area of assessment

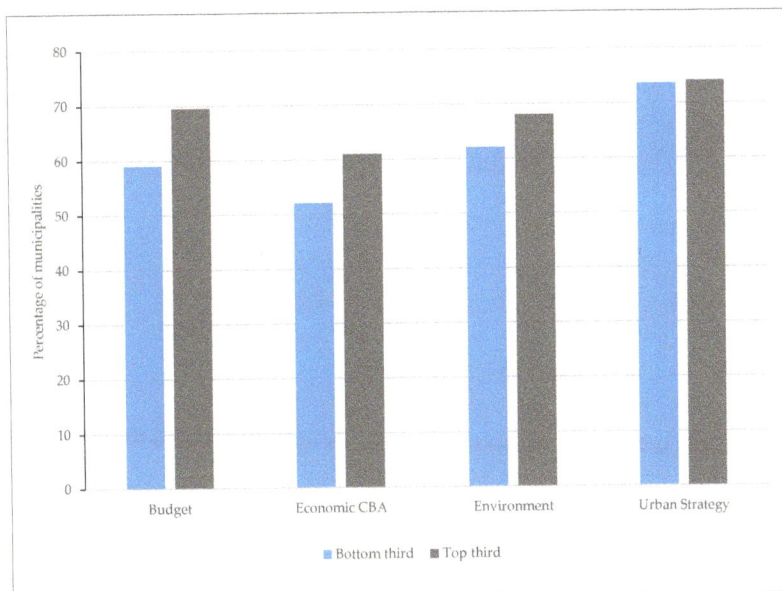

b. Importance of assessment

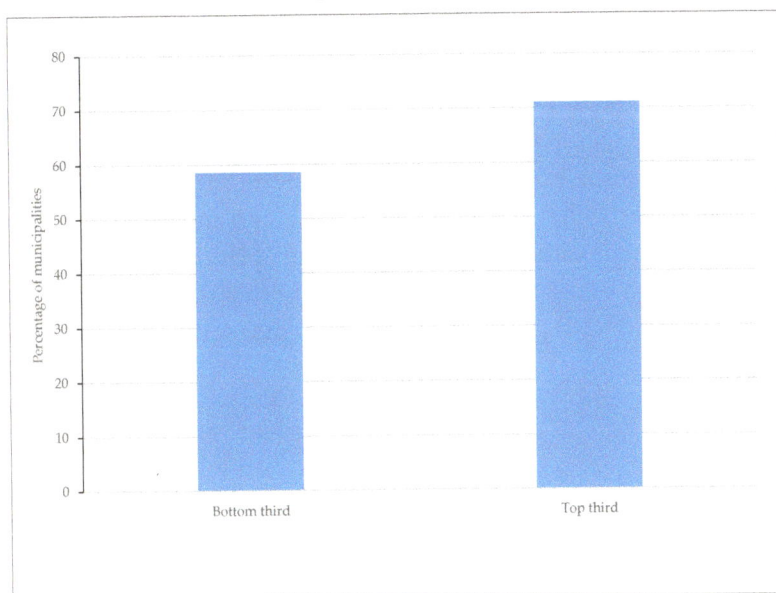

Fig. 10 Independent assessment of projects and infrastructure quality

Note: bottom/top third refers to the third of municipalities reporting the lowest (highest) average infrastructure quality relative to the country mean. Panel a. reports the share of municipalities that respond "always" or "frequently" to the question "Before going ahead with an infrastructure project, do you carry out an independent assessment of ...?". Panel b. reports the share of municipalities that respond "critical" or "important" to the question "And how important would you say are the results of the independent assessment/s when deciding whether or not to go ahead with a project?" *Source of data*: EIB Municipalities Survey 2017. *Figure created by the authors.*

The sluggish investment performance cannot be explained by saturation effects, but rather reflects underinvestment. Notably, spillovers to new infrastructure investment for the business sector continue to remain high. Moreover, one in three municipalities state that recent investment volumes have been below their needs. In some parts of Europe (particularly in weaker regions), this share is even higher.

Sound project selection, preparation and implementation are key to addressing infrastructure gaps, in disadvantaged and leading regions. Evidence suggests that a key obstacle to more investment is access to funding. However, infrastructure investment is also often hampered by limited implementation and planning capacity (Oprisor et al. 2015). To ensure the efficient use of available funds, sound infrastructure governance is key. A comprehensive analysis of all economic and social costs and benefits should thus accompany any spending increase (Kline and Moretti 2014). Application procedures for EU funds can be used to promote the comprehensive use of cost-benefit analysis.

The EU's upcoming Multiannual Financial Framework provides an opportunity to address the identified infrastructure gaps through a coherent policy mix. The first proposal of the European Commission (EC) includes important steps in this direction (European Commission 2018). Notably a countercyclical investment support scheme is envisaged, to avoid a lasting decline in infrastructure investment after economic downturns. Moreover, the EC proposal aims to strengthen the link between EU funding and respect for the rule of law. It also includes proposals to expand the Reform Support Programme, which offers technical and financial support for reforms. Such initiatives can ensure that infrastructure planning, governance and funding go hand in hand. The EIB has traditionally worked towards delivering such coherent policy solutions. Notably, the EIB combines the financing of projects with high socioeconomic returns, including those with high risks, with technical assistance solutions.

References

Calderon, C. and Serven L. (2014) *Infrastructure, Growth and Inequality: An Overview.* Washington, DC: World Bank, http://documents.worldbank.org/curated/en/322761468183548075/pdf/WPS7034.pdf

EIB (2017) *EIB Investment Report 2017/2018: From Recovery to sustainable growth.* Luxembourg: European Investment Bank, https://www.eib.org/attachments/efs/economic_investment_report_2017_en.pdf

EIB (2018) *EIB Investment Report 2018/2019: Retooling Europe's Economy.* Luxembourg: European Investment Bank, https://www.eib.org/attachments/efs/economic_investment_report_2018_en.pdf

EPEC/Eurostat (2016) "A Guide to the Statistical Treatment of PPPs". Report. Eurostat and the European PPP Expertise Centre, https://www.eib.org/attachments/thematic/epec_eurostat_statistical_guide_en.pdf

European Commission (2017a) "Government Investment in the EU: The Role of Institutional Factors". Report on Public Finances in EMU, Directorate General Economic and Financial Affairs (DG ECFIN), European Commission, https://ec.europa.eu/info/sites/info/files/economy-finance/ip069_iv_government_investment_in_the_eu.pdf

European Commission (2017b) *My Region, my Europe, our Future: Seventh Report on Economic, Social and Territorial Cohesion*. Brussels: European Commission.

European Commission (2018) *A Modern Budget for a Union that Protects, Empowers and Defends the Multiannual Financial Framework for 2021–2027*. Communication from the Commission, COM(2018), 2 May 2018. Brussels: European Commission, https://eur-lex.europa.eu/legal-content/EN/TXT/?uri=COM%3A2018%3A321%3AFIN

Kline, P. and E. Moretti (2014) "People, Places, and Public Policy: Some Simple Welfare Economics of Local Economic Development Programs", *Annual Review of Economics* 6(1): 629–62.

Oprisor, A., G. Hammerschmid, and L. Löffler (2015) *The Hertie School — OECD Global Expert Survey on Public Infrastructure*. Berlin: Hertie School of Governance.

Revoltella, D. and P.-B. Brutscher (2018) "Infrastructure Investment in Europe: New Data, Market Dynamics, Policy Actions, and the Role of the European Investment Bank", in *Finance and Investment: The European Case*, ed. by C. Meyer, S. Micossi, M. Onado, M. Pagano and A. Polo (Oxford: Oxford University Press), pp. 299–316.

Revoltella, D., P.-B. Brutscher, A. Tsiotras and C. T. Weiss (2015) "Linking Local Business with Global Growth Opportunities: The Role of Infrastructure", *Oxford Review of Economic Policy*, 32(3): 410–30, https://doi.org/10.1093/oxrep/grw019

World Economic Forum (2017a) *World Economic Forum Global Competitiveness Indicators*. Geneva: World Economic Forum.

World Economic Forum (2017b) "Migration and its Impact on Cities". Report in collaboration with PwC, October, http://www3.weforum.org/docs/Migration_Impact_Cities_report_2017_HR.pdf

2. Public Investment and Capital in France

Mathieu Plane[1] and Francesco Saraceno[2]

Introduction

Public investment in France has seen contrasting trends in recent decades. While it was rather dynamic until the late 2000s, a real inflection took place at the turn of 2010, when the fiscal stance changed, and a substantial part of the adjustment was achieved by reducing capital expenditure. Indeed, the reduction of public investment has contributed to 30% of fiscal consolidation even though investment only represented 6% of public expenditure. The share of public investment on GDP, that was largely above 4% since the 1960s (Figure 1), has fallen below that level in 2011; it averaged 3.4% of GDP since then, its lowest level since 1952. Despite the commitment of President Emmanuel Macron to put in place a large investment plan on the five-year period of his term, and the will to preserve local governments' investment by constraining only their current expenditure, the share has not recovered yet. This sustained weakness in general government investment raises the question of the evolution of public capital in France. This is relevant because it provides an historical picture of the assets cumulated over time by the government (and of their composition), the counterpart of its public debt.

How did public capital in France evolve since the late 1970s? What are its main characteristics and how is it measured? Which public institutions hold this capital? How did investment flows and depreciation shape it? What is the net position of public administrations today? This chapter will address these questions by tracing the historical evolution of public assets, both financial or non-financial, and by looking into the components of public capital. We will look at general government figures as well as their components (central government plus local government and social security administrations). We will specifically investigate non-financial assets, especially fixed assets that represent the accumulation of public investment net of its depreciation.

1   Observatoire Français des Conjonctures Économiques — OFCE SciencesPo Paris.
2   Observatoire Français des Conjonctures Économiques — OFCE SciencesPo Paris; School of European Political Economy — Università Luiss Guido Carli Roma.

    https://doi.org/10.11647/OBP.0222.02

What is referred to as public capital covers a wide variety of assets, such as land, residential buildings, ports, dams, roads but also intellectual property rights. It is necessary to break down the "wealth of the State" into these different components to understand its dynamics considering, as we will show below, that price (most notably land prices) and volume effects may play a significant role in explaining the evolution of the different components, and of aggregate figures.

The data we use are from the INSEE national accounts, which are public; our analysis covers the period 1978–2018. INSEE reports the consolidated level (General Government, GG) and its components, distinguishing between the central government (CG), local governments (LG), social security administrations (SSA) and other government agencies (OGA).

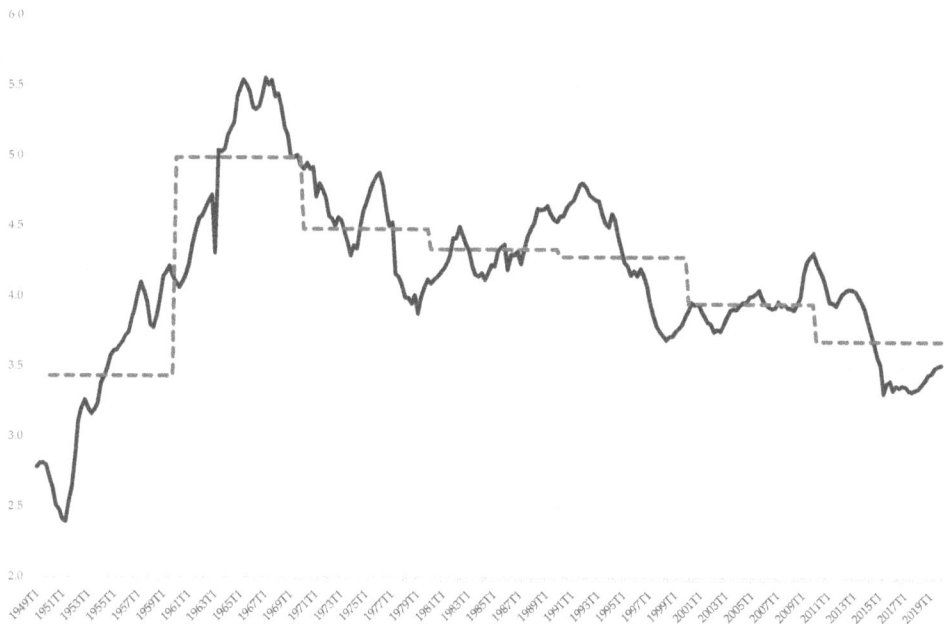

Fig. 1 General government investment rate (as a percentage of GDP).

Source of data: Insee. Figure created by the authors.

In section 2.1. we will look at the evolution of government net wealth from the late 1970s to the present day. Consistently with the general aim of this volume, we will then focus, in section 2.2., on the stock of non-financial assets held by the government. Section 2.3. will detail the gross and net (of depreciation) flows of capital for different types of assets, documenting a shift from material to immaterial investment. After this essentially descriptive assessment, we will analyse, on the basis of a multi-sectoral macroeconomic model (Callonnec et al. 2013, 2016), the impact on the growth rate of different macro sectors, of a permanent increase of public investment. Based on this, we will give an assessment of public capital needs in different sectors of the French economy.

2.1. The Net Wealth of Public Administrations

In 2018, the consolidated public sector had a positive net wealth (Table 1). Total assets represented 148.5% of GDP, of which 89.9% for non-financial assets and 58.6% for financial assets. Financial liabilities totalled 135.7% of GDP. The net worth in 2017 was therefore 12.9% of GDP, around 4,500 euros per capita. (47,650 of debt and more than 52,000 of assets, including 31,600 non-financial assets).

Table 1 Decomposition of General Government Net Wealth

	As a % of GDP			In euros per head
	1978	*2007*	*2018*	*2018*
Non-financial assets	60.8	90.4	89.9	31592
Financial assets	62.7	52.6	58.6	20585
Financial liabilities	78.6	84.9	135.7	47654
Net worth	49.6	58.1	12.9	4523

Source of data: INSEE, authors' calculations.

While still positive, consolidated net wealth is today at an all-time low, a level that is mostly explained by the financial and economic crisis. Indeed, after reaching a record level in 2007 (58.1% of GDP), it has lost 45 points of GDP in the space of eleven years. The reasons for this sharp drop are to be found on the net financial liabilities (debt) side that increased substantially while non-financial assets remained broadly constant (Figure 2).

This net worth is unevenly distributed among different levels of government. Indeed, it is very positive for local administrations (62% of GDP in 2018), very negative for the central government (-63.9% of GDP) and slightly positive for social security administrations and other government agencies (7.7% and 7.4% respectively). Broadly speaking the central government, that runs recurrent public deficits, has accumulated public debt; low-debt local governments hold non-financial assets, be it land, buildings or civil engineering works. With the economic and financial crisis, from 2008 on, the net worth of the central government deteriorated considerably (it lost 44 points of GDP between 2007 and 2018), as public deficits and debt increased. On the other hand, the net worth of local governments remained high and relatively stable over the same period due to a stable value of non-financial assets and of their debt. This follows a decade (1998–2007) in which the value of non-financial assets increased by almost 30 percentage points of GDP, due to the sharp increase in land and real estate prices (mostly held by local governments), while debt remained constant.

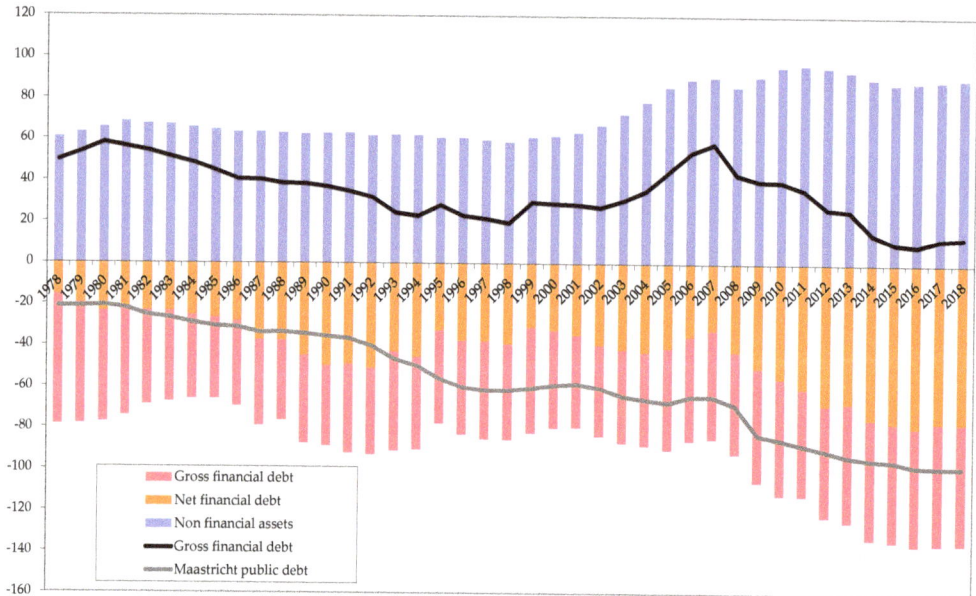

Fig. 2 Evolution of General Government Net Wealth as a percentage of GDP

Source of data: Insee. Figure created by the authors.

2.2. Evolution of Public Non-Financial Assets

In 2018 non-financial assets (NFAs) of the general government represented 61% of total assets and accounted for 90% of GDP. These can be further divided into fixed capital (produced NFAs), which are the result of past public investments, and land (non-produced NFAs).

Fixed assets account for 53% of GDP, mostly civil engineering works and non-residential buildings (43% of GDP). The remaining (10% of GDP) are public housing, machinery and equipment, weapons systems and intellectual property rights. Non-produced-NFAs account for 39% of total assets (37% of GDP) most of which (98%, or 36.2% total assets) are constituted of land owned by the general government. Unlike fixed assets, non-produced NFAs do not depreciate, and their evolution depends mainly on land prices.

From the late 1970s to the late 1990s, the value of public NFAs fluctuated, between 60% and 70% of GDP. Then, from 1998 to 2011, it increased by 38 points of GDP, reaching 96% of GDP in 2011. Over the past six years, this value has fallen by 7 points of GDP, and in 2018 its level was close to 2006. Most of the increase (around 90%) in the value of total NFAs can be attributed to the increase in the value of non-produced NFAs, that went from 8% of GDP in 1998 to almost 40% in 2011 (Figure 3). The large increase in valuation of non-produced NFAs is largely explained by the revaluation of built land prices, and not by an increase of volume (investment flows). There are a number of possible explanations for land price increases, which was by no means a

French phenomenon. A scarcity of undeveloped land, either because of insufficient supply or because it is subject to retention, tends to drive up its price (for details, see Levasseur 2013). The retention of land is due to several factors: increased retention in the ascendant phase of the cycle enhanced by the fact that in France there are no statistical databases which produce information on the non-built land (its location and the sale price previously recorded for land of equivalent quality), low cost of keeping undeveloped land, etc. Furthermore, price increases could be traced to the long-term agglomeration effects of economic agents trying to exploit positive externalities (as long as these are not more than compensated by congestion costs). Another structural reason is to be found in land use regulations (especially in urban areas), that empirical research has shown to play a major role in explaining rationing in the real estate and land market.

Besides these long-term trends, contingent factors such as expansionary monetary policies in the early 2000s, and the increase of private debt, probably played a role in explaining land price dynamics and the related increase in the valuation of non-produced NFAs.

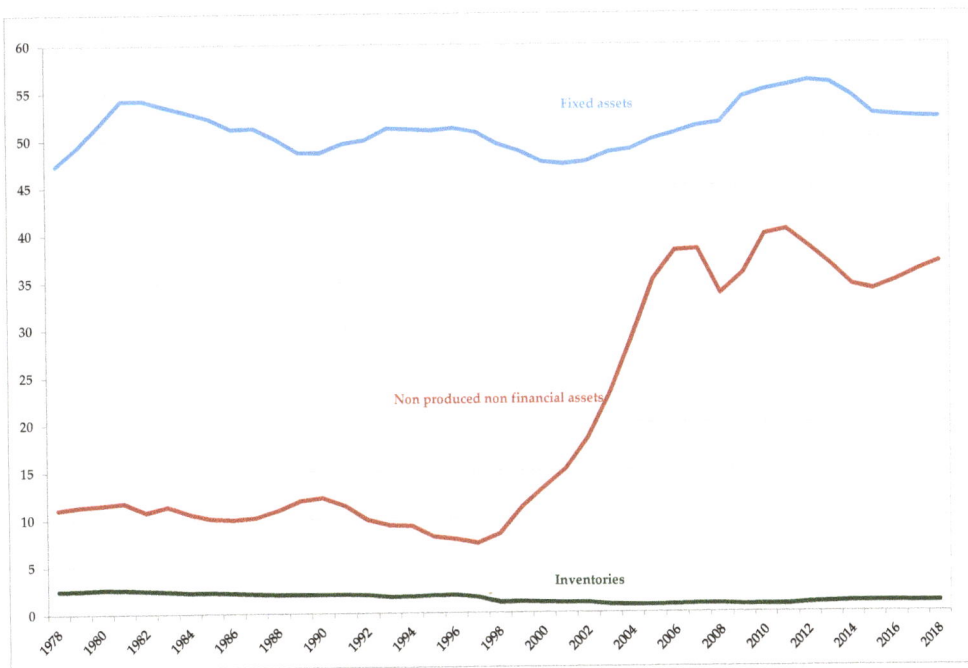

Fig. 3 Decomposition of public non-financial assets as a percentage of GDP

Source of data: Insee. Figure created by the authors.

2.2.1. The value of fixed assets remained constant

Fixed capital is given by the past accumulation of realized investments, net of depreciation. Between the end of the 1970s and 2018, the value of fixed assets held by the general government ranged from 47% to 53% of GDP, showing significantly lower volatility than the value of non-produced NFAs. This is because fixed assets experience much smaller price fluctuations than land. Between 1998 and 2018, the value of fixed assets grew by 2.7% of GDP, ten times less than the value increases of non-produced NFAs.

"Non-residential buildings" account for 28% of fixed assets (14% of GDP in 2018). These are buildings that are not intended for residential purposes, such as warehouses and industrial buildings, commercial buildings, performance halls, schools, hospitals, etc. The evolution of their value sees a decrease in the 1980s and 1990s (from 14% of GDP to 11% in 2000), then a steady increase until 2013 (to 16% of GDP). The last few years have seen a contraction, as for most other items, and in 2018 their value stands at 14% of GDP like in the early 1980s but their share in fixed assets is currently higher than before the crisis of 2008. It should be noted that around three quarters of these assets are owned by local governments.

Civil engineering works, other than non-residential buildings, account for more than half (54%) of fixed assets held by the general government. "Other civil engineering works," in the INSEE accounting classification, corresponds to everything but buildings. This category includes, for example, highways, roads, streets, railways, airfield runways, bridges, tunnels, waterways and water lines, ports, dams and other hydraulic works, communication and transmission of electricity, pipes and cables of urban networks; but also includes maintenance costs of roads, of sewerage systems and the works related to sites' clearing and preparation. Like non-residential buildings, the vast majority of "other civil engineering works" (76%) are owned by local governments. The evolution over time of this class of assets makes no exception. The stock of "other civil engineering works" in value peaked in 1982, approaching 30% of GDP; this period marks the end of the long catching up phase of the post-Second World War period. Subsequently, its value declined (while remaining relatively high) to fluctuate between 26% and 28% of GDP over the period 1985–2000. At the turn of 2000, the value of the stock of "other civil engineering works" increased steadily to a high point in 2012, at 30% of GDP. Since 2012, its value has declined significantly, to reach 28% of GDP in 2018 and its share in fixed assets currently represent 3 percentage points less than in 2007.

Since 1978 — but also since 2007 — it has been the non-residential buildings, and to a lesser extent the intellectual property rights, which have seen the major increase of their share in fixed assets. By contrast, the share of weapon systems and of civil engineering works has decreased (since 1978 and 2007 respectively).

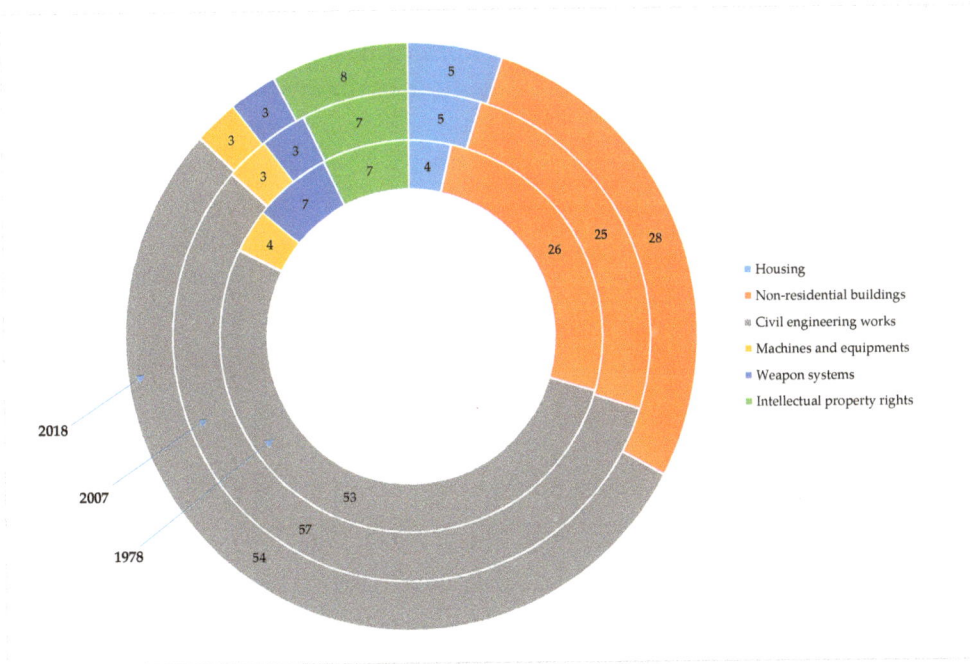

Fig. 4 Fixed assets by item (as a percentage of fixed assets) in 1978, 2007 and 2018

Source of data: Insee. Figure created by the authors.

2.3. The Dynamics of Gross Investment

The previous section showed a substantial stability of the public capital stock, whose dynamics for most categories followed the long cycles of economic activity. The only exceptions were non-produced NFAs, whose increase in value was mostly driven by land prices. Nevertheless, stock analysis only gives a partial picture: while non-produced NFAs account for 40% of the value of the total stock of capital, they account for less than 3% of NFA flows (i.e. gross public investment, in the terminology of national accounts). In fact, 97% of these flows are accounted for by fixed assets. And when we turn our attention to flows, valuation effects do not play any role.

As we said above, the flow of fixed assets, i.e. gross investment, has declined sharply since 2011. It has stood between 3.3% and 3.5% of GDP since 2015, its lowest level since the early 1950s. In 2018, 29% of general government gross investment consisted of "non-residential buildings", 29% of "other civil engineering works", 27% of "intellectual property rights" (of which 22% are research and development and 5% are software and databases), 7% are "machines and equipment," 3% are "weapon systems" and 2% is "housing".

Most of these items had similar dynamics over time, with peaks in the early 1990s, and since then either constant levels or a steady decline (especially since the global financial crisis). Two items nevertheless warrant further consideration. The first is investment in "intellectual property rights", of which more than 80% is research and development expenditure. It increased significantly during the 1980s, from 0.7% of GDP in 1980 to 1% in 1990. Over the past thirty years, it averaged 0.9% of GDP, the value it had in 2018. Finally, investment in "other civil engineering works" was high in the 1980s through to the early 1990s, ranging from 1.3% to 1.5% of GDP. From the mid-1990s to 2013, it has swayed between 1.1% and 1.3% of GDP. But, since 2014, it has shrunk leading to a historically low level in 2015–2018 (1% of GDP). Overall, except for intellectual property rights, all components of public investment are at historic lows and it is "civil engineering works" that have experienced the greatest decline.

2.4. Net Flows of Fixed Assets Give Another (and Different) Picture

The earlier description of investment (the fixed asset flow) by asset type captures gross investment. However, the most relevant measure must include capital depreciation. Indeed, considering the net flow of fixed assets (net investment) gives information on whether the stock of capital is expanding or shrinking, abstracting from the effects of revaluation of the existing stock. Thus, if gross investment is larger (smaller) than the depreciation of capital (consumption of fixed capital, CCF, in national accounts' nomenclature), then net investment is positive (negative) and the stock of capital increases (decreases). Unlike fixed assets, non-produced NFAs (land) and inventories may experience changes in value but are not subject to consumption of fixed capital. CCF only applies to fixed assets.

Historically, net flows of non-produced NFAs and inventories are relatively stable, with the sum of the two hovering between -0.1 and 0.2 % of GDP over the period 1979–2018. Changes in the net flow of non-financial assets are the result of the net flow of fixed assets. Over the period from the late 1970s to the first half of the 1990s, general government net investment was strong, averaging more than 1% of GDP per year (Figure 5). It even experienced a strong boom over the period 1987–1992, averaging above 1.4% of GDP per year. From 1993 to 1998, general government's net investment declined sharply, reaching 0.5% of GDP in 1998, a decrease of 1% of GDP in the space of six years. Like in other European countries, this is mostly due to the effort to meet the Maastricht criteria in the run up to the Euro: the cyclically adjusted deficit for France decreased from 4.6% of GDP in 1993 to 1.8% in 1998. Past this phase, net investment recovered, then fluctuated between 0.7 and 0.9 % of GDP over the 2000–2010 period, without ever returning to the level observed during the 1980s and the first half of the 1990s. But it is mainly from 2011, following the global financial crisis that net investment experiences a break. Between 2010 and 2015, it dropped from 0.7% of GDP to zero, and has since remained at a very low level (between 0 and 0.1% of GDP). It is the lowest level since the late 1970s when the wealth accounts were introduced.

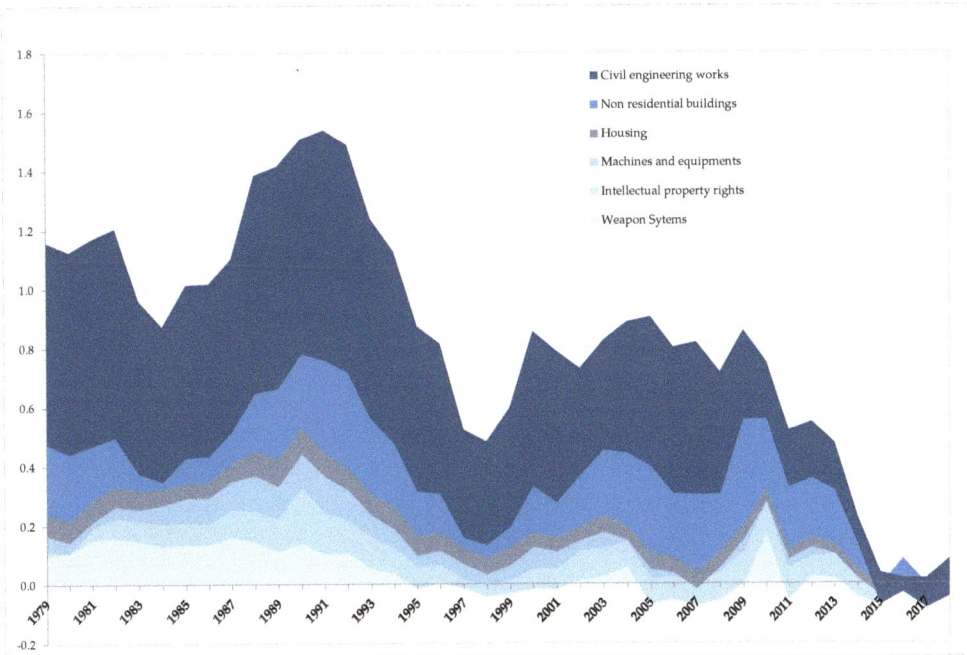

Fig. 5 Net General Government investment by component as a percentage of GDP

Source of data: Insee. Figure created by the authors.

Thus, since 2015, France has spent about 0.8 percentage points of GDP (about 19 billion in constant 2018 euros) less on net investment than it did during the period 2000–2010, and 1.5 points (approximately 35 billion in constant 2018 euros) less than during the period 1990–1992.

Looking at the components, the main determinants of the net investment dynamics described above are "other civil engineering works" and, to a lesser extent, "non-residential buildings". Net investment in "non-residential buildings" has gone through various cycles since the late 1970s; over the past decade has declined sharply (like most other government expenditures) and has reached historically low levels: since 2015 it has averaged -0.1% of GDP, meaning that since 2015 the stock of "non-residential buildings" decreased. Overall, "other civil engineering works" has been the main determinant of fluctuations in the net flow of fixed assets. For these investments we can distinguish three periods: the first — from the late 1970s to the first half of the 1990s — is characterized by a high level of net investment, close to or above 0.6% of GDP for almost every year and with peaks in 1991–1992 (0.8% of GDP). The second period — from 1995 to 2008 — is characterized by an intermediate level ranging from 0.4% to 0.5% of GDP per year. Finally, from 2010, net investment in "other civil engineering works" has constantly decreased, reaching 0.1% of GDP since 2014.

If we look at the evolution of net investment by level of government, we can learn four lessons. The first is that the net investment in "other civil engineering works" of Other Governments Agencies (OGA) is low and relatively stable over the period 1979–2015. Secondly, while the central government contributed positively, albeit weakly, to net investment, during the period ranging from 1987 to 1992, it gradually reduced its engagement. From 1995 to 2004, the investments made by the central government barely offset the depreciation of existing capital and, since 2005, the central government net investment has moved into negative territory, with the exception of 2010 (when, as a part of the stimulus plan following the 2008 Global Financial Crisis, significant investments in weapons systems were made). Thus, since 2005, the stock of fixed capital owned by the central government has decreased. It is in fact very clear, and this is the third remark, that local governments have historically been the main contributors to net government investment. However, since 2007 — on the one hand, with the Global Financial Crisis that reduced own resources levied by local governments, and, on the other hand, with the reduction of endowments to local governments that followed fiscal consolidation — net investment by local governments has collapsed from 0.8% of GDP in 2007 to 0% in 2016. In 2017 and 2018, it recovered slightly respectively to 0.1% and 0.2% of GDP, a level that barely offsets the destruction of capital by the central government and by social security administrations. Finally, social security administrations (SSA), that historically are not a major investor, but which posted a positive net investment over the period 1978–2014 (0.1% of GDP on average) have been destroying fixed capital for the past four years, with negative net investment for the first time in four decades.

The picture that emerges from the analysis of stocks and flows is rather consistent and gives two main messages: the first is that public investment and the stock of capital hve been largely affected by the macroeconomic cycle. In the two significant phases of consolidation, the run-up to the euro in the 1990s and the aftermath of the sovereign debt crisis, investment was strongly reduced. Especially in the latter case, net investment turned negative of zero for all levels of government, thus reducing the stock of capital that is today at an all-time low. The second message, that emerges in particular from the analysis of stocks, is that in spite of these trends in investment, the capital stock in France is still significant (and larger than in other countries, as the other chapters of the *Outlook* show). One might ask then if the effort of consolidation, and the disproportionate burden that it has laid on public investment, at least led to more sustainable public finances.

2.4.1. Since 2009, debt has not been used to finance an accumulation of assets

If we compare the evolution over the last twenty years of non-financial assets net flows in relation to the primary net financial flow (financial assets — financial liabilities — interest expenses) which we consider here as a proxy of the net worth, two sub-periods emerge clearly (Figure 6). The first, which runs from 1996 to 2008, can be seen as a period in which the additional public net financial debt (excluding interest expense) was more than offset by the net accumulation of non-financial assets, leading to a positive net value on this period, which means that the general government stock of wealth has increased in value over this period, even abstracting from price effects. The second period, which runs from 2009 to 2018, describes a new pattern in which the net debt increase is no longer offset by an increase in public non-financial capital, generating a sharp deterioration in government net worth. The economic and financial crisis led to a sharp increase in public debt. In 2011, France embarked on a process of fiscal consolidation: while on one side it has partly reduced new financial commitments, on the other side it has been more than offset by a reduction in the net accumulation of non-financial assets. This is further proof of the fact that the burden of fiscal consolidation was disproportionately laid on the shoulders of public investment. The sharp reduction in net worth therefore casts doubts on the effectiveness of fiscal consolidation in strengthening the public finances outlook for France.

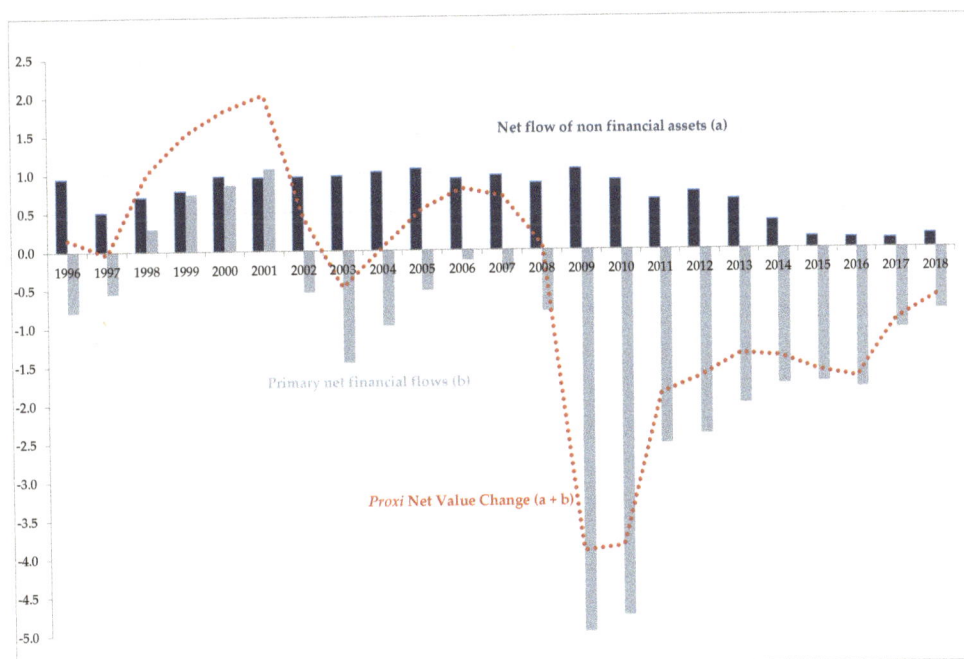

Fig. 6 Net flow of non-financial assets and primary net financial flows as a percentage of GDP

Source of data: Insee. Figure created by the authors.

2.5. Assessing the Impact of an Investment Push in France

2.5.1. A quantification of investment needs for France

According to a report of the French entrepreneurial association MEDEF (2015), which, as of today, represents the most comprehensive attempt to assess the French public capital gap, the network infrastructure needs for France would be €50 bn per year for five years, half of which would be financed by the general government, the rest being shared between public and private companies (Table 2).

Transportation is an important part of the network infrastructure, and its needs are estimated as €28 bn per year, almost two thirds of which are funded by the general government. More than half of that (€15 bn) would be absorbed by the extensive road network. The maintenance of the rail network and the construction of a high-speed line would represent €7 bn. The rest corresponds to infrastructures related to other public transportation: airports, ports and fluvial works.

Table 2 Network infrastructure needs per year for France for five years

General government: 25.1	Public companies: 13.8	Private companies: 11.2
Transports: 17.7	Transports: 8.1	Transports: 2.0
Water: 4.0	Energy: 5.7	Water: 5.0
Energy: 2.3		Digital: 2.0
Digital: 1.0		Gas: 2.2
Electric charging stations: 0.1		

Note: values in euro bn. *Source of data*: MEDEF (2015).

Power distribution networks are also high on the agenda, representing €8 bn, with funding from the public electric company (ERDF) and from the general government. These figures would take into account the introduction of Linky smart meters and the adaptation of the network-connected objects and new technologies.

A special effort should be made for water, estimated to cost €9 bn each year (funded in equal parts by the general government and private companies) according to the association "Canalisateurs de France". The maintenance of pipelines is particularly urgent: in France, more than 20% of the potable water introduced into the network is lost, causing an important economic cost. In total, notes the MEDEF, costs (economic, among others) of non-action could exceed those of investment.

Finally, the coverage of the entire French territory with ultra-high-speed internet would require €3 bn a year; in this case, two thirds of funding would have to come from private companies and one third from the general government.

The report numbers are most probably underestimated, as stated by the authors themselves, to the extent that they do not integrate the totality of the investments necessary to carry out the ecological transition or prevent natural or climatic hazards (rising waters, storms, floods etc.). Investment needs for the digital transition are also most probably underestimated. Thus, these figures are to be seen as a lower bound.

2.5.2. The macroeconomic impact of an investment shock

Based on the OFCE's Three-Me macro-sector model (OFCE 2016), we simulated a permanent increase of 1 point of GDP (approximately €23 bn) in public investment. This amount roughly corresponds to the infrastructure investment needs to be funded out of the general government, that have been put forward in the MEDEF report. Three-ME (Multi-sector Macroeconomic Model for the Evaluation of Environmental and Energy policy) is a macroeconomic model. It has been built on a calibration of the French economy. Its main purpose is to evaluate the medium- and long-term impact of public choices on the economy at the macroeconomic and sectoral levels. Three-Me exhibits the main features of neo-Keynesian models: a slow adjustment of effective quantities and prices to their notional level; an endogenous money supply; a Taylor rule and a Phillips curve. Compared to standard multi-sector CGEs, this has the advantage to allow for the existence of suboptimal equilibria, characterized by the presence of involuntary unemployment. Furthermore, production and consumption structures are represented with a generalized CES function which allows for the elasticity of substitution to differ between each couple of inputs or goods.

In the medium term, i.e. over a five-year horizon, an increase in public investment of 1% of GDP would generate a gain of 1.2% of GDP (a value of the multiplier that is in the same ball park as the consensus in the literature, see Gechert's 2015 meta-analyis) and would create or safeguard 290,000 jobs (Table 3); this would reduce the unemployment rate in France by 1 point.

Table 3 Impact of a 1% of GDP increase in public investment on GDP
and employment in France

	1 year	2 years	3 years	4 years	5 years
GDP	0.9	1.0	1.1	1.2	1.2
Value Added	0.9	1.0	1.1	1.1	1.1
Employment (in '000s)	120.5	213.7	269.4	290.8	286.5

Source of data: Modèle Three-Me, OFCE.

Quite logically, the first sector to benefit from an increase in public investment would be construction, with 46% of the jobs created (Table 4). The increase in activity in that sector would also have a crowding-in effect on all other sectors that are experiencing an increase in their added value and job creation. Note that these effects are particularly pronounced in sectors with low import content and little chances of delocalization (construction and services).

Table 4 Sectoral impact of a 1% of GDP increase in public investment

	Domestic employment (in full-time equivalents)		Added value (in %, volume)	
	1 year	**5 years**	**1 year**	**5 years**
Agriculture, forestry and fishing	+ 760	+ 1 010	+ 0.3	+ 0.3
Manufacture of food products, beverages and tobacco	+ 530	+ 2 480	+ 0.2	+ 0.5
Other manufacturing	+ 12 970	+21 480	+ 0.9	+ 0.7
Construction	+ 63 500	+132 180	+ 7,5	+ 7.8
Transport	+ 2 000	+ 1 960	+ 0.3	+ 0.2
Mainly market services	+ 40 430	+ 106 050	+ 0.6	+ 0.9

Source of data: Modèle Three-Me, OFCE.

2.6 Conclusion

This chapter showed that France did not escape the recent trend of most European countries, towards a drastic downsizing of its public capital stock. In spite of the rhetoric of the time, national accounts data show that the 2008 Global Financial Crisis was not countered with a public investment push: the sharp increase of debt between 2007 and 2017 did not correspond to an accumulation of public capital. On the contrary, investment paid the heaviest toll in the subsequent consolidation phase, when both expenditure reduction by the central government, and cuts in transfers to local administrations (the largest owner of non-financial assets) resulted in a significant loss of public capital. Thus, in the space of a decade, the French general government saw its net investment drop to negative levels, and its net worth decrease by 50 points of GDP, to an all-time low in 2018. An even greater source of concern is that the previous increase of the net worth, in the years 2000s, is mostly attributed to a price effect of non-produced non-financial assets (land and real estate).

Investment needs in network infrastructure are important (transport, energy, water, digital etc.) and public investment deficiencies of course have important macroeconomic consequences both in the short and in the long run. We highlighted the results from OFCE (2016) that state how a 1% public investment push would have important growth effects (with a multiplier above 1) in the short and medium run. Yet, it is in the long run that the multiplier associated with public investment is larger than the overall expenditure multiplier. Stabilizing the flow of investment is crucial to maintain a public capital stock that is a necessary complement to private investment (Creel et al. 2015).

The European institutional setting has played a role in the widespread reduction of investment expenditure. The exclusive focus on structural deficit built into European rules has introduced a strong bias against capital spending, since investment is easier to cut than current expenditure. We documented how, already in the run up to the introduction of the euro, in the 1990s, the drop of structural government deficit in France went through a drastic cut of net investment. The same happened in the past decade. The bias against public investment leads to a chronic deficiency of public capital, barely compensated by government action in good times.

Thus, France makes no exception to the general trend documented in this Report, even if in levels its capital stock remains relatively high with respect to its partners. This leads to an obvious conclusion: the introduction of a Golden Rule excluding public investment from the deficit limits, similar to the one implemented in the UK by Chancellor of the Exchequer Gordon Brown in the 1990s (for details, see Creel et al., 2009), would certainly help fill the investment gap. The new rule would require countries to balance their current budget, while financing public capital accumulation with debt. Investment expenditure, in other words, would be excluded from deficit calculation, a principle that timidly emerges also in the current Commission practices. Such a rule would stabilize the ratio of debt to GDP, it would focus efforts of public consolidation on less productive items of public spending, and would ensure intergenerational equity (future generations would be called to partially finance the stock of public capital bequeathed to them). Last, but not least, especially in the current situation, putting in place such a rule would not require treaty changes, and it is already discussed, albeit timidly, in EU policy circles. Furthermore, a broad definition of investment would allow to coordinate the policies of Member States towards growth enhancing items, and could even be an important piece of a renewed European industrial policy (Saraceno 2017, Ducoudré et al. 2019).

The current environment of low interest rates, that is bound to persist into the medium term (Summers 2014) is an additional reason to try to fill the public investment gap that was progressively dug in the past decades. In a recent issue of the World Economic Outlook, the International Monetary Fund (IMF 2014) went as far as defining a public investment boost, in the current environment of scarce public capital and low interest rates, as self-financing (a 'free lunch').

Furthermore, the preceding pages show the importance of properly measuring capital. Thus, it seems increasingly crucial to be able to distinguish, within the balance sheet, between the capital account and the operating account (in which it seems sensible to add a structural/cyclical division), to understand the past dynamics of debt and its use. We are pursuing this work.

References

Callonnec, G., G. Landa, P. Malliet, F. Reynès and Y. Yeddir-Tamsamani (2013) "A Full Description of the Three-ME Model: Multi-Sector Macroeconomic Model for the Evaluation of Environmental and Energy Policy". OFCE Working Paper Report, https://www.ofce.sciences-po.fr/pdf/documents/threeme/doc1.pdf

Callonnec, G., G. Landa Rivera, P. Malliet, F. Reyns and A. Saussay (2016) "Les propriétés dynamiques et de long terme du modèle Three-ME: Un cahier de variantes", *Revue de l'OFCE* 149(5): 47–99, https://doi.org/10.3917/reof.149.0047

Creel, J., P. Hubert and F. Saraceno (2015) "Une analyse empirique du lien entre investissement public et privé", *Revue de l'OFCE* 144(8): 331–56, https://doi.org/10.3917/reof.144.0331

Creel, J., P. Monperrus-Veroni and F. Saraceno (2009) "Fiscal Policy Is Back in France and the United Kingdom!", *Journal of Post Keynesian Economics* 31(4): 645–67, https://doi.org/10.2753/pke0160-3477310407

Ducoudré, B., M. Plane, X. Ragot, R. Sampognaro, F. Saraceno and X. Timbeau (2019) "Refonte Des Règles Budgétaires Européennes", *Revue de l'OFCE* 158(4): 307–30, https://doi.org/10.3917/reof.158.0307

Gechert, S. (2015) "What Fiscal Policy Is Most Effective? A Meta-Regression Analysis", *Oxford Economic Papers* 67(3): 553–80, https://doi.org/10.1093/oep/gpv027

IMF (2014) "Legacies, Clouds, Uncertainties", *World Economic Outlook*, October, https://www.imf.org/en/Publications/WEO/Issues/2016/12/31/Legacies-Clouds-Uncertainties

Levasseur, S. (2013) " Éléments de réflexion sur le foncier et sa contribution au prix de l'immobilier", *Revue de l'OFCE* 128(2): 365–94, https://doi.org/10.3917/reof.128.0365

MEDEF (2015) "Les infrastructures de réseau au service de la croissance". Report by MEDEF, December, https://www.fntp.fr/sites/default/files/content/publication/vf_rapport_infrastructures_-_25_11_15.pdf

OFCE (2016) "Investissement public, capital public et croissance". Report edited by X. Ragot and F. Saraceno, https://www.ofce.sciences-po.fr/pdf-articles/actu/Rapport-FNTP-01-12.pdf

Saraceno, F. (2017) "When Keynes Goes to Brussels: A New Fiscal Rule for the EMU?", *Annals of the Fondazione Luigi Einaudi* 51(2): 131–58.

Summers, L. H. (2014) "U.S. Economic Prospects: Secular Stagnation, Hysteresis, and the Zero Lower Bound", *Business Economics* 49(2): 65–73, https://doi.org/10.1057/be.2014.13

3. Public Investment in Germany

The Need for a Big Push

Sebastian Dullien,[1] Ekaterina Jürgens[2]
and Sebastian Watzka[3]

Introduction

For a number of years, Germany has been at the centre of the European debate about increasing public investment. With record-large current account surpluses, increasing public investment in Germany has often been seen as a possible remedy to imbalances in the euro area (OECD 2016; IMF 2018). Within Germany, the debate has focused on insufficiencies of the public capital stock and especially public infrastructure and has intensified over time (Expertenkommission 2015; Bardt et al. 2019), with the federation of German trade unions (DGB) and the federation of German industries (BDI) jointly endorsing a big, debt-financed, ten-year investment programme in November 2019.

This chapter takes a closer look at public investment in Germany. It first describes the development of German public investment and the German public capital stock over the past decades (section 3.1.), then defines quantitatively and qualitatively needs for public investment (section 3.2.) and gives a first model-based evaluation on the economic effects of a debt-financed, ten-year €450 bn public investment programme (section 3.3.) both on the German economy and on other euro area countries.

3.1. The German Public Capital Stock

After the unification boom at the beginning of the 1990s, public investment in Germany has steadily declined. Net public investment (gross public investment minus depreciations) dropped from almost 1% of GDP in the early 1990s to around 0.2% of

---

1   Hochschule für Technik und Wirtschaft — HTW Berlin; Institut für Makroökonomie und Konjunkturforschung — IMK.

2   Institut für Makroökonomie und Konjunkturforschung — IMK.

3   Institut für Makroökonomie und Konjunkturforschung — IMK.

https://doi.org/10.11647/OBP.0222.03

GDP towards the end of the decade and turned negative in 2004. Since then, it has been hovering around zero (Figure 1). As a consequence, while Germany's population and GDP have still been growing, its public capital stock net of depreciation has been stagnating for the past two decades (Figure 2), resulting in a falling ratio of public capital stock to GDP. Lately, increases in public investment spending have led to a slight increase in the net investment-to-GDP ratio, but the increase has been too small to stop the declining trend in the public capital stock to GDP.[4]

The stagnation of the public capital stock has become a problem for the economy at large. While the large bulk of overall investment takes place in the private sector, government investment plays a decisive role. Government investment provides important public goods and is often complementary in private production and investment. State-owned infrastructure, such as transport networks and energy grids, is a crucial factor affecting potential output and productivity growth (Baxter and King 1993; Clemens, Goerge and Michelsen 2019).[5] It is hence plausible that the weakness in private sector fixed capital formation in Germany is at least partly a consequence of insufficient public investment.

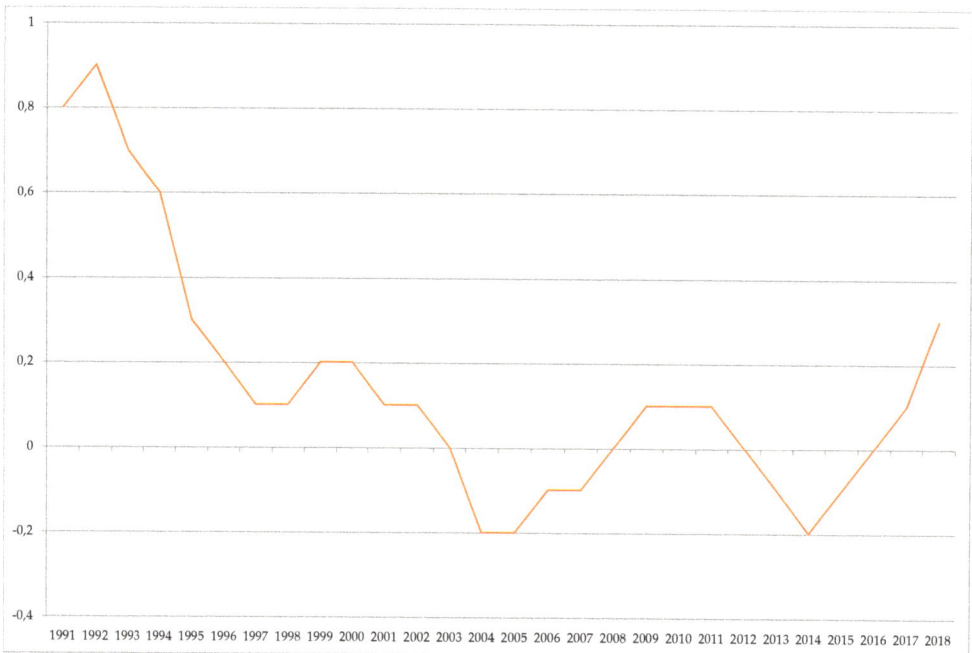

Fig. 1 Net public investment in Germany, in percentage of GDP, 1991–2018

Source of data: Destatis 2019. Figure created by the authors.

---

4   Given reasonable assumptions about the trend growth of German GDP, net public investment of 0.6 % of GDP are necessary to keep the public capital stock-to-GDP ratio constant. See Dullien (2017).

5   Clemens, Goerge and Michelsen (2017) find that 1 bn euro of public investment in Germany will increase private investment by around 1.1 bn euro after around five years.

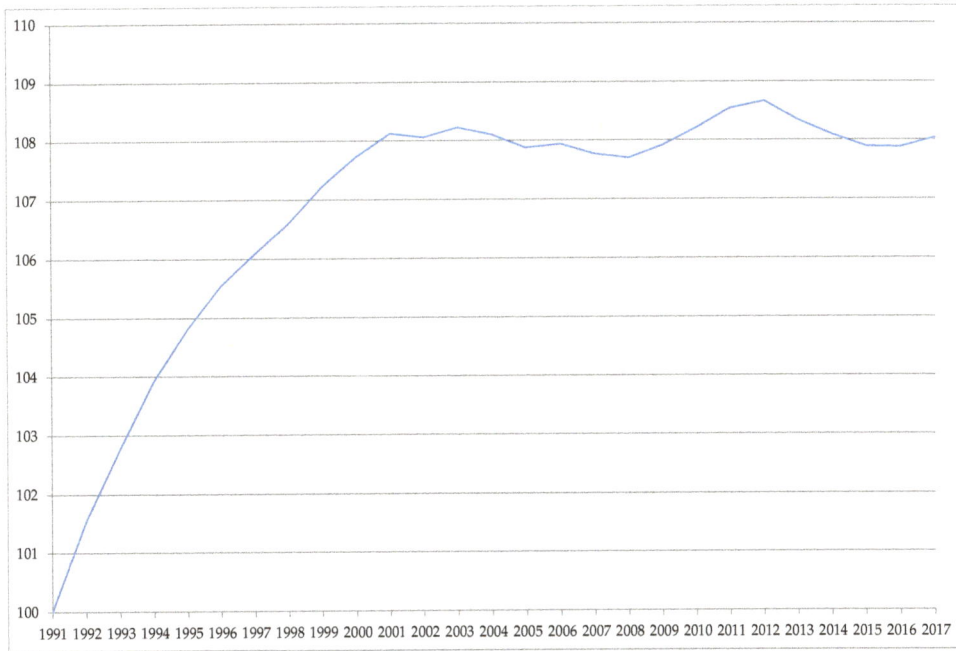

Fig. 2 Net capital stock in Germany from 1991–2018, in constant prices (index, 1991 = 100)

Source of data: Destatis 2018. Figure created by the authors.

In particular, transport infrastructure is a fundamental factor for economic growth. Insufficiently maintained and expanded, it can lead to delays in passenger and goods transport. In the case of Germany, while the gross stock of publicly owned structures (a large part of which is transport infrastructure) has only marginally grown since the beginning of the decade, passenger as well as freight vehicle and railway traffic expanded considerably, both in absolute and per-capita terms (Figure 3). For example, the overall freight mileage on German roads increased by 16.6% between 2010 and 2017, while the economy grew by only 13.7%.[6] Moreover, this data probably even underestimates the degree of underinvestment, as the gross capital stock concept ignores the wear and tear of the roads and bridges.

For evaluating the quality of German infrastructure, it is important to keep in mind that vast parts of it were built during the major construction programs in the 1970's in the West and in the 1990's in the East. For example, almost half of all motorway bridges (measured by surface area) were built between 1965 and 1975 (Bundesministerium für Verkehr und digitale Infrastruktur 2016, p. 2). Those bridges were not designed to carry today's heavy traffic and would require a complete overhaul even if they had been properly maintained over the last decades (which often has not been the case).

---

6   One reason for the disproportional increase for transport services has been the eastward expansion of the European Union and Germany's central geographical location within the EU.

All in all, expanding traffic volumes are pushed through an outdated transport infrastructure of deficient quality. This is also felt by the German business sector: in a recent survey, two thirds of German companies stated that their business was regularly hindered by deficiencies in the public infrastructure, especially by unsatisfactory traffic conditions (Grömling and Puls 2018).

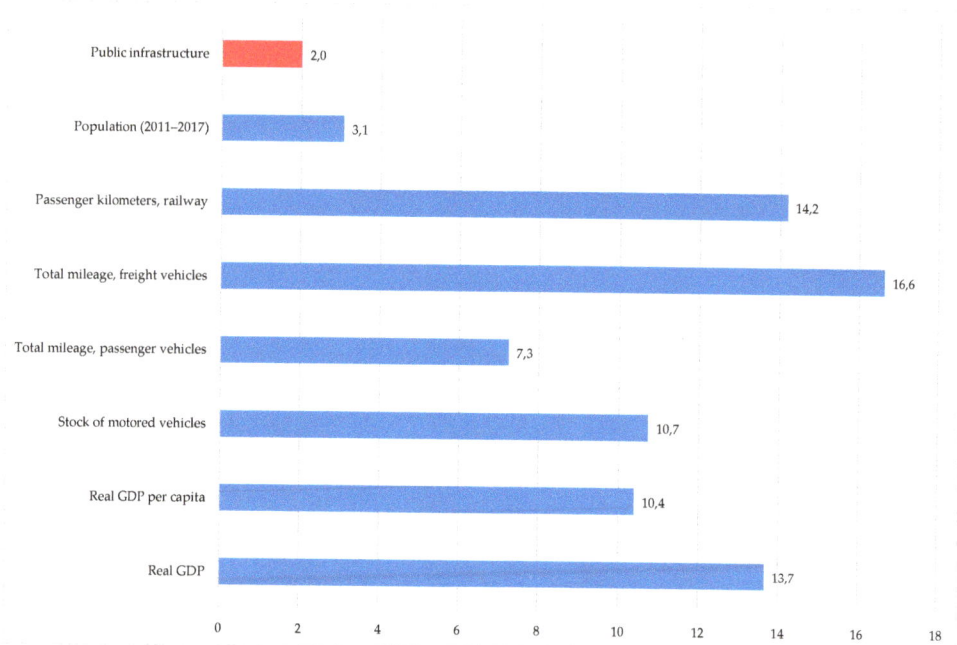

Fig. 3 Development of various economic indicators in Germany, percentage change 2010–2017
Source of data: Dullien and Rietzler (2019). Figure created by the authors.

The poor development of the German public investment of the last decades can be traced back to several, partly interlinked causes (Bardt et al. 2019).

First, from a politician's point of view, cutting infrastructure investment has the advantage that citizens usually only become aware of the infrastructure deterioration with a delay. So, especially when confronted with the need of cutting public deficits, investment cutbacks can become a preferred choice and might therefore be implemented before taxes are raised or other government expenditure is cut.

Second, economists and officials for a long time assumed an imminent decline in Germany's working population and potential GDP growth rate, which did not materialize. A smaller economy would have needed a smaller capital stock, and debt dynamics would have been more toxic under more pessimistic growth assumptions. As a consequence, third, the so-called debt brake ("Schuldenbremse") was written into the German constitution which limits structural public sector deficits to 0.35% of GDP, replacing the former Golden Rule of public finance which allowed the government to borrow for investment purposes.

Fourth, welfare reforms shifted the fiscal burden of unemployment towards the municipalities. As in Germany, the municipal level is in charge of maintaining a large part of road infrastructure, public transport, schools and other local infrastructure, this further squeezed out public investment. This trend has been aggravated by the fact that the *Länder* (the federal states) had to move towards balanced budgets under the debt brake and have hence cut their respective transfers to the municipalities' budgets.

In a nutshell, due to fiscal consolidation pressure, investment in public infrastructure has been greatly neglected in Germany in recent decades. This has resulted in the deterioration and depletion of Germany's public capital stock that does not anymore meet the requirements of a modern economy.

3.2. Quantifying Investment Needs

In addition to the gradual closing of the accumulated infrastructure gap, imminent challenges for the German economy require massive additional investments. Decarbonization in accordance with the Climate Action Plan 2050 will need additional spending on the expansion of renewables, modernization of the energy and transport networks, as well as making existing residential buildings more energy-efficient. To cushion demographic change, it is necessary to invest more in early childhood education and care. Early childhood education increases people's chances of a productive participation in the economy later in life, while childcare makes it possible to boost the current labour force participation by enabling both parents to work.

In what follows, we outline the rough estimation of the magnitude of the required public investment in Germany in the upcoming decade, adopted from Bardt et al. (2019). The term "investment" is used here in a broad sense, so that it also includes government measures to promote private investment (such as subsidies for energy-efficient building refurbishment) or spending on human capital development, which is not accounted for as public investment in the national accounts. The concept of public investment is thus defined as government expenditures capable of increasing the production potential of the German economy in the future or of generating long-term net returns to the economy as a whole. As the counterfactual scenario, we assume a price-adjusted continuation of the investment positions listed in the government budget 2019.

Indeed, every attempt of such a comprehensive calculation is vulnerable to critique. For example, one can argue that suggested figures in specific areas are too high or too low. However, our estimations are based on well-founded studies of individual sectors and, most important, the goal of this exercise is only to deliver a convincing first idea of the rough monetary size of the overall economic challenge to be addressed.

For a ten-year horizon, our estimate of the investment requirements in Germany (based on Bardt et al. 2019) includes:

- Repair and modernization of public infrastructure: the municipal panel of the public KfW bank states an investment need of €138.4 bn (Kreditanstalt für Wiederaufbau 2019). For this paper, it is assumed that the infrastructure gap should be closed within ten years.

- Significant expansion of early childhood education and full-day schooling is desirable and economically efficient from a demographic point of view. Over ten years, the necessary investment adds up to €50 bn for the improvement of early childhood education, as well as €9 bn for the construction and €25.5 bn for the operation of full-day schools (Krebs and Scheffel 2019).

- Expansion of the local public transport is necessary to enable decarbonization. Currently, infrastructure projects of around €8.2 bn have been registered or accepted for financing via the Municipal Transport Financing Act (Gemeindeverkehrsfinanzierungsgesetz — GVFG). If investment were to be financed from existing funds provided under the GVFG, it would take twenty-four years to complete these projects. In order to ensure their finalization within the next decade, larger funds are required. According to surveys among providers of local public transport, €15 bn are needed here (Verband Deutscher Verkehrsunternehmen 2017). All in all, investment needs sum up to approximately €20 bn in this sector.

- The long-distance and freight services of the German railway (Deutsche Bahn) also require a massive modernization and capacity expansions. The necessary investment adds up to €60 bn. In addition, an expenditure of approximately €20 bn is needed for the maintenance and refurbishment of German highways.

- In comparison to other rich countries, Germany lags behind in both financing of universities and promotion of research and development. Overall, additional expenditure of €2.5 bn per year should be budgeted to modernize universities and strengthen research funding.

- There is currently a housing shortage in many large German cities. Yet, estimates for the demand for residential dwellings in the coming years differ. Ralph Henger and Michael Voigtländer (2019) expect that, due to the current construction activity, the housing market will gradually relax. However, Till Baldenius, Sebastian Kohl and Moritz Schularick (2019) conclude that the lack of housing will continue until 2030, especially in metropolitan areas. Either way, at least €1.5 bn per year are needed as additional public incentive for housing construction.

- In Germany, the telecommunication network coverage is poor by international standards, particularly outside big cities. A country-wide expansion of broadband internet would cost 60 to €100 bn (Expertenkommission 2015), a

5G network expansion some €60 bn more. Much of these expenses are likely to come from private telecom operators. Still, public funding is crucial to mend the patches in digital infrastructure. We assume that a government spending of €20 bn will be necessary in the coming ten years.

- The decarbonization of the German economy poses a particular challenge. Current studies show that, in sum, between €1700 bn (Dena 2018) and €2300 bn (Gerbert and others 2018) will be required to reduce the German economy's carbon emissions by 95% until 2050. If one takes the lower limit of the estimated cost and distributes the total expenditure over the entire period up to 2050, further assuming that the state bears approximately 15% of the costs, then a public investment need of approximately €7.5 bn per year results.

Table 1 summarizes the above calculation. All in all, public investment needs sum up to a volume of at least €450 bn over the next ten years. The required financing is thus not excessively large in relation to the German economic output. Spread over the years, this would average an annual additional expenditure of around €45 bn, which corresponds to approximately to 1.3% of GDP.

There is no good economic reason why the type of investments listed above should be paid from the current year's budget. On the contrary, as the investments benefit many generations to come, it is reasonable to spread also the cost over several generations. For example, decarbonization will lead to a massive reduction in Germany's energy import bill. Today's expenditure will thus be offset by saved costs in the future. Similarly, improvements in early childhood education today are expected to translate into higher employment, higher productivity and higher incomes in the future.

Moreover, current financing conditions for Germany are extremely favourable, such that long-term bond (with maturity of at least ten years) yields are negative. In other words, Germany would not have to pay back the full amount of debts taken on today. At the same time, the German government debt-to-GDP ratio has been steadily decreasing in the recent years and is about to fall below the 60% benchmark. Combined with the long-term productivity effects of the above described public investment, it is advisable to enable debt-financing of the investment program. It would be inefficient and unfair to burden the current generation with the entire cost of the restructuring of the economy. Much worse, it would be greatly dangerous to forgo current and future opportunities because of fear of an increase in public borrowing.

The actual fiscal policy framework — including the debt brake, the Stability and Growth Pact and the Fiscal Compact — should therefore be used (and, if necessary, modified) in a way that the financing of investment requirements becomes possible through new borrowing. From the economic point of view, it makes sense to follow a Golden Rule which exempts investment — at least up to a fixed amount — from the deficit limit, as in Truger (2016).

Table 1 Public investment requirements in Germany

	Sum over 10 years, base year prices (bn €)
Infrastructure investment on municipal level	
Updating of existing local infrastructure	138
Public transport	20
Education	
Early childhood education	50
Development of full-day schooling	9
Operation of full-day schooling	25
Funding of universities and R&D	25
Housing investment	
Public sector share	15
Interregional infrastructure	
Broadband internet/5G	20
Railway	60
Highways	20
Decarbonization	
Public sector share	75
Total	**457**

Source of data: Bardt et al. (2019).

There are two possibilities for the technical implementation of such a Golden Rule. Firstly, it would be conceivable to change the German constitution. Secondly, one could use the room for flexibility built in the debt brake so that debt financing of new investment becomes feasible. For example, a separate legal entity (fully owned by the federal government) could be established as a federal investment fund for development goals, responsible of precisely defined investment tasks. This entity could be allowed to borrow while its debt is not counted under the German debt brake. The local authorities could then lease the corresponding capital goods from this fund against payment of the financing costs and depreciation. In this way, an amendment of the constitution would not be necessary.

The European budget rules would count such an entity to the public sector, but since Germany's public debt is expected to fall under the 60% benchmark, the usual fiscal rules will be relaxed, so that the limit for the medium-term structural deficit rises from 0.5% to 1% of GDP. Moreover, Germany could (and should) lobby at the European level for an exemption from new borrowing for certain types of growth enhancing green investment.

3.3. Macroeconomic Implications of a Public Investment Program in Germany

It is important to consider the potential macroeconomic effects of such a large investment program for Germany, and its spillover effects for the rest of the euro area. In this section, we use a modified version of the NiGEM model developed by the National Institute of Economic and Social Research (NIESR)[7] to come up with some first evaluations.

In line with current market-based EONIA forecasts (European Central Bank 2019), our baseline forecast assumes that the ECB's monetary policy stance will remain accommodative for a prolonged period of time. Specifically, we assume ECB interest rates to remain zero well into the 2020s and thereafter slowly rise to 1%. From a fiscal policy perspective, our baseline forecast fully adheres to the German debt brake, so that budget deficits are ruled out. This restriction is removed for the shock scenario.

The scenario for our proposed €450 bn debt-financed public investment program is modelled as follows: quarterly public investment is assumed to be €11.25 bn (about 1.5% of GDP) higher vis-à-vis our baseline forecast starting in the first quarter of 2020 and remaining so over a period of ten years. Importantly, we model this additional public spending as entirely debt-financed. In addition, we assume the ECB's policy rate to remain constant at the baseline rate.

The government investment program triggers an increase in accumulation of both public and private capital. The capital build-up acceleration peaks at the end of the investment program with the overall capital stock being 4% higher than in the baseline.

The simulated investment program results in a significant boost to the German economy with GDP initially increasing slightly above 1% vis-à-vis the baseline and about 0.9% (again vis-à-vis the baseline) on average during the public investment program span (Figure 4). Importantly, GDP remains persistently higher, also after the end of the investment program. Due to the increased overall capital stock, potential output increases and remains sustainably higher even beyond 2029, reaching a level of about 1.5% above the baseline in 2029.

As mentioned above, the investment program is assumed to be completely debt-financed with tax rates kept constant. The evolution of the government debt ratio under the debt-financed public investment program together with the debt ratio of our baseline forecast is shown in Figure 5. Relative to the baseline, the reduction of the debt-to-GDP ratio slows significantly. However, despite the additional borrowing, the ratio continues to fall and constantly stays on the modest level of just above 50%

---

7   NiGEM is a comprehensive multi-country simulation and forecasting model for the global economy with detailed country models for all OECD countries as well as numerous emerging nations. See also nimodel.niesr.ac.uk/. We use a slightly modified version with re-estimated import equations for Germany, France, Italy and Spain (see Behrend et al. 2019).

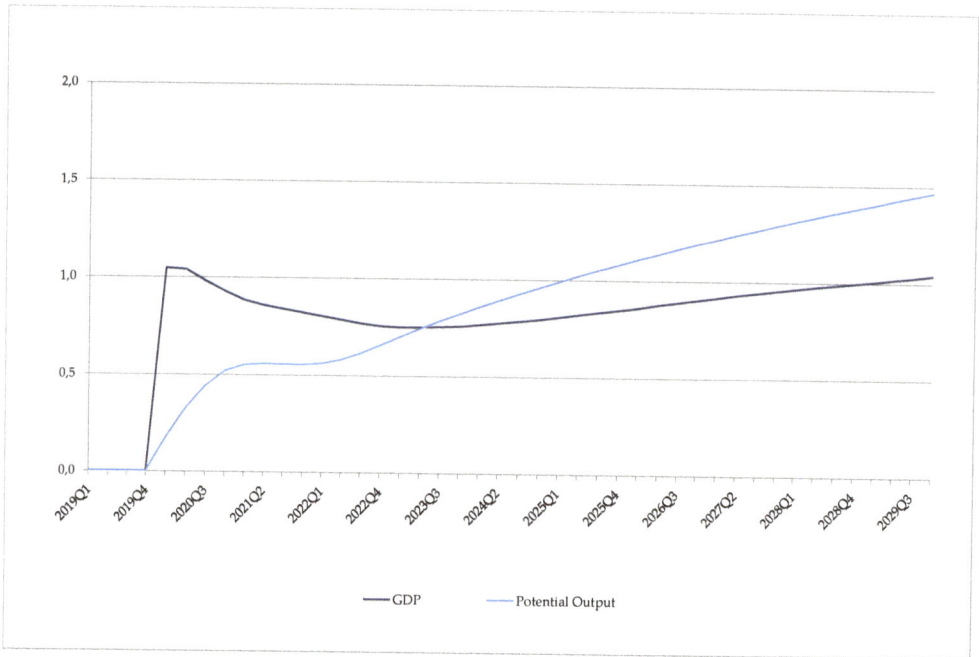

Fig. 4 German GDP and potential output increase, level difference in %

Source of data: NiGEM. Figure created by the authors.

of GDP (Figure 5). Hence, the simulation shows that it is possible to implement a comprehensive public investment program without jeopardizing debt sustainability.

Another important result of our simulation is that the program in fact leads to a reduction in the German current account surplus which falls by almost 1.3 percentage points. The rebalancing is possible through a stark increase in imports, whereas exports essentially remain unchanged.

Last but not least, the investment expenditure triggers positive spillover effects on other euro countries. The main beneficiaries of the German fiscal expansion seem to be the nearest small open economies, such as Belgium, Netherlands and Austria (Figure 6). These countries experience a substantial boost to GDP which increases by 0.2 to 0.45% vis-à-vis baseline GDP over the duration of the investment program. GDP in the euro area in total will be positively affected by around 0.4%, again vis-à-vis the baseline.

All in all, the proposed debt-financed public investment plan has the potential to bring about substantial and continuous boost to economic activity in Germany, stimulating domestic demand in the short run and increasing the country's public and private capital stock in the long run. In addition, our results indicate that such an investment program would considerably rebalance the German current account bringing it in line with levels agreed on under the European Commission's Macroeconomic Imbalance Procedure. Moreover, positive spillover effects are likely to

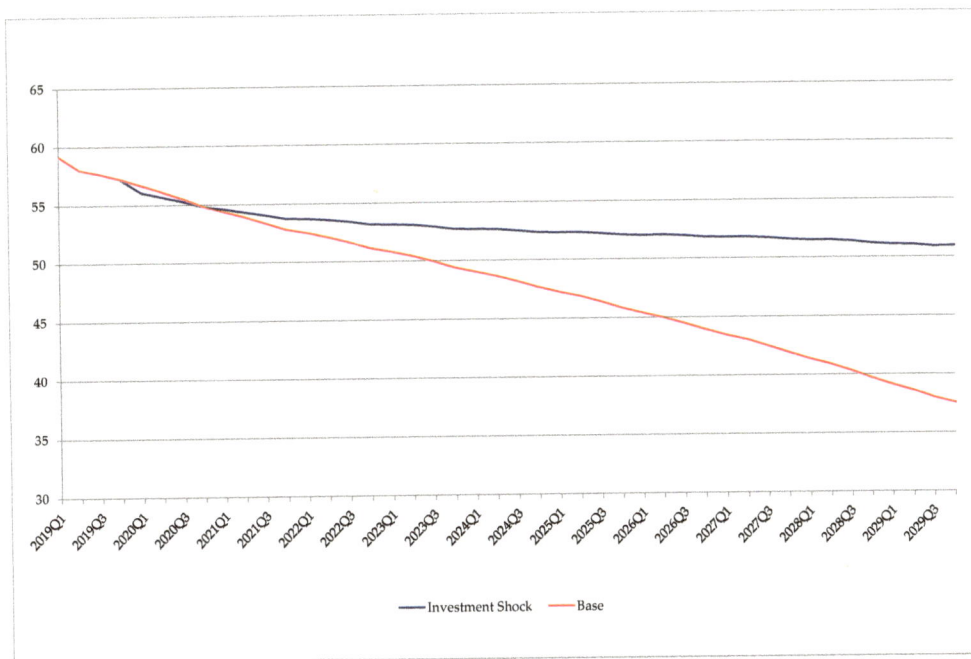

Fig. 5 Government debt, in percentage of GDP

Source of data: NiGEM. Figure created by the authors.

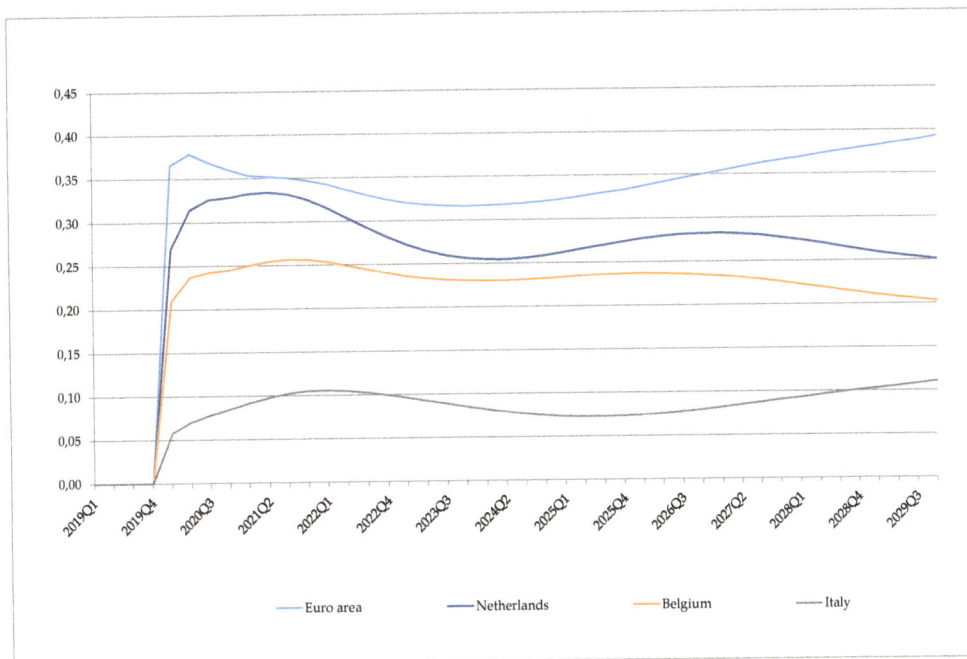

Fig. 6 GDP of selected countries and euro area, deviation from baseline, level difference in percent

Source of data: NiGEM. Figure created by the authors.

follow in the rest of the euro area. Crucially, the investment program does not have to impede the soundness of the German public finance.

Conclusion

This chapter has argued that the stagnating German public capital stock poses significant risks for future economic growth of the country. Various indicators point at severe and persistent underinvestment, a significant part of which can be traced back to lack of funding. Additional investment needs have been estimated to be roughly €450 bn over the coming decade. As simulations show, such a program could be entirely debt-financed while keeping the German debt-to-GDP ratio below the Maastricht threshold of 60% of GDP. Moreover, it would significantly lift both German potential and actual GDP. It would also contribute to bring Germany's current account surplus from its currently very high levels of 7–8% to below 4%, bringing it in line with the levels set by the European Commission's Macroeconomic Imbalances Procedures. Whilst the spillover effect to other European economies would be limited, they will nevertheless be felt positively and might even be reinforced if other European governments follow the German example and also start modernizing their public capital stocks.

A potential obstacle might be existing fiscal rules such as the German debt brake, but at least for a significant part of the investments needed, technical solutions such as public entities devoted to investments could allow some sort of debt-financing. Beyond what is possible under current fiscal rules, a reform of the legal framework should be considered, given that it has been designed under the assumption of persistently much higher interest rates compared to what we have been observing in the past years, and given that sticking to current fiscal rules while neglecting much needed public investment might carry high welfare costs.

References

Baldenius, T., S. Kohl and M. Schularick (2019) *Die neue Wohnungsfrage: Gewinner und Verlierer des deutschen Immobilienbooms.* Bonn: Macrofinance Lab, https://pure.mpg.de/rest/items/item_3070687_1/component/file_3070688/content

Bardt, H., S. Dullien, M. Hüther and K. Rietzler (2019) "Für eine solide Finanzpolitik: Investitionen ermöglichen!", *IMK-Report* 152.

Baxter, M. and R. G. King (1993) "Fiscal Policy in General Equilibrium", *American Economic Review*, 83(3): 315–34.

Behrend, A., K. Gehr, C. Paetz, T. Theobald and S. Watzka (2019) *Europa kann es besser: Wirtschaftspolitische Szenarien für stabileres Wachstum und mehr Wohlstand.* Bonn: Friedrich-Ebert-Stiftung, http://library.fes.de/pdf-files/fes/15862.pdf

Blanchard, O. (2019) "Public Debt and Low Interest Rates", *American Economic Review*, 109(4): 1197–229, https://doi.org/10.1257/aer.109.4.1197

Bundesministerium für Verkehr und digitale Infrastruktur (2016) "Stand der Ertüchtigung von Straßenbrücken der Bundesfernstraßen", https://www.bmvi.de/SharedDocs/DE/ Anlage/StB/bericht-stand-der-modernisierung-von-strassenbruecken-2016.pdf?__ blob=publicationFile

Clemens, M., M. Goerge and C. Michelsen (2019) "Öffentliche Investitionen sind wichtige Voraussetzung für privatwirtschaftliche Aktivität", *DIW-Wochenbericht* 31: 537–43, https:// www.diw.de/documents/publikationen/73/diw_01.c.670904.de/19-31-3.pdf

Dena (2018) *dena-Leitstudie Integrierte Energiewende: Impulse für die Gestaltung des Energiesystems bis 2050*. Berlin: Deutsche Energie-Agentur GmbH (dena), https://www.dena.de/fileadmin/ dena/Dokumente/Pdf/9261_dena-Leitstudie_Integrierte_Energiewende_lang.pdf

Destatis (2018) "Anlagevermögen nach Sektoren ab 1991 bis 2017 — Stand: August 2018", https:// www.destatis.de/DE/Themen/Wirtschaft/Volkswirtschaftliche-Gesamtrechnungen- Inlandsprodukt/Publikationen/Downloads-Vermoegensrechnung/anlagevermoegen- sektoren-5816101187004.html

Destatis (2019) "Investitionen — 2. Vierteljahr 2019", https://www.destatis.de/DE/Themen/ Wirtschaft/Volkswirtschaftliche-Gesamtrechnungen-Inlandsprodukt/Publikationen/ Downloads-Inlandsprodukt/investitionen-pdf-5811108.html

Dullien, S. (2017) *A New "Magic Square" for Inclusive and Sustainable Economic Growth: A Policy Framework for Germany to Move Beyond GDP*. Bonn: Friedrich-Ebert-Stiftung.

Dullien, S. and K. Rietzler (2019) "Verzehrt Deutschland seinen staatlichen Kapitalstock? — Replik", *Wirtschaftsdienst* 99(4): 286–91, https://doi.org/10.1007/s10273-019-2445-5

Earthman, G. I. (2017) "The Relationship between School Building Condition and Student Achievement: A Critical Examination of the Literature", *Journal of Ethical Educational Leadership*, 4(3): 1–16.

European Central Bank (2019) "Economic Bulletin 06/2019", https://www.ecb.europa.eu/pub/ economic-bulletin/html/eb201906.en.html

Expertenkommission (2015) *Stärkung von Investitionen in Deutschland: Abschlussbericht*. Berlin: Bundesministerium für Wirtschaft und Energie, https://www.bmwi.de/ Redaktion/DE/Publikationen/Studien/staerkung-von-investitionen-in-deutschland. pdf?__blob=publicationFile&v=11

Gerbert, P., P. Herhold, J. Burchardt, S. Schönberger, F. Rechenmacher, A. Kirchner, A. Kemmler and M. Wünsch (2018) "Klimapfade für Deutschland", https://www.zvei.org/fileadmin/ user_upload/Presse_und_Medien/Publikationen/2018/Januar/Klimapfade_fuer_ Deutschland_BDI-Studie_/Klimapfade-fuer-Deutschland-BDI-Studie-12-01-2018.pdf

Grömling, M. and T. Puls (2018) "Infrastrukturmängel in Deutschland: Belastungsgrade nach Branchen und Regionen auf Basis einer Unternehmensbefragung", *IW-Trends* 45(2): 89–105.

Henger, R. and M. Voigtländer (2019) "Ist der Wohnungsbau auf dem richtigen Weg?: Aktuelle Ergebnisse des IW-Wohnungsbedarfsmodells", *IW-Report* 28.

Hüther, M., "10 Jahre Schuldenbremse: Ein Konzept mit Zukunft?", *IW Policy Paper* 3

IMF (2018) "Germany: Staff Concluding Statement of the 2018 Article IV Mission", https:// www.imf.org/en/News/Articles/2018/05/14/Germany-Staff-Concluding-Statement-of-the- 2018-Article-IV-Mission

Krebs, T. and M. Scheffel (2017) *"Öffentliche Investitionen und inklusives Wachstum in Deutschland"*, Bertelsmann Stiftung, Inklusives Wachstum für Deutschland, https://www.

bertelsmann-stiftung.de/fileadmin/files/BSt/Publikationen/GrauePublikationen/NW_OEffentliche_Investitionen_und_inklusives_Wachstum.pdf

Kreditanstalt für Wiederaufbau (2019) "KfW-Kommunalpanel 2019", https://www.kfw.de/PDF/Download-Center/Konzernthemen/Research/PDF-Dokumente-KfW-Kommunalpanel/KfW-Kommunalpanel-2019.pdf

OECD (2016) *OECD Economic Surveys: Germany 2016*. Paris: OECD Publishing.

Rachel, L. and L. Summers (2019) "On Secular Stagnation in the Industrialized World", *NBER Working Paper* w26198, https://doi.org/10.3386/w26198

Truger, A. (2016) "The Golden Rule of Public Investment — a Necessary and Sufficient Reform of the EU Fiscal Framework?", *IMK Working Paper* 168.

Verband Deutscher Verkehrsunternehmen (2017) "Deutschland mobil: Handlungsempfehlungen für die 19. Legislaturperiode des Deutschen Bundestages", https://www.vdv.de/neue-mobilitaet-fuer-ein-mobiles-land.pdfx

World Bank (2019) "Gross Fixed Capital Formation in % of GDP, Years 1970 to 2018", https://data.worldbank.org/indicator/NE.GDI.FTOT.ZS?end=2017&most_recent_value_desc=true&start=1970

4. Public Investment Trends across Levels of Government in Italy

Floriana Cerniglia[1] and Federica Rossi[2]

Introduction

Italy, over this last decade, has experienced the worst economic crisis in its history. A double recession, during which GDP contracted by approximately 9%, was followed by weak and stunted expansion: from 2013 to the present day, less than half of the ground lost has been regained. As a result of the crisis, Italy has seen a real slump in investments. In this context, there is mounting pressure for greater public investment to stimulate economic activity in the short run and to impact the potential for long-term economic growth.

As a result of the severe economic and financial crisis, Italy has had to implement extraordinary actions to contain and reduce its public debt. Public investment has been curtailed the most, with respect to other categories of expenditure. Sub-national governments (Regions, Provinces and Municipalities) have been forced to implement quite stringent containment measures. According to the Parliamentary Budget Office (Ufficio Parlamentare di Bilancio (UPB)), from 2009 to 2016 the primary expenditure of central government increased by 5.7%, while the primary expenditure of sub-national governments decreased by 7.2%.

It has not been easy for Italian sub-national governments to implement the necessary fiscal adjustments since they have been subject to continuously changing fiscal rules and regulations. From 2010–2015, Italian sub-national governments were subject to the so-called Internal Stability Pact. According to this law, sub-national administrations were only allowed to spend revenues collected during the fiscal year, while savings accumulated over the previous years were "frozen" at the Central Treasury in Rome. This created the need for a budget surplus. However, since the existing, immediately available, public revenues were just enough to cover the current expenditure, public

---

1 Director of CRANEC — Facoltà di Scienze Politiche e Sociali, Università Cattolica, Milano

2 CRANEC — Università Cattolica, Milano.

     https://doi.org/10.11647/OBP.0222.04

investments collapsed. And unfortunately, sub-national investments account for more than half of overall public investments.

Moreover, in 2016, the Internal Stability Pact was substituted by a new fiscal rule (law 164/2016) which requires a non-negative budget. Under this new framework, the control of debt once again prevails over the aim of relaunching investments, since debt (the main source for financing public investment) and the use of surpluses are excluded from calculating the "final budget" (Giorgiantonio et al. 2018). Another change was the introduction of vertical/horizontal National Agreements and Regional Agreements (also known as Solidarity Agreements). These measures do not allocate new financial resources for investment, but only increase the sub-governments' budget-margins. This does allow for greater public capital expenditure in specific strategic sectors (i.e., school buildings, the prevention of hydro-geological risk, post-earthquake reconstruction). Moreover, the National Agreements support the development policies of disadvantaged local governments (e.g. small municipalities), while Regional Agreements aim to optimize the use of budget-margins at multiple levels of government, consolidated at the regional level. Unfortunately, the Solidarity Agreements in general have had little success, with the exception of Lombardy and Emilia Romagna (Sciancalepore 2017; Ferretti et al. 2018).

This chapter aims to provide a run-through of the public investment trends across levels of government in Italy from 2000 to 2017. We consider the breakdown of public investment by levels of government as quite important. Since the reform of the Italian Constitution in 2001, the interactions between levels of government in Italy has become increasingly challenging. Coordination challenges between the central government and sub-national governments in running current and capital expenditures as well as the financing of local expenditures (both current and capital) remain unsolved problems, which most obviously impact the time required to make an investment. As stressed by Lee Mizell and Dorothée Allain-Duprè (2013), since sub-national governments are important actors when it comes to implementing public investment strategies for economic growth, it is important to develop good practices in terms of institutional arrangements. For instance, it must be clearly established "who is responsible for what." An effort in this direction has been pursued over the last years, as just mentioned above; and these types of interventions have ensured that, at least for some municipalities, investment resources stopped declining (Ferretti et al. 2019).

The chapter is organized as follows: section 4.1. provides an overview of major trends in public capital expenditure, including local and national public companies, which in Italy are significant contributors to public investment. We focus in particular on investment data on infrastructure, machinery and equipment funded by public expenditure.

The focus is on both the central government and sub-national governments and on investments made by public companies at the national and local levels. This overview is possible considering the "Conti Pubblici Territoriali" dataset (hereafter CPT), released by the Italian Agency for Territorial Cohesion. The dataset covers annual data, in nominal terms, of revenues and expenditures by the Italian Public Administration (PA) and by the Enlarged Public Administration (Enlarged PA). Notice that the PA includes the *central government* plus *local governments* and *regional governments*.[3] Data on the Enlarged Public Administration includes the PA described above plus national and local public companies and utilities.[4]

Considering that the last available data date back to 2017, in section 4.2. we present more recent data taken from 2018, 2019, 2020 budget laws concerning regulatory interventions and proposals to increase public investment. Section 4.3. provides some final remarks and concludes with policy prescriptions.

4.1. Public Investment in Italy

Over the past seventeen years, public expenditure by the Italian PA has steadily grown from 46.5% of GDP in 2000 to 48.7% of GDP in 2017, with a peak of 51% in 2013. The growth is mainly due to total current expenditure excluding interest (from 36.2% of GDP in 2000 to 41.1% of GDP in 2017). As for gross fixed capital formation, the GDP ratio was 2.8% in 2000 and 2.1% in 2018, with a peak of 3.7% in 2009).[5] Consequently, Italy's infrastructure gap has widened. The "Global Infrastructure Outlook" (published in 2017) calculated for Italy, with reference to seven sectors (electric energy, roads, railroads, telecommunication, water, ports and airports), an annual infrastructural investment need (for the period 2016–2040) of $67 bn, a much higher level of public investment made in 2018.

Real GDP has also declined: -1.4% from 2008–2012, and 0% from 2013–2016.[6] Even though a precise assessment of the macroeconomic effects on growth of an increase in public investment is shrouded with uncertainty (as is well known, the size of the multiplier depends on many factors), estimates by the Bank of Italy indicate that, for

---

3   The *central government* includes the State, Cassa Depositi e Prestiti, ISTAT, ISAE, ENEA, CNR, INFN, ENIT, ICE, AGEA, CRI, CONI, ANAS, Social security institutions, ENAV, Patrimonio dello Stato S.p.a., EQUITALIA, Customs and Monopolies Agency; *local governments* include provinces, municipalities, metropolitan cities, agencies and institutions linked to provinces or municipalities, sub-regional tourism promotion institutions, universities, chambers of commerce, mountain communities, port authorities, national parks; *regional governments* include regional administrations, public health providers (ASL), hospitals, agencies and institutions linked to regions, regional agencies for promoting tourism. CPT data are cash flows. Notice that all budgetary data for each level of government are presented according to both a functional and an economic classification and — most importantly — data are consolidated, namely net of intergovernmental financial flows such as transfers among levels of government. See Conti Pubblici Territoriali (2007).

4   A caveat is required here: for purely operational purposes, CPT has chosen the threshold of 30% for public shareholdings, below which it is generally presumed that public control does not exist. Concerning CPT data on investment by public companies: both private and purely public financial resources can be used to contribute to investments.

5   See http://www.bdap.tesoro.it/sites/openbdap/cittadini/contabilitanazionale/ContiSatellite/Investi mentiFissiLordi/Pagine/ccn_inv_consuntivo.aspx

6   See European Commission (2020), Table 1.1., p. 15.

the Italian case, the multiplier is greater than one (Busetti et al. 2019). The positive effect on growth will also determine a decrease of the debt/GDP ratio. The scenario that a sustained public investment stimulus would create sizeable output effects and positive cross-border spillovers is simulated in the Country report on Italy 2020.[7]

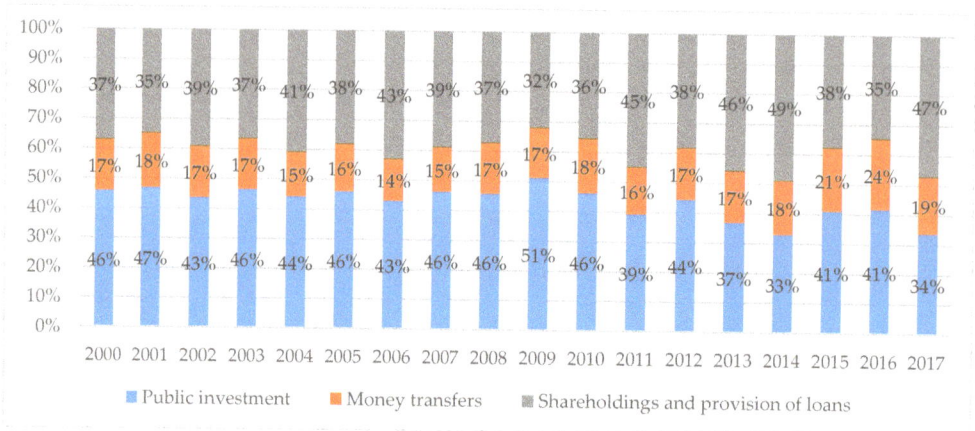

Fig. 1 Enlarged PA: public capital expenditure components (%)

Source of data: Conti Pubblici Territoriali. Figure created by the authors.

In what follows, we shall focus on public capital expenditure, which consists of three components: i) public investment, broken down as infrastructure expenditure, and machinery and equipment expenditure; ii) money transfers, for example to private companies, public institutions, etc; and iii) shareholdings and the provision of loans.

The shares for each component of the Enlarged PA are shown in Figure 1. On average, public investment accounts for 43%, money transfers for 18% and shareholdings and provision of loans for 39%.[8]

Figure 2 shows the trends of public capital expenditure[9] without shareholdings and the provision of loans by national and local public companies and by the PA.

Since 2009, public capital expenditure by the PA has had a negative trend, and it plummeted to only 1.8% of GDP in 2017. Public capital expenditure by national and local public companies, on the other hand, has had a positive trend: from 1.3% of GDP in 2000, to 2.2% of GDP in 2017.

---

7   See European Commission (2020), Box 3.1., p. 23.
8   Focusing only on PA capital expenditure: public investments on average accounted for 35% of capital expenditure, money transfers accounted for 23%, and shareholdings and loans for 41%. For further details and data, see Cerniglia and Rossi (2020).
9   In this chapter, we focus exclusively on flows of public capital expenditure and public investment. For an overview of the stock of public capital, please refer to: International Monetary Fund, Investment and Capital Stock Dataset, 2017, which estimates that the Italian infrastructural endowment was about 56% over GDP in 2015 (Spain's was 57%, Germany's 48% and France's 72%); the first census (2011) of the Public Administration's real estate holdings (http://www.dt.tesoro.it/it/attivita_istituzionali/patrimonio_pubblico/censimento_immobili_pubblici/rapporti_annuali_immobili/); and Banca d'Italia (2019), pp. 217–20.

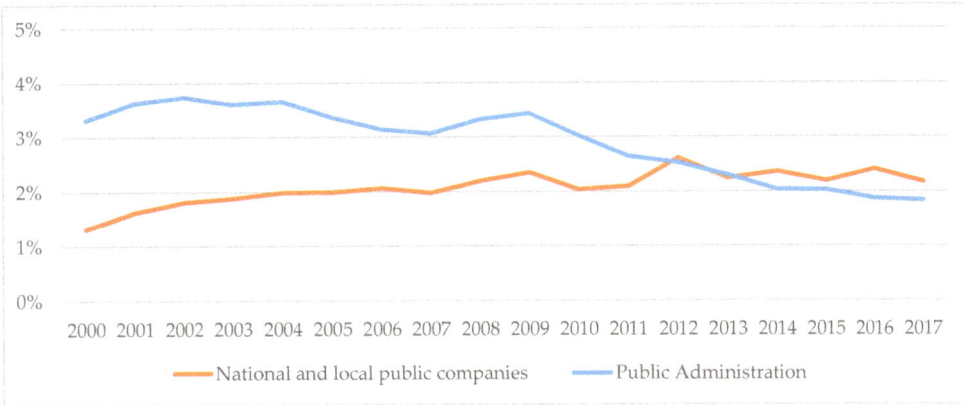

Fig. 2 Public capital expenditure (percentage of GDP) in Italy

Source: Conti Pubblici Territoriali. Figure created by the authors.

In 2000 the PA's public capital expenditure was almost €40.9 bn in absolute value, and that of national and local companies was €16.2 bn. In 2017, it was respectively €31.4 bn and €37.2 bn.

As the boost to economic growth comes from investment — which, as stated above for the period considered accounts for on average almost 43% of public capital expenditure by Enlarged PA — we believe it is important to break down this figure and provide more details. We shall do that by focusing on the public investment trend (Figure 3) and the weights of the PA and of public companies (Figure 4).

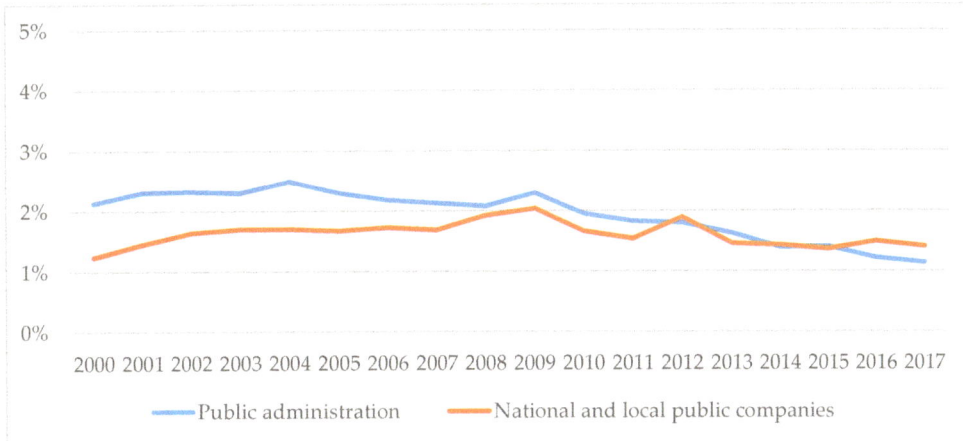

Fig. 3 Public investment as percentage of GDP

Source of data: Conti Pubblici Territoriali. Figure created by the authors.

Over the past seventeen years, 54% (on average) of public investments in Italy were made by the PA, while 46% by national and local public companies.

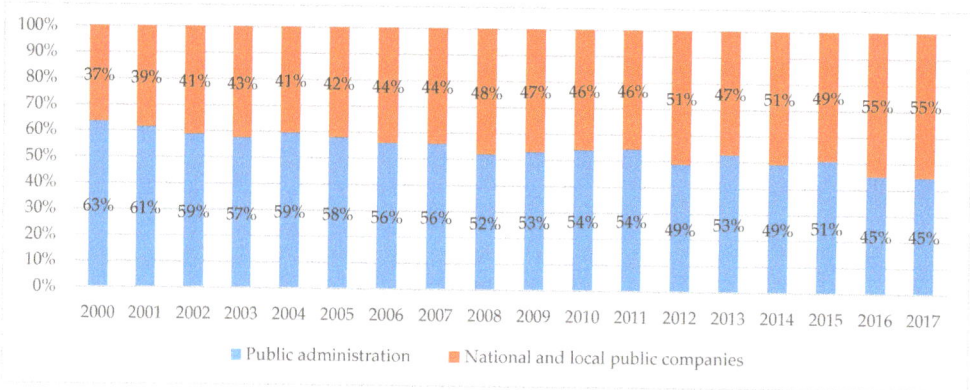

Fig. 4 Public investment by PA and public companies (%)

Source of data: Conti Pubblici Territoriali. Figure created by the authors.

Looking at the trend as a percentage of GDP (Figure 3), three periods can be identified):[10] i) 2000–2004 — with an increase in investments by both the PA (from 2.1% to 2.5% of GDP) and public companies (from 1.2% to 1.7% of GDP); ii) 2004–2009 — investments by the PA ranged from 2.3% to 2.5% of GDP, while investments by public companies increased from 1.7% to 2% of GDP; iii) 2009–2017 — with a fall in PA investments (from 2.3% of GDP in 2009 to 1.1% of GDP in 2017) and a decrease in public companies' investments (from 2% of GDP in 2009 to 1.4% of GDP in 2017, excluding a positive peak in 2012).

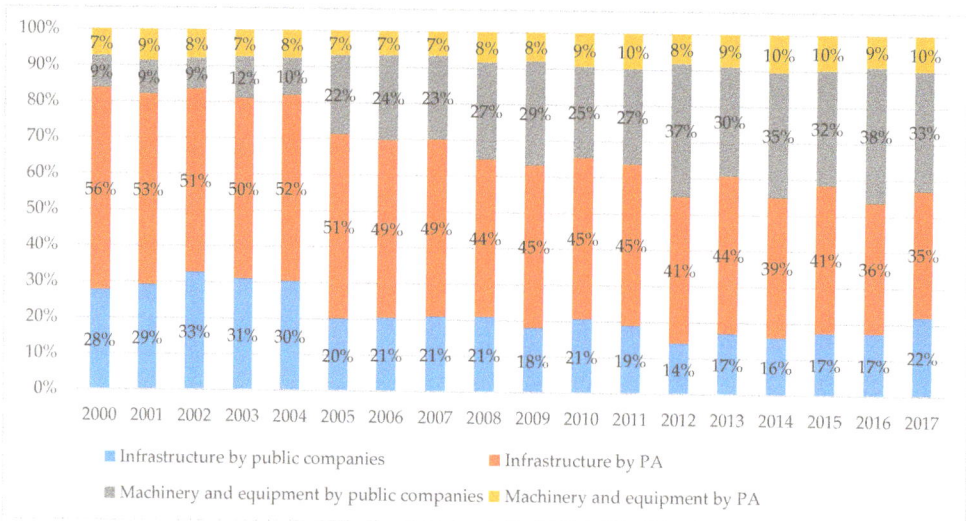

Fig. 5 Public investment components (%)

Source of data: Conti Pubblici Territoriali. Figure created by the authors.

10　Consider these additional figures: investment by public companies in 2000 were €15.2 bn, while in 2017 they were €24 bn. Investments made by the PA were €26.3 bn in 2000 and €19.5 bn in 2017.

Moreover, public investments consist of different components which are reported in Figure 5: on average, infrastructure investments by the PA and public companies accounted for 69%, while machinery and equipment investments accounted for 32%.

The PA predominantly invested in infrastructure (on average, 46%), while, from 2005 onwards, public companies increasingly invested in machinery and equipment. Let us provide a few examples in monetary terms: for instance, in 2017, investments in infrastructure by the PA amounted to €15.2 bn, investment in machinery and equipment by PA amounted to €4.2 bn; investment in infrastructure by public companies amounted to €9.6 bn, investment in machinery and equipment by public companies amounted to €14.4 bn.

Since sub-national governments have a crucial role in Italy, it is interesting to figure out the contribution of each level of government and of public companies to the Enlarged PA. Figure 6 speaks for itself: public investment was primarily made by sub-national governments (local and regional governments, on average 41%) followed by national public companies (30%), and local public companies (15%).

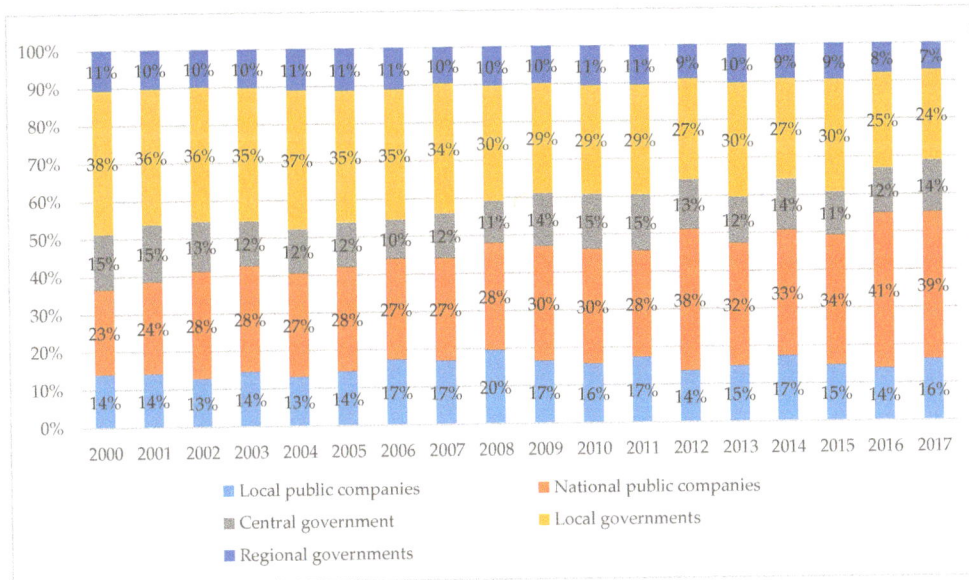

Fig. 6 Public investment by PA levels of government and by public companies (%)

Source of data: Conti Pubblici Territoriali. Figure created by the authors.

To have a deeper understanding of the period considered, Figure 7 shows the evolution of the annual growth rates of public investment considering in turn central government and sub-national levels of government as well as public companies (both national and local). Between 2001 and 2009, the annual growth rate remained positive, with the exception of 2005 (-2.8%). Excluding 2012 (when an increase in investments by national public companies compensated for the decrease in investment by the other actors), the annual growth rate of public investment remained negative until 2017.[11] It must be pointed out that the reduction in investment by sub-national governments and national public companies contributed the most to this negative trend in public investments over the period considered. Not only in Italy, but also in most OECD countries (see OECD 2017) —more than half of public investments occurred at the sub-national level. However, in the economic literature, an issue which needs investigation is to estimate the effect of capital (de)centralization on economic growth. An attempt has been made by Cerniglia et al. (2017) with reference to Italy. The findings are that decentralization in current expenditure has no effect on economic growth, whereas a critical mass of decentralized capital expenditure may have a positive effect. Results suggest a positive role for local governments in creating conditions for effective public investments.

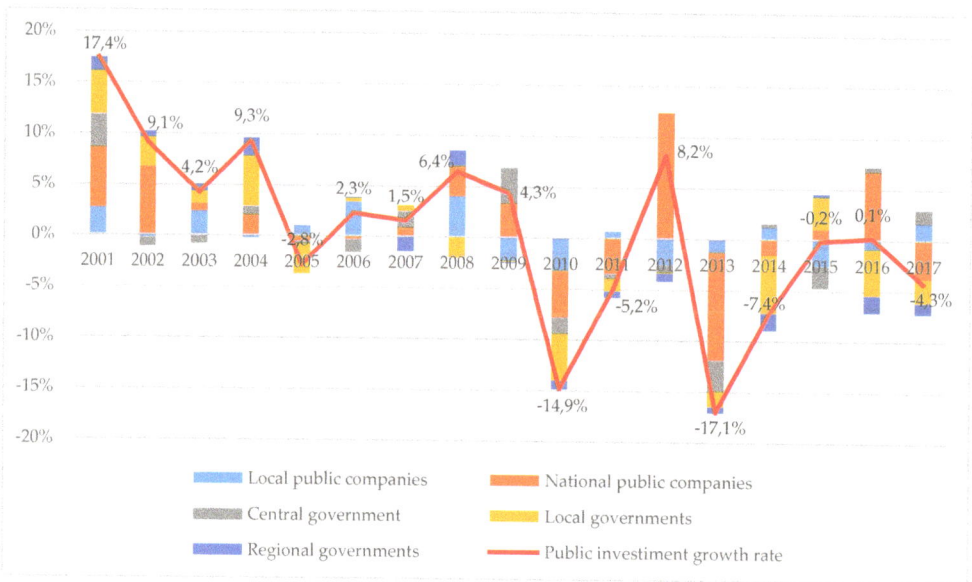

Fig. 7 Contributions to public investment growth by PA and public companies (%)

Source of data: Conti Pubblici Territoriali. Figure created by the authors.

Finally, it may be useful to look at specific sectors of investment. Figures 8 and 9 show the average shares over the 2000–2017 period for public companies and the PA respectively.

---

11   Notice that in 2015 data indicate the extraordinary expenditure reporting due to the 2007–2013 European Structural Funds programme.

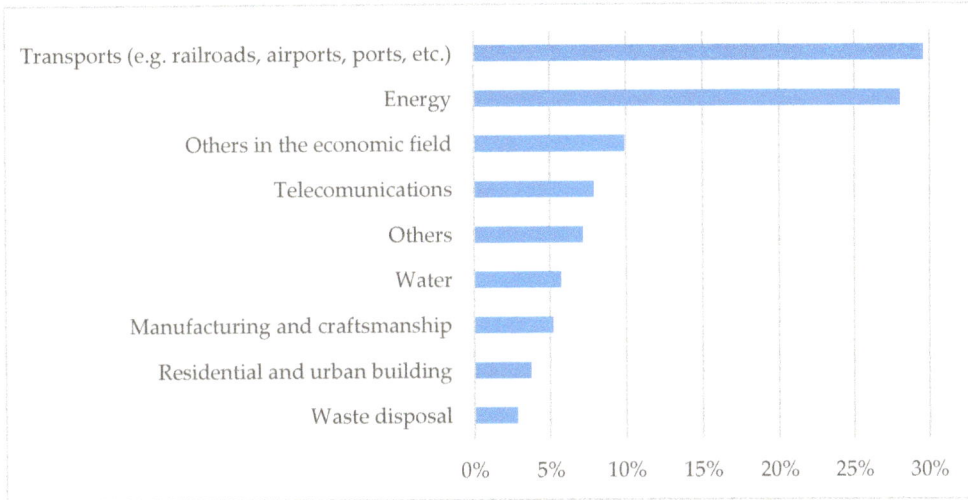

Fig. 8 Investment by public companies by sector (%)

Source of data: Conti Pubblici Territoriali. Figure created by the authors.

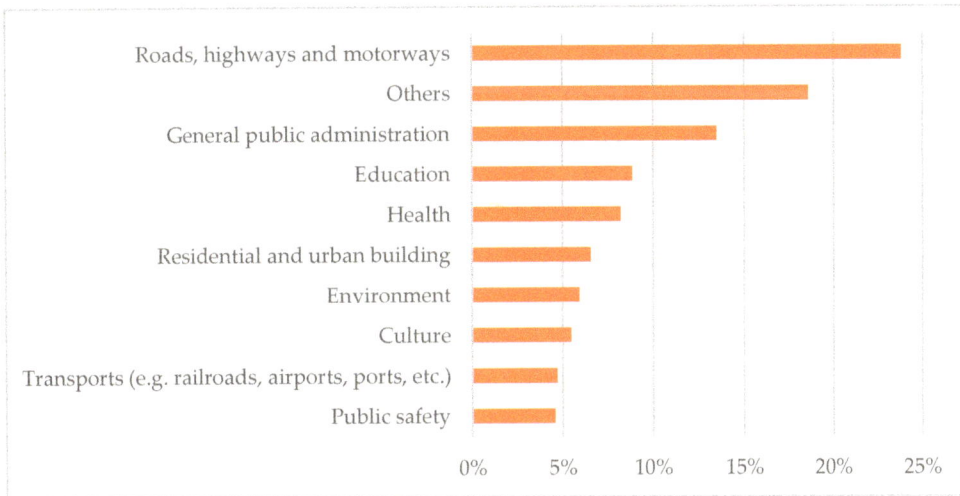

Fig. 9 PA investment by sector (%)

Source of data: Conti Pubblici Territoriali. Figure created by the authors.

First, we can highlight that public companies and the PA invest in different sectors.[12] Indeed, the majority of investments by public companies were in transports[13] (30%, or on average €7.2 bn per year), energy (28%, or on average €6.9 bn per year), others in

---

12   . The Global Infrastructure Outlook (Global Infrastructure Hub (2017)) calculated the annual infrastructure investment needs for Italy, for the 2016–2040 period. The annual estimates for the seven sectors are as follows: 15$ bn for electric energy, 12.3$ bn for roads, 19.6$ bn for railroads, 8.1$ billion for telecommunication, 3.5$ bn for water, 4.6$ bn for ports and 1.1$ bn for airports.

13   The building, running and maintenance costs of the following transportation infrastructures: rail, maritime, aviation, lake, river, including ports, airports, stations and freight villages.

the economic field (10%, or on average €2.5 bn per year), telecommunications (8%, or on average €1.9 bn per year) and water (6%, or on average €1.4 bn per year). While the majority of investments by the PA went to roads, highways and motorways (24%, or on average €6.9 bn per year), general public administration (13%, or on average €3.9 bn per year), education (9%, or on average €2.6 bn per year), health (8%, or on average €2.4 bn per year) and residential and urban buildings (7%, or on average €1.9 bn per year). Other somewhat relevant sectors include the environment (6%), other transports (5%), culture (5%) and public safety (5%).

4.1.1. Public investments across regions

Italy's regional divide remains large, and sadly, it continues to grow. The population in the southern regions (or "Mezzogiorno") is almost 34% of the total population, but in 2018, its share of GDP amounted to almost 22.3%,[14] in 2000 it was 24.7%. In the last decade, public expenditure has decreased in the southern regions.[15] Since public investment is a powerful instrument to promote convergence across regions, it is fundamental to consider its territorial distribution. We do so in the present section. It should be noted that data include both ordinary and additional resources (i.e., from the European Union Funds). This explains the positive trend for some of the years in the Mezzogiorno.

Table 1 shows the shares of public investment and public capital expenditure (without shareholdings and provision of loans) in the Mezzogiorno, considering both the Enlarged PA and PA. In 2017 only 30% of the public investment by the Enlarged PA was devoted to the Mezzogiorno (€11.6 bn — in constant 2010 euros), overall, during the period considered (2000–2017), the share was always below 34% (with the exception of 2015). On the other hand, in 2017, 36.4% of the public investment made by the PA were devoted to the Mezzogiorno (€6.04 bn — in constant 2010 euros). The largest share (44.5%) of public investment made by PA in the Mezzogiorno in 2015 can be exclusively ascribed to the expenditure reporting of the 2007–2013 European Structural Funds programme.

Disparities across regions still emerge if we look at per capita investments. Figure 10 shows the relation between per capita GDP in euro and per-capita public investment by the PA in 2016. In the bottom-left part of the graph, we see that the Mezzogiorno area is characterized by low per capita GDP and low per capita public investment, while the upper-right part shows the three Northern regions with the highest GDP and per capita investments in Italy.

---

14   See SVIMEZ (2019). Notice also that per capita GDP (2010 price) in 2018 was €31.498 in the Central-Northern area and €17.436 in the Mezzogiorno. North-Central Italy includes the following Italian regions: Piemonte, Lombardia, Liguria, Valle d'Aosta, Emilia Romagna, Trentino Alto Adige, Veneto, Friuli-Venezia Giulia, Lazio, Marche, Toscana and Umbria. The Mezzogiorno consists of: Abruzzo, Basilicata, Calabria, Campania, Molise, Puglia, Sardegna and Sicilia.
15   See SVIMEZ (2019); Ufficio Parlamentare di Bilancio (2017); and Conti Pubblici Territoriali (2019, p. 17).

Table 1 Public investment and public capital expenditure shares in Mezzogiorno by the PA and Enlarged PA

Year	Public investment		Public capital expenditure	
	% Mezzogiorno Enlarged PA	% Mezzogiorno PA	% Mezzogiorno Enlarged PA	% Mezzogiorno PA
2000	31.5	34.1	35.9	39.2
2001	30.8	35.1	36	40.8
2002	29.3	33.6	34.6	39.7
2003	26.8	30.4	32.2	37
2004	27	31.6	31.7	36.7
2005	27.7	32.8	31.5	36.7
2006	27.8	33.7	32.2	36.3
2007	27.4	32.4	29.9	33.9
2008	29.2	35.4	30.3	33.6
2009	27.6	33.8	30.1	34.8
2010	30	35	30.9	32.6
2011	30.1	34.5	33.1	35.7
2012	31.3	36.4	32.4	34.1
2013	30.4	35.4	32.8	34.1
2014	30.5	37.5	33	35.8
2015	35.9	44.5	36.9	40.9
2016	32.4	38.6	34	34.1
2017	30	36.4	31.8	31.9

Source of data: Conti Pubblici Territoriali.

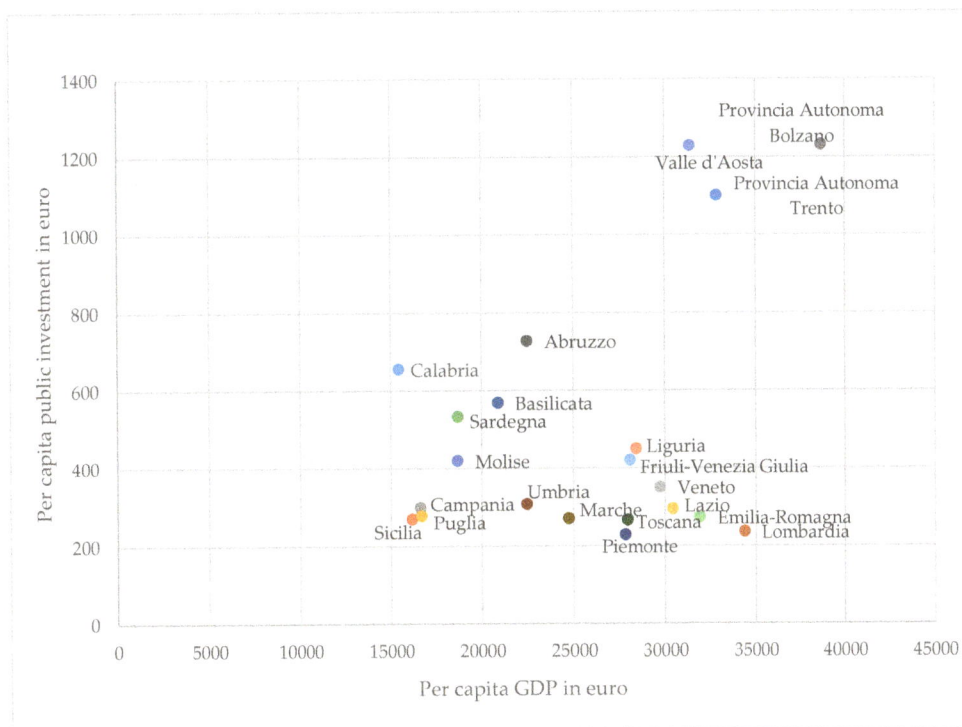

Fig. 10 Per capita public investment by the PA, and per capita GDP by Italian regions in 2016

Source of data: Conti Pubblici Territoriali. Figure created by the authors.

Figure 11 shows the distribution of public investment by the PA and by public companies, GDP and population for each Italian Region in 2017: Lombardia is the region with the highest population concentration (17%), GDP (22%) and investments by the PA (12%). If we look at investments made by public companies, the main beneficiary is Lazio (21%), followed by Lombardia (16%), Emilia Romagna (9%) and Veneto (8%). In all of the Mezzogiorno area, the shares of investment by the PA are higher than the shares of investment by public companies.[16]

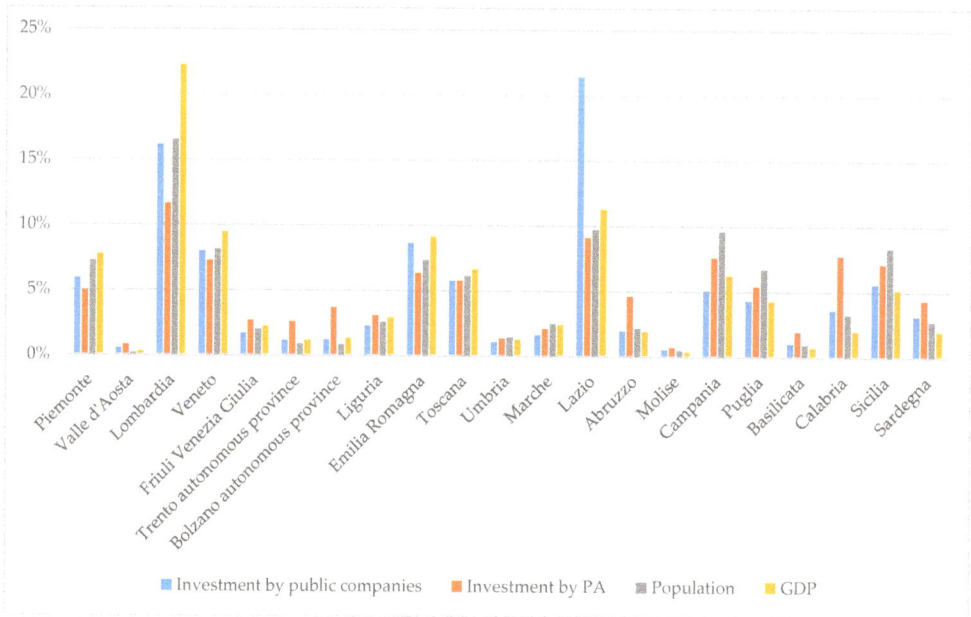

Fig. 11 Population, GDP and public investment by PA and public companies shares by Italian regions in 2017 (%)

Source of data: Conti Pubblici Territoriali. Figure created by the authors.

The issue of having shares of public investments in North-Central Italy and the Mezzogiorno that proportionally reflect the population in those areas, has been a serious political concern these last years. Two aspects are at stake: i) investments by public companies have been incredibly low in the Mezzogiorno, with few exceptions;[17] ii) if we exclude resources coming from EU funds, the proportion of public investment

---

16   For an overall picture of annual data see Cerniglia and Rossi (2020). Moreover, SVIMEZ (2019, pp. 483–84) provides indexes on transportation infrastructure (highways, roads etc.) in relation to the population by region. For example, the Italian infrastructure index for 2015 was 116.0 overall, but 156.5 for the North Central regions, and barely 38.6 for the Mezzogiorno. In other words, the Mezzogiorno has seen a constant decrease in investments in public works from 1970 to 2018. This means that while the nation-wide decrease was 2%, the Mezzogiorno had a whopping 4.6% cut, but investments for the Central Northern regions contracted by only 0.9% (SVIMEZ 2019, p. 488).

17   See CPT (2019, p. 46). For instance, the Ferrovie dello Stato (the Italian Railway Network) reduced the shares of expenditure in the Mezzogiorno in 2017 from 34.7% to 29.1%; in 2013, the share was 14.3%.

in the Mezzogiorno is much lower that 34%.[18] Indeed, when analysing the breakdown of public capital expenditure between North-Central Italy and the Mezzogiorno, it is important to distinguish between ordinary and additional resources. The CPT data presents the so-called Single Financial Framework ("Quadro Finanziario Unico (QFU)"), which estimates the shares of both ordinary and additional resources attributed to the two macro-areas. For instance, CPT data show that in 2017 the public capital expenditure of the PA was around €32.548 bn.[19] However, only €27.600 bn were ordinary resources and of this amount about €6.04 bn went to the Mezzogiorno. Therefore, the Decree-Law n.243/2016 and Law n.18/2017 introduced the "34% clause", meaning that this proportion (net of additional resources) is the amount of capital expenditure that should be allocated to the Mezzogiorno since the population in this area is around 34%. The 2019 Budget (Law n.145/2018) modifies the aforementioned Law n.18/2017 extending the "34% clause" also to public companies (Anas and the Italian Railway Network).

Very recently, an appreciable emphasis on the regional divide, caused also by a lack of public investments by the government, was highlighted in "Piano Sud 2030".[20] According to this document, in order to allow the Mezzogiorno to reach its 34% benchmark, €5.600 bn in ordinary capital expenditure need to be given from 2000 to 2022.

4.2. 2018, 2019 and 2020 Budgets: The Financial Resources for Public Investments

Additional funds for public investment were allocated in the 2018, 2019 and 2020 Budget Laws.[21] The main instrument for managing public investments in the 2017 and 2018 Budgets was the Fund for Investment, Financing and Infrastructural Development (Investment Fund, from here on). The 2017 Budget (Law n.232/2016) established this Fund with an initial endowment of €47.55 bn spread over fifteen years: €1.9 bn in 2017, €3.15 bn in 2018, €3.5 bn in 2019 and €3 bn for each following year from 2020 to 2032. The 2018 Budget (Law n.205/2017) added €36.1 bn to the Investment Fund for the period from 2018 to 2033. Therefore, the Fund's financial endowment rose to €83.7 billion spread over the 2017–2033 period. Also, both the 2017 and 2018 Budgets allowed local governments, in good financial conditions, to use budget surpluses and take out new loans (limiting the allocation of the resources for investments). The Investment Fund should have become the cornerstone of the Italian infrastructure policy, but it accumulated numerous setbacks, which deeply limited the impact of the investments, as compared to the Government's forecasts. Other negative aspects are the extremely

18   See Tortorella (2019).
19   Of this amount €10.402 (30.9%) goes to the Mezzogiorno.
20   Ministro per il Sud e la Coesione territoriale (2020).
21   Further details on these budget laws can be found in Cerniglia and Rossi (2020).

long time-lags for the actual allocation of funds, and the uncertainty derived from the Constitutional Court case (n.74/2018), which found certain constitutional-related problems in the law establishing the Fund. Notwithstanding, the Fund does contain effective and policy measures, for example: bridging the technical-organizational gap of public administrations in planning and evaluating public investments and simplifying the regulatory framework (in particular, the Public Procurement Code and the fiscal rules for local authorities). The 2019 Budget (Law n.145/2018) establishes a new Fund with the aim of relaunching the central governments' investments and the country's economic development. The total budget package is €43.6 bn for the 2019–2033 period (broken down as follows: €740 mn in 2019, €1.26 bn in 2020, €1.6 bn in 2021, and €40 bn spread over the 2022–2033 period). In addition, the 2019 Budget has established a Fund for re-launching local government infrastructure investments: €2.78 bn for 2019, €3.18 bn for 2020, €1.255 bn for 2021 and €27.88 billion spread over the 2022–2033 period (for a total of €35.095 bn). Furthermore, the Government has decided to consider small public works (for ordinary and extraordinary maintenance) a priority. In order to address the problem of an existing technical-organizational gap between public administrations in planning and evaluating public investments, the Government has planned to create various agencies. A new temporary agency, InvestItalia, has the aim of supporting the initiatives of the Prime Minister in the political and administrative management of public and private investments. In particular, InvestItalia analyses and evaluates investment programmes for tangible and intangible infrastructures; determines the feasibility of investment projects; and supports public administrations in implementing investment plans and programmes. Finally, it also identifies obstacles and critical issues related to the implementation of investments and implements the appropriate solutions to overcome them. InvestItalia should work alongside the Centrale per la progettazione delle opere pubbliche, which is supposed to support central and local governments in the following fields: designing the proposal for the public work, managing the procurement procedures, and providing economic and financial evaluations of the works and technical assistance to the administrations involved in public/private partnerships. These two new temporary agencies should cooperate with "Strategia Italia", an economic control room instituted by the so-called "Genova Decree" (d.l. n.109/2018). Strategia Italia verifies the state of implementation of infrastructure investment plans and programmes, in particular those related to hydrogeological instability, and the seismic vulnerability of public buildings and environmental degradation. Moreover, it proposes suitable solutions to overcome obstacles or delays. The Government has also prepared two sets of measures to support investments. The first is the so-called "Growth Decree-Law" (n.34, 30 April 2019), has introduced measures to stimulate capital accumulation and private investments. The second instrument, "Sblocca Cantieri" (d.l. n.32/2019, converted into Law n.55/2019), aims to speed up procurements, especially in the field of public works, by overcoming some weaknesses of the Public Procurement Code. Sub-contracting procedures have also been simplified, for instance the threshold for the sub-contracts have been increased to 40% of the total amount of the procurement, and the requirement to indicate the list of sub-contractors in the tender has been eliminated till 31 December 2020. Finally, one of the most significant measures in the 2020 Budget (Law n.160/2019) is the establishment of the Fund for relaunching central government investments: around €110 mn in the first year, €400 mn in the second year and €770 mn in the third year. The 2020 Budget will provide resources up to 2034, with a budget of €22 bn for the 2020–2034 period. In particular, the Fund aims to finance investments which improve environmental sustainability (e.g. reduction of emissions, increase of energy efficiency) and, more generally, innovation. This Fund has the same characteristics as the one (with the same name) established by the 2019 Budget. The 2020 Budget also allocates some resources for investments by local administrations, especially for municipalities. Indeed, the Budget assigns resources to every municipality, based on its population (from €5,000 for the municipalities with up to 5,000 inhabitants, to €250,000 for municipalities with at least 250,000 inhabitants), for an overall total of €235 mn in 2020, €400 mn in 2021 and €500 mn in 2022. These resources aim to support small investments in the fields of energy efficiency and sustainable territorial development. Another new aspect of the 2020 Budget which is worth mentioning is the so-called Green New Deal, with an endowment of €470 mn for 2020, €930 mn for 2021 and €1.4 bn euro to be distributed over the 2022–2023 period. Moreover, the 2020 Budget has strengthened the 34% clause in favour of the Mezzogiorno: according to this budget, the additional resources are excluded from the computation of the 34%.[22]

4.3. Conclusions and Some Policy Prescriptions

As underlined throughout the chapter, there has been a dramatic decline in public investment in Italy since 2009, implying a substantial investment gap. This decrease has mainly been driven by the decrease in investments by local governments, which have historically accounted for roughly 60% of the country's overall public investments.

However, Italy is not only facing a strained situation, where smaller and smaller amounts of financial resources are allocated to public investment. Indeed, one of its main obstacles is transforming the allocated financial resources into actual construction sites: a gap between the planned expenditure for investment and the results exists. The situation is particularly critical regarding suspended public works. Since April 2018, Associazione Nazionale Costruttori Edili (ANCE) has monitored (through www. sbloccacantieri.it) the infrastructure works throughout the country, which are delayed or suspended, due to complex procedures, suffocating bureaucracy, impediments linked to the application of the Public Procurement Code or lack of financial resources, as well as political vetoes, which call into question the start and/or continuation of already planned works.

---

22   For further details see Ufficio Parlamentare di Bilancio (2020).

Between April 2018 and January 2019, ANCE identified 574 suspended works worth approximately €39 bn (ANCE 2019). Looking at their territorial distribution, 380 works (66% of the total, worth about €25 bn) were located in the Northern regions; 62 works (accounting for €9 bn) were in Central Italy and 132 works (the remaining €5 bn) were in the Mezzogiorno.

Regarding the size of the suspended sites, 544 are small-medium sized, worth €2.6 bn; 30 are above the €100 mn threshold (for a total value of €36.4 bn) and mainly concern the construction of new transport infrastructures or the modernization of existing ones, aimed at improving the territory's competitiveness. In addition, there are relevant works underway to improve citizens' health and safety, such as hospitals and projects which limit hydro-geological instability. Projects greater than €100 mn are mainly concentrated in Northern Italy (17 works account for €24 bn), five works (€8.2 bn) are in Central Italy and eight projects (€3.5 bn) are in the South.

Concerning unfinished work, "Anagrafe delle opere incompiute" (managed by the Ministry of Infrastructure and Transport, according to Law 214/2011) identified 647 public works, which were started, but not completed, for a total value of almost €4 bn at the end of 2017. Among the causes of the stalemates, a lack of funds is indicated in more than half of the cases (a phenomenon that includes slowdowns in the supply of resources).

In conclusion, the limited effectiveness of relaunching economic growth policies is not ascribable to a single factor, but rather lies in the coexistence of several elements. Certainly, the accounting harmonization process has introduced innovations in the management of resources, which have not been completely transposed by administrations, and thus influence their spending capacity. Indeed, the changes to fiscal rules require time to be assimilated by the institutions, especially since their investment capacity, after years of inactivity, has been further weakened by employment turnover (ANCE 2019).

Another element to consider is the implementation of the new Public Procurement Code, and more generally, the excessive bureaucracy and the complex institutional and regulatory framework, which together lead to innumerable obstacles for the actual creation of public infrastructure.

To sum up, policy prescriptions, coming from the main findings of our analysis are as follows:

- Since one of the main causes reported by Anagrafe delle opere incompiute is the lack of funds, an appropriate management of time mismatches in the availability of resources, which come from different sources, is necessary.

- Addressing greater public investments in the Mezzogiorno area, in order to reduce the infrastructure gap. In particular, it is important to avoid the substitution effect between ordinary and additional resources. Indeed, additional resources have often replaced ordinary ones in recent years, rather than being added to them.

- Unlocking the turnover of PA personnel and the resources dedicated to professional training, in order to rebuild the technical skills within the administration.

- Establishing a precise and clear governance framework, which excludes overlaps and conflicts of competences between institutions and levels of government.

- Improving the quality of infrastructure projects.

- The reconstitution of a complete and reliable regulatory framework (interventions on Public Procurement Code, the role of the Italian Anticorruption Authority (ANAC) and of Corte dei Conti).

- Rationalizing the entire process of public procurement, in particular by eliminating the inefficiencies creating long 'idle times'.

- Paying attention to the maintenance of public infrastructures: the available empirical evidence suggests that, in Italy, the provision of infrastructure is inadequate, or is at risk of becoming so, due to a lack of maintenance.

For Italy, implementing a massive investment program over the next years is a key challenge that needs to be addressed in order to improve GDP growth. But, how might it be financed, given the current concerns regarding Italy's public finances? As stated by other authors in the above report, the obvious and necessary conclusion is the introduction of a Golden Rule, which excludes public investments from the deficit limits.

References

ANCE (2019) *Osservatorio congiunturale sull'industria delle costruzioni. Gennaio 2019.* Rome: EDILSTAMPA Srl, https://www.ance.it/docs/docDownload.aspx?id=48610

Assonime (2018) *Politica delle infrastrutture e degli investimenti: come migliorare il contesto italiano, Note e Studi 6/2018.* Milan: Assonime, http://www.assonime.it/Stampa/Documents/rapporto%20assonime.pdf

Banca d'Italia (2019) "Relazione annuale. Anno 2018", https://www.bancaditalia.it/pubblicazioni/relazione-annuale/2018/index.html

Boitani, A., and G. Mele (2019) "Investimenti pubblici e bassa crescita", in *Inclusione, produttività, crescita. Un'agenda per l'Italia*, ed. by Carlo Dell'Arringa and Paolo Guerrieri (Rome: AREL, Il Mulino, 2019), pp. 201–33.

Busetti, F., C. Giorgiantonio, G. Ivaldi, S. Mocetti, A. Notarpietro and P. Tommasino (2019) "Capitale e investimenti pubblici in Italia: misurazione, effetti macroeconomici, criticità procedurali", *Questioni di economia e finanza* 520, https://www.bancaditalia.it/pubblicazioni/qef/2019-0520/QEF_520_19.pdf

Cerniglia, F., R. Longaretti and A. Michelangeli (2017) "Decentralization of Public Spending and Growth in Italy. Does the Composition Matter?", *CRANEC Working Paper* 4, https://ideas.repec.org/p/crn/wpaper/crn1704.html

Cerniglia, F. and F. Rossi (2020) "The Slump of Public Investment in Italy and the Role of the Different Levels of Government. An Analysis on the Last Two Decades", *CRANEC Working Paper* 2.

Conti Pubblici Territoriali (2007) "Unità di valutazione degli investimenti pubblici — '*Guida ai Conti Pubblici Territoriali (CPT). Aspetti metodologici e operativi per la costruzione di conti consolidati di finanza pubblica a livello regionale*'", http://old2018.agenziacoesione.gov.it/it/cpt/

Conti Pubblici Territoriali (2018) *Relazione annuale CPT 2018. Politiche nazionali e politiche di sviluppo a livello territoriale*. Temi CPT 7. Rome: Agenzia per la Coesione Territoriale, http://old2018.agenziacoesione.gov.it/opencms/export/sites/dps/it/documentazione/CPT/Temi/RapportoCPT_2018.pdf

Conti Pubblici Territoriali (2019) *Relazione annuale CPT 2019 Politiche nazionali e politiche di sviluppo a livello territoriale*. Temi CPT 11. Rome: Agenzia per la Coesione Territoriale, https://www.agenziacoesione.gov.it/wp-content/uploads/2019/11/Temi_11_RapportoCPT_2019.pdf

EIB (2017) *EIB Investment Report 2017/2018: From Recovery to Sustainable Growth*. Luxembourg: European Investment Bank, https://www.eib.org/attachments/efs/economic_investment_report_2017_en.pdf

European Commission (2020) "Country Report Italy 2020, Brussels, 26.2.2020, SWD(2020) 511 Final", https://ec.europa.eu/info/sites/info/files/2020-european_semester_country-report-italy_en.pdf

Ferretti, C., G. F. Gori and P. Lattarulo (2018) "Finanza locale e investimenti negli anni della crisi", in *La finanza territoriale. Rapporto 2018*, ed. by IRES Piemonte, IRPET, SRM, PoliS Lombardia, IPRES and Liguria Richerche (Soveria Mannelli: Rubbettino), pp. 43–59, https://www.sipotra.it/wp-content/uploads/2019/03/La-finanza-territoriale-Rapporto-2018.pdf

Ferretti, C., G. F. Gori and P. Lattarulo (2019) "Il superamento del patto di stabilità e la disponibilità dell'avanzo favoriranno gli investimenti dei comuni?", in *La finanza territoriale. Rapporto 2019*, ed. by IRES Piemonte, IRPET, SRM, PoliS Lombardia, IPRES and Liguria Richerche (Soveria Mannelli: Rubbettino), pp. 15–37, http://www.irpet.it/wp-content/uploads/2019/11/pubblicazione_finanza_2019.pdf

Giorgiantonio, C., A. Pasetto and Z. Rotondi (2018) "La dotazione infrastrutturale: i nodi da affrontare nella nuova legislature", in *La finanza pubblica italiana*, ed. by Giampaolo Arachi and Massimo Baldini (Bologna: Il Mulino), pp. 211–35.

Global Infrastructure Hub (2017) "Global Infrastructure Outlook. Infrastructure Investment Needs. 50 Countries, 7 Sectors to 2040", https://cdn.gihub.org/outlook/live/methodology/Global+Infrastructure+Outlook+-+July+2017.pdf

Ministro per il Sud e la Coesione terriotriale (2020) "Piano Sud 2030, Sviluppo e coesione per l'Italia", http://www.ministroperilsud.gov.it/media/1997/pianosud2030_documento.pdf

Mizell, L. and D. Allain-Duprè (2013) "Creating Conditions for Effective Public Investment: Sub-National Capacities in a Multi-Level Governance Context", *OECD Regional Development Working Papers* 2013(04), https://doi.org/10.1787/5k49j2cjv5mq-en

Montanaro, P. (2011) "La spesa per infrastrutture in Italia: dinamica recente, confronto internazionale e divari regionali", in *Le infrastrutture in Italia: dotazione, programmazione, realizzazione*, Seminari e convegni (Rome: Banca d'Italia, 2011), pp. 187–218, https://www.bancaditalia.it/pubblicazioni/collana-seminari-convegni/2011-0007/7_infrastrutture_italia.pdf

OECD (2017) *Effective Public Investment across Levels of Government. Italy.* Paris: OECD, https://www.oecd.org/effective-public-investment-toolkit/Italy.pdf

Realfonzo, R. (2019) "100 miliardi di sottoinvestimento pubblico e deficit di competitività. L'Italia ha bisogno di politiche industriali", *Economia e Politica* 18(2).

Sciancalepore, C. (2017) "Le intese regionali nella regola fiscale del pareggio di bilancio: esperienze e prospettive future", *Irpet Note e contributi* 9, http://www.irpet.it/wp-content/uploads/2018/01/orff-9_2017-intese_reg-li-regola-fiscale-pareggio-bilancio_sciancalepore-11-17.pdf

SVIMEZ (2019) *Rapporto SVIMEZ 2019 sull'economia e la società del Mezzogiorno. Il Mezzogiorno nella nuova geografia europea delle disuguaglianze.* Rome: Svimez, http://lnx.svimez.info/svimez/wp-content/uploads/2019/11/rapporto_svimez_2019_sintesi.pdf

Tortorella, W. (2019) "Il Mezzogiorno e quota 34%. L'esigenza di una norma chiara", *Economia e Politica* 18(2).

Ufficio Parlamentare di Bilancio (2017) "Audizione del Presidente dell'Ufficio Parlamentare di bilancio in merito alla distribuzione territoriale delle risorse pubbliche per aree regionali", http://www.upbilancio.it/wp-content/uploads/2017/11/Audizione_22_11_20171.pdf

Ufficio Parlamentare di Bilancio (2018) *Il contributo dei sottosettori delle Amministrazioni pubbliche al contenimento della spesa* Rome: Ufficio Parlamentare di Bilancio, http://www.upbilancio.it/wp-content/uploads/2018/09/Focus_10_2018.pdf

Ufficio Parlamentare di Bilancio (2019) *Rapporto sulla politica di bilancio 2019.* Rome: Ufficio Parlamentare di Bilancio.

Ufficio Parlamentare di Bilancio (2020) *Rapporto sulla politica di bilancio 2020* Rome: Ufficio Parlamentare di Bilancio.

5. Trends and Patterns in Public Investment in Spain

A Medium- and Long-Run Perspective

José Villaverde[1] and Adolfo Maza[2]

Introduction

In the last decade, the Spanish economy experienced its most acute crisis since the end of the Second World War. GDP, employment and unemployment were deeply affected after the 2008 Global Financial Crisis and, although the economy registered a certain recovery from 2014 onwards, the levels of these three variables have not made up for the lost ground; that is to say, all of them still remain below pre-crisis levels. Because of this, there have been calls from various quarters for the government (at the central, state and local levels) to play a much more active role in the economy, mainly by means of increasing public spending.

There are several reasons justifying these appeals. As is well known, according to both theoretical and empirical analysis (Aschauer 1989; Abiad et al. 2015; DeJong et al. 2017, among others) there is a positive relationship between the rate of growth of an economy and productive government spending and, more specifically, public investment. This relationship takes place both in the short and long run; in the short run, because public investment adds to aggregate demand; in the medium and long run, because this spending increases the productive capacity of the economy.

Considering the relevance that public investment has for economic growth, this chapter unveils (some of) its main characteristics in Spain. In section 5.1., it pays attention to the levels, evolution and composition of public investment over the period 2000–2017; here, the Spanish performance is compared with that of six key reference areas: the European Union (EU), the euro area (EA) and the four largest economies in the EU (France, Germany, Italy and the United Kingdom). In section 5.2., the focus

---

1   Departamento de Economía — Universidad de Cantabria.
2   Departamento de Economía — Universidad de Cantabria.

https://doi.org/10.11647/OBP.0222.05

of the analysis changes in two respects: on the one hand, it refers just to Spain and to a much longer sample period (from 1964 to 2014); on the other hand, attention is paid not only to public investment but also to the public capital stock. Section 5.3. presents the main conclusions.

5.1. Trends and Patterns of Public Investment in Spain in the EU Context, 2000–2017

In line with the empirical literature on the topic, total (private plus public) investment and public investment are most commonly approximated through gross fixed capital formation and general government gross fixed capital formation. Using Eurostat's annual government financial statistics as the source of information for these variables, Table 1 shows that, in this respect, Spain experienced a pro-cyclical trend throughout the sample period. While the average rate of growth of total investment in the country between 2000 and 2008 was 4.6%, it fell to an astonishing -6.2% from 2007 to 2014, before gaining momentum, once again, in the next sub-period (2014–2017) with an average increase of 3.6% per year. For the whole period, the average growth rate of investment in Spain was a mere 0.7%; this rate is higher than that of Italy and the UK, both of which recorded negative figures, but similar to that of the EA and lower than those for France, Germany and the whole of the EU.

Expressed as a percentage of GDP, Spanish real total investment experienced a trend similar to the one mentioned above, from an initial level of 25.4% in 2000 to a final level of 21.6% in 2017, with a maximum of 29.6% in 2007 and a minimum of 20% in 2013. Although the trend was rather alike for each one of the six reference areas, two points need to be highlighted. First, the ratio "investment/GDP" was, up until 2010, much higher in Spain than in any other of the benchmarking areas. Second, the decrease in the ratio in the aftermath of the financial crisis was, as in the absolute value of the investment, much greater in Spain than in any one of those six areas.

Regarding public investment, the main trait is that its evolution clearly differs from that of total investment. As shown in the first two blocks of Table 1, there are at least three important differences to account for. First, public investment grew faster than total investment over the boom years of the sample period (2000–2008); second, public investment did not evolve as well as total investment over the next two sub-periods of crisis and recovery; and third, public investment experienced an average annual decline of 1.6% while, as mentioned, total investment increased by an average of 0.7%. Putting it in other words, this means that private investment (see the third block of Table 1) in Spain performed worse than public investment during the boom time but much better over the next years (see second and third periods of Table 1).

Overall, the ultimate result of all the aforementioned developments imply that there have been some changes in the share of public investment in total investment in Spain. First, it remained rather stable between 2000 and 2007; then, it increased rapidly in 2008 and, in particular, in 2009; finally, it decreased very sharply over the next eight

Table 1 Gross Fixed Capital Formation: growth rate (%)

		2000–2008	2008–2014	2014–2017	2000–2017
Total	Euro area	2.0	-2.5	2.9	0.7
	European Union	2.4	-1.9	2.7	1.1
	France	2.4	-1.0	2.1	1.3
	Germany	0.5	0.6	2.0	0.9
	Italy	1.5	-5.2	2.5	-0.6
	Spain	4.6	-6.2	3.6	0.7
	United Kingdom	-1.6	0.5	0.1	-0.6
Public	Euro area	2.7	-3.2	0.6	0.2
	European Union	2.7	-2.1	0.2	0.5
	France	1.3	-0.7	-1.0	0.1
	Germany	0.6	0.9	3.7	1.4
	Italy	1.6	-5.6	-2.6	-1.9
	Spain	6.1	-11.5	-0.1	-1.6
	United Kingdom	6.2	-0.2	-1.8	2.4
Private	Euro area	1.9	-2.3	3.2	0.8
	European Union	2.3	-1.9	3.2	1.1
	France	2.7	-1.0	2.7	1.5
	Germany	0.4	0.5	1.8	0.8
	Italy	1.5	-5.1	3.2	-0.4
	Spain	4.3	-5.4	4.0	0.9
	United Kingdom	-2.8	0.6	0.5	-1.0

Source of data: Eurostat database. Table created by the authors

years, reaching a minimum of 9.6% in 2017. Although public investment in the EU, the EA and the four EU largest economies followed a similar pattern to that of Spain, two points need, once more, to be underlined. On the one hand, none of them experienced such an abrupt increase of public investment from the onset of the financial crisis and such a huge decrease in the consecutive years. On the other hand, although in four of them (the exceptions being Germany and, above all, the UK) the share of public investment in total gross capital formation diminished between 2000 and 2017, the decline was sharpest by far in Spain.

As mentioned in the introduction to this chapter, there tends to be a close and positive correlation between public investment and GDP; there is no doubt, however, that this is quite often disrupted, especially at crisis times, simply because public investment is, everywhere, the most volatile component of aggregate demand. As depicted in Figure 1, this is precisely the case of Spain: against an average of some 3.5%, the share of public investment over GDP has varied greatly over time, in particular immediately after the eruption of the crisis.[3] Initially representing 3.6% of GDP in 2000,

---

3   It is also important to note that, on average, public investment in Spain accounted for 8.4% of public expenditure; this average, however, masks the fact that the evolution of the ratio followed the shape of an inverted U, with a maximum of 11.9% in 2007 and a minimum of 4.6% in 2016.

one of the highest values among the reference areas, it increased somewhat steadily to 5.1% in 2009. However, from then on, and because of the efforts imposed to consolidate the very weak Spanish public finances,[4] the share began to decrease continuously (the only transitory exception, and by a little margin, was 2015) to the much lower level of 2.1% in 2017. Once again, despite the fact that this was also roughly the trend followed in all reference areas, it must be pointed out that the extent of the changes (both upwards and downwards) was, as a norm, much higher in Spain than in any one of these areas. Additionally, it must be said that over the boom years of the sample period all reference areas, with the only exception of France — which recorded ratios very like those of Spain — registered levels of public investment that, as shares of their respective GDP, were much smaller than the Spanish ones. Throughout the crisis years, however, things changed dramatically for Spain, to the point of becoming the country in which the fall in public investment as a percentage of GDP was the highest.

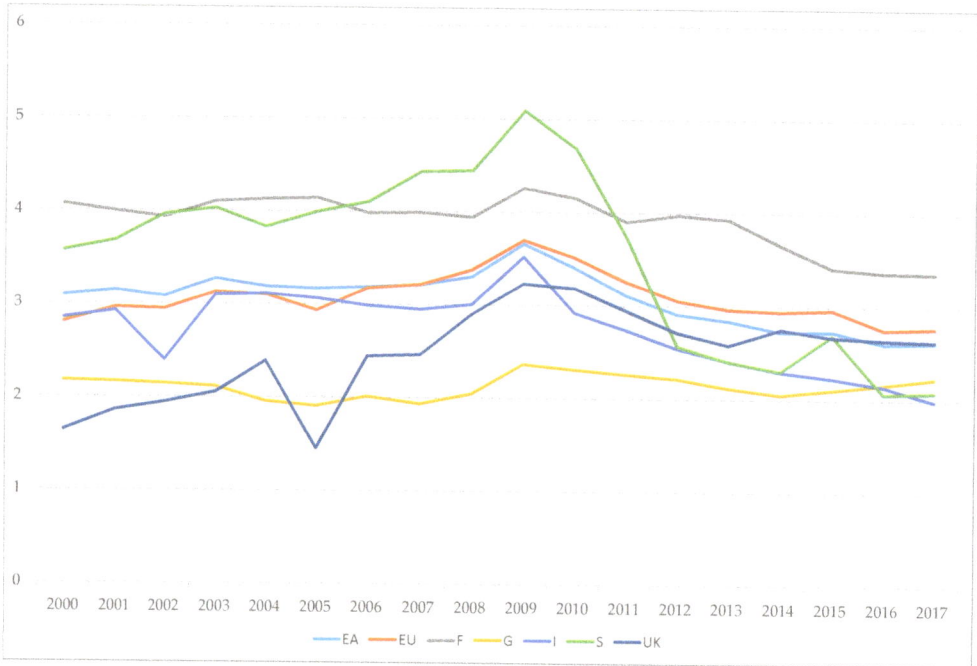

Fig. 1 Public investment effort: public investment over GDP (%)

Note: EA = euro area; EU = European Union; F = France; G = Germany; I = Italy; S = Spain; UK = United Kingdom. *Source of data*: AMECO database. Figure created by the authors.

Although all public investment contributes to fostering economic growth, not all of its components do it in the same way; in particular, empirical evidence shows that investment in transport infrastructure and investment in R&D are the items that

---

4   According to the Bank of Spain, "the contribution of public investment to the recent fiscal consolidation process has exceeded its weight in spending" (Perez and Sotera 2017, p. 4).

contribute the most to the aggregate productivity of the economy. In this respect, it is convenient to remember that, as stressed by the OECD, "investment spending has a high multiplier, while quality infrastructure projects would help to support future growth, making up for the shortfall in investment following the cuts imposed across advanced countries in recent years" (OECD 2016, p. 6).

Therefore, it is always appropriate to ask in which areas or activities does the Spanish Government invest?[5] To answer this question it is convenient to make use of the Classification of the Functions of Government (COFOG), which distinguishes between ten categories: General public services (01), Defence (02), Public order and safety (03), Economic Affairs (04), Environmental protection (05), Housing and community amenities (06), Health (07), Recreation, culture and religion (08), Education (09) and Social protection (10). Considering this classification, it can be seen (Figure 2) that in Spain, and indeed everywhere else, public investment in Economic affairs — which mainly refers to infrastructure — gets, on average for the whole sample period, the

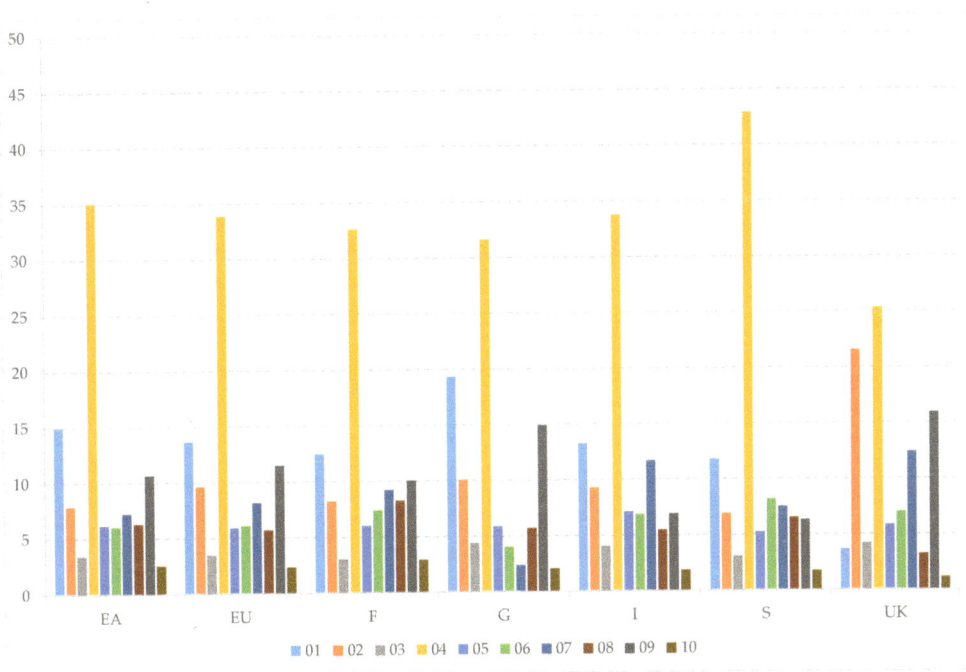

Fig. 2 Distribution of public investment by type of asset: average for the period 2000–2017 (%)

Note: EA = euro area; EU = European Union; F = France; G = Germany; I = Italy; S = Spain; UK = United Kingdom. 01 = General public services; 02 = Defence; 03 = Public order and safety; 04 = Economic affairs; 05 = Environmental protection; 06 = Housing and community amenities; 07 = Health; 08 = Recreation, culture and religion; 09 = Education; 10 = Social protection. *Source of data*: Eurostat database. Figure created the by authors.

---

5   Although here we do not pay attention to the distribution of public investment by different levels of government, it is worth remembering that, in Spain, the shares of the central, state and local governments were, on average for the period 2000–2017, 31.1%, 42.3% and 26.6%.

highest share: specifically, in Spain it accounts for around 43% of total public investment. Additionally, it should also be appreciated that Spain is the country in which this item is the most important; while in the EU and the EA, the average share of it was 33.8 and 35%, respectively, in all the other four countries of reference the share was even lower, with the UK registering the lowest value (25.3%). This notwithstanding, public investment in Economic Affairs was, after Housing, Social protection and Recreation, culture and religion, in Spain the item that suffered the largest fall in the aftermath of the Great Recession; on average, it declined by 8.9% per year between 2008–2017. Because of this, the share of Economic affairs in total public investment lost about ten percentage points in the last years of the sample period, from a maximum of 48.6% in 2011 to a minimum of 38.8% in 2017.

5.2. Public Investment and Public Capital in Spain: A Long-Term Perspective

Having examined in the previous section the dynamics and main characteristics of public investment in Spain relative to that of the whole EU, the EA and the four largest economies in the EU, over the period 2000–2017, we change our focus in this section in two respects. First, we now pay attention not only to public investment but also to the public capital stock in the country; and second, we adopt a much longer time perspective, as the sample covers a period of some fifty years, from 1964 to 2014. All data used in this section are taken from the Valencian Institute of Economic Research (IVIE) dataset on public capital.[6]

According to Figure 3, two main characteristics concerning investment have to be stressed. First, both total and public investment roughly followed the same pattern over time. They grew moderately until the mid-1980s, they accelerated their rate of growth from then on to the second half of the 2000s (in particular public investment), and they experienced an abrupt decline since then up to 2014. Second, the share of public investment in total investment experienced many ups and downs around an average of 11.2%. Here several sub-periods are clearly noted. From 1964 to 1980, the ratio, although very volatile, stood around 9%. The arrival of democracy in Spain, the integration of the country into the EU, and the sharing of power between the central and regional governments brought about a huge increase in the ratio to the point that it reached maximum values in the neighbourhood of 17% at the beginning of the 1990s. Afterwards, the ratio declined for a period of about five years to stabilize approximately at 11% for the whole next decade, between 1996 and 2006. Finally, it experienced a huge rise after the crisis outbreak to reach, in 2009, a near maximum of around 16%. Unfortunately, and once again as a result of the fiscal consolidation

---

6   Specifically, the database used is 'Stock and Capital Services' (https://www.ivie.es/en_US/bases-de-datos/capitalizacion-y-crecimiento/el-stock-y-los-servicios-de-capital/).

efforts previously mentioned, it decreased markedly from then on to a level close to the minimum of the 1970s; in fact, between 2008 and 2014 public investment in Spain fell by nearly 60%, which implies a negative rate of growth of 13.8% per year.

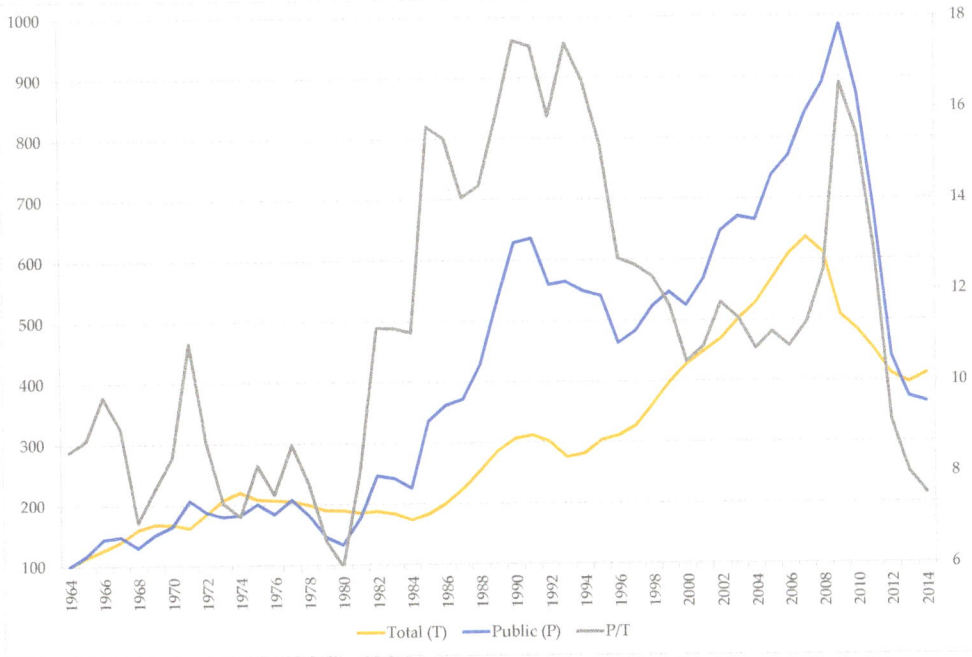

Fig. 3 Investment (1964 = 100): total and public

Note: the ratio P/T is measured (in percentage points) in the right-hand axis. *Source of data*: IVIE database. Figure created by the authors.

This last point is confirmed (Figure 4) if we consider the evolution of the public investment effort, as measured once again by the "public investment/GDP" ratio, over time. This ratio, being between 2 and 2.5% for over the first twenty years of the sample period, increased very rapidly in the second half of the mid-1980s to reach a maximum above 4%. Afterwards, it declined also very sharply until the mid-1990s to keep a level around 3% up to the 2008 Global Financial Crisis, when it increased to achieve, once more, a level of 4%; this, however, was only a very transitory increase as in 2010 it began to decrease to reach a level of just 1.5% in 2014. On average, the public investment effort in Spain has been 2.8%.

Figure 5 shows the distribution of public investment by type of assets. Although IVIE offers a very rich classification, we have reduced it to just five types for reasons of simplicity: Dwellings, Non-residential structures (Infrastructures), Transport equipment, Machinery and other equipment,[7] and Intangible assets (Information and

---

7   Considering its limited relevance, we have included "Biological property assets" within the "Machinery and other equipment".

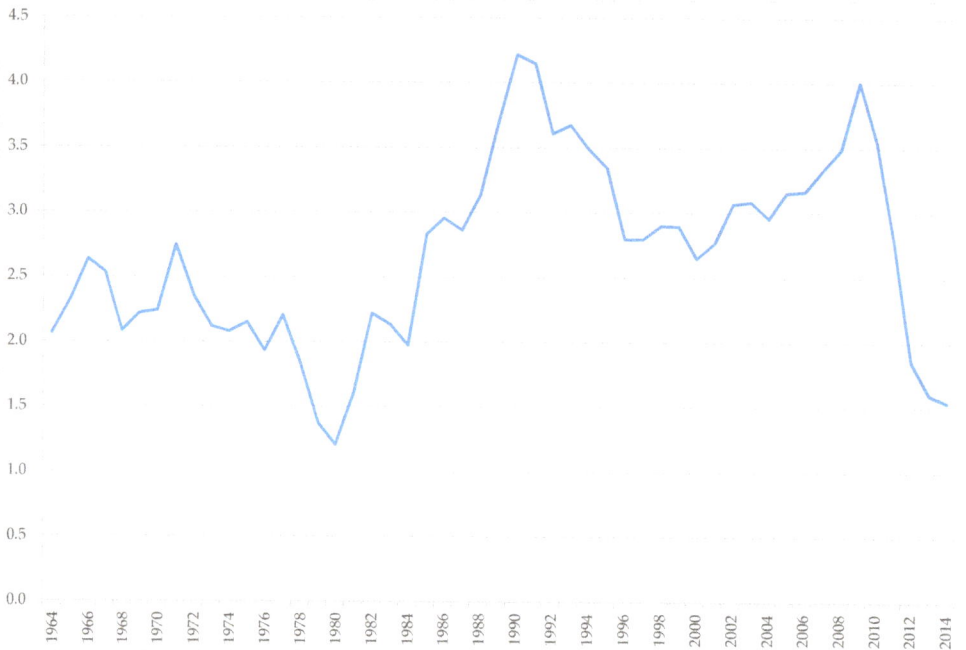

Fig. 4 Public investment effort: public investment over GDP (%)

Source of data: IVIE database. Figure created by the authors.

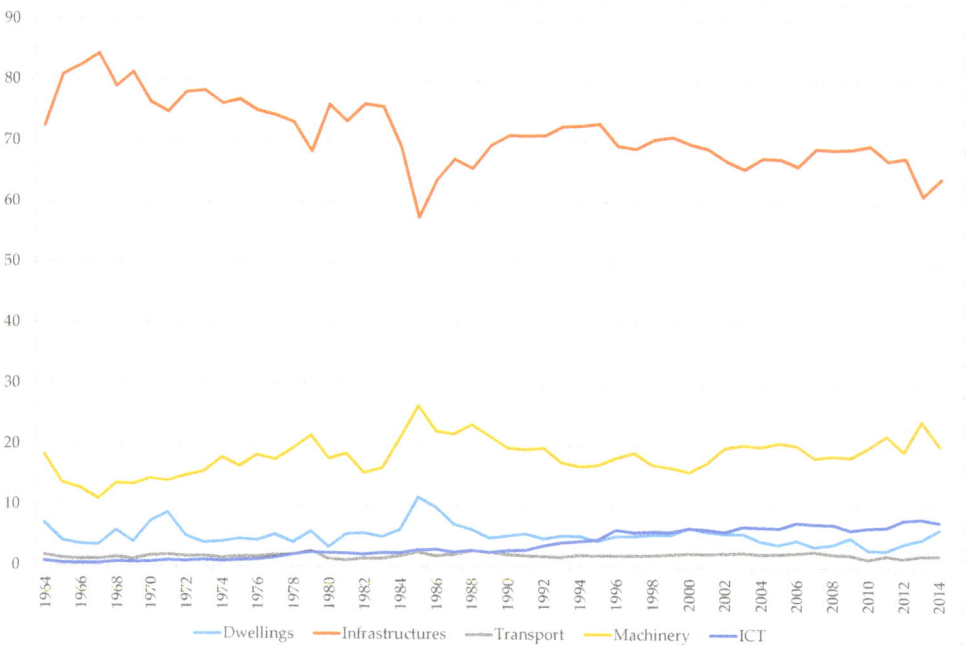

Fig. 5 Distribution of public investment by type of asset (%)

Source of data: IVIE database. Figure created by the authors.

communication technology, ICT). As can be seen, the lion's share of public investment corresponds to one single asset, Infrastructures, to which roughly between 60 and 80% of total public investment is devoted. Additionally, Machinery and other equipment is also relevant, as it contributes to around 20% of total public investment. Albeit still very low in relative terms, it is important to note that the share of public investment in Intangible assets grew slowly but steadily until the beginning of the nineties but that, since then, it has grown more rapidly, reaching levels of around 8% in the last final years. In fact, investment in Intangible assets grew much more rapidly than any other type of public investment; it is also true, however, that this investment is the one that was most negatively affected by the outbreak of the crisis (its annual average rate of growth between 2008 and 2014 was -12.9%).

As is well known, the stock of capital of an economy is the result of investment accumulation and de-accumulation over time. As mentioned before, in addition to offering information about investment, IVIE also provides information about the stock of capital (both net and productive) in the economy. Net capital is the result of net investment accumulation while productive capital is equal to net capital minus the loss of capital efficiency due to the ageing of capital assets. As the estimation of the loss of efficiency always implies making some arguable assumptions and, additionally, the evolution of net and productive capital has moved along very similar paths, here we decided to focus exclusively on net capital (referred to henceforth in short, as simply "capital").

Total and public capital in Spain increased a lot over time. Initially and until the mid-1980s, both grew steadily at a similar rate, but afterwards public capital rose much faster. Consequently, the share of public over total capital was very stable over the first twenty years of the sample period at a level of 8%; afterwards, however, it increased sharply to up a maximum of around 12% in the mid-1990s, to remain stable since then at a level between 11 and 12%. Regardless, this performance cannot obviate the fact that public capital suffered a little decrease during the crisis years: while, taking 1964 as the base year with a value of 100, the index rose from 100 to 804.5 until 2011, it declined from 2011 to 2014 to a level of 764.3.

When we consider the ratio public capital/GDP (Figure 6), the most salient trait is that, after long periods of relative stability (1964–1980 and 1994–2008), it increased very markedly. That is to say, the two most expansionary phases took place, roughly, between 1980 and 1995; and immediately after the burst of the Great Recession. Consequently, the ratio rose from slightly more than 20% of GDP in 1980 to around 36/37% at the end of the sample period. Regarding public capital per inhabitant, its evolution differs from that of net capital over GDP in that now, with the exception of the first fifteen years of the sample, the ratio increased almost continuously over time. In any case, its evolution mimics that of public capital/GDP in that the average for the second half of the period (close to €8,000 per inhabitant) was much higher than that for the first (€3,500).

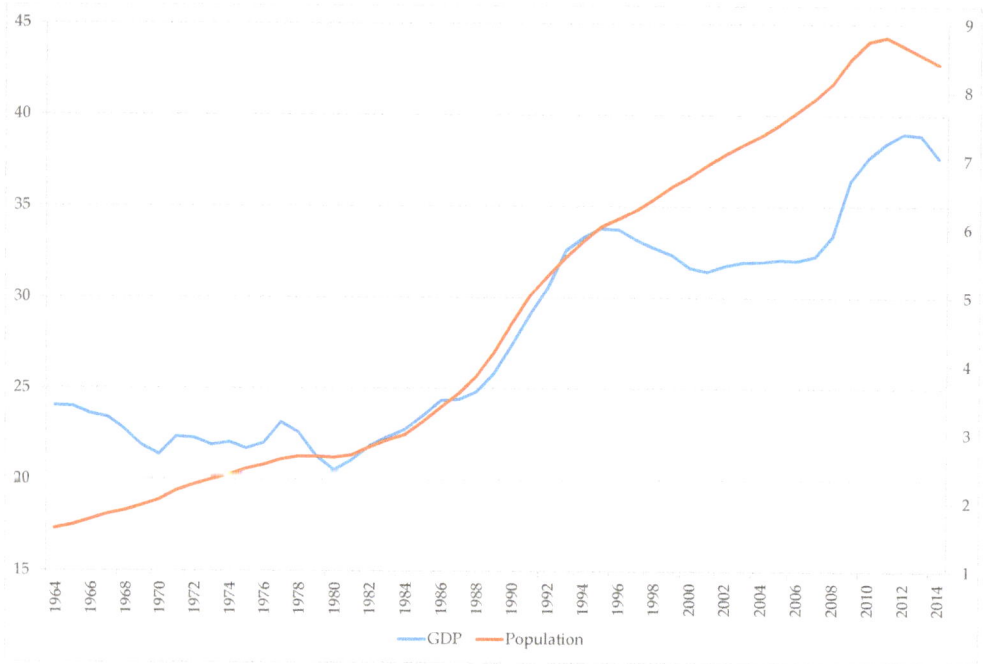

Fig. 6 Public capital ratios: over GDP (%) and population (thousand euros per inhabitant)

Note: the ratio public capital/population (in thousand euros) is measured on the right-hand axis. *Source of data*: IVIE database. Figure created by the authors.

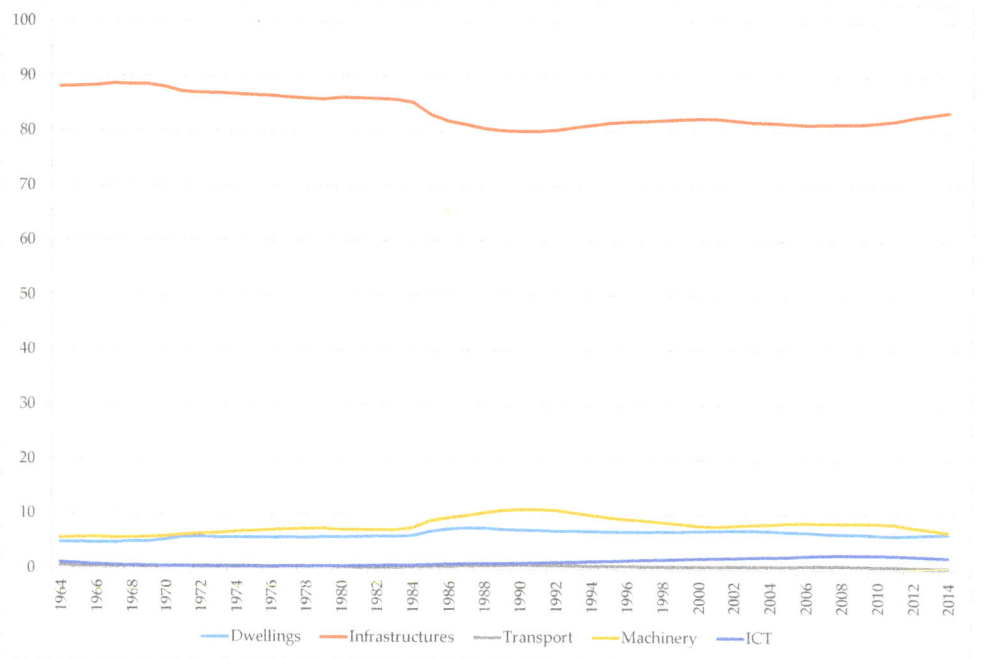

Fig. 7 Distribution of public capital by type of asset (%)

Source of data: IVIE database. Figure created by the authors.

Regarding the distribution of the public capital stock by type of asset (Figure 7), it is important to stress that, naturally, it is much in line with that of the public investment previously mentioned. Once again, it happens that Infrastructures is, by far, the most important type of capital asset of the five here considered; it represents, on average, nearly 84% of public capital. As is obvious, this implies that the other types of capital assets contribute with very low percentages to the total; in particular, these contributions were of some 8% for Machinery, 6.3% for Dwellings, 1.3% for ICT, and 0.6% for Transport equipment. What cannot be seen in Figure 7, is that there are three additional relevant characteristics related to this distribution. First, as expected, all types of capital assets increased in net terms over time. Second, ICT is the type of capital asset that grew more rapidly since the early 1990s (between 1990 and 2007/2008 it grew at an average yearly rate of 8.9%). Third, capital for all types of assets declines (in three out of the five cases very abruptly) from the outbreak of the financial crisis.

5.3. Conclusions

Like some other European countries, namely Greece, Spain was hit badly by the 2008 Global Financial Crisis. Because of this, the country faced some important constraints in its public finances; namely, public investment experienced a severe blow after the outbreak of the crisis. In fact, during the period 2000–2007, Spain was the country that registered the second highest increase in public gross fixed capital formation among the five biggest European countries, a rate (6.8% per year) that was also much higher than that of the EU (2.3%) and the euro area (2.6%). However, over the next period, 2008–1013, the situation changed completely: public investment dropped, on an annual basis, at a rate close to 11%. Thus, Spain became the country that suffered the most acute decline in public investment among the big five.

In relative terms, the situation did not improve. Although Spanish GDP also registered a large drop in the aftermath of the recession, public investment decline was even larger. Therefore, the ratio "public investment/GDP", that had been among the highest of the EU, also recorded an intense fall to the point of becoming one of the lowest of the EU. In fact, from being at a level closer to or over 4% between 2000 and 2009 (when it reached a maximum over 5%), the ratio decreased to a minimum of around 2% in 2016 and 2017.

From the point of view of the asset composition of public investment, two results are worth mentioning. On the one hand, the Economic affairs category is clearly the most important category, even to a much higher extent than in any of the reference areas: it represents, on average, around 43% for Spain against less than 35% in both the EU, the euro area and the other four big countries. On the other hand, the share of this category of investment declined, because of the crisis, from 2007/2008 onwards.

However, a longer, although less updated, time perspective (1964–2014) offers a somewhat different picture of the evolution of public investment in Spain. After having experienced a more or less stable increase between 1964 and 1980 (it rose from an index of 100 to one of 200), this type of investment scored an impressive increase in the next decade, to reach an index level over 600. The first half of the 1990s was more turbulent (the index declined below 500), but afterwards and up until 2008 it achieved another impressive increase, registering an index value close to 1000. Unfortunately, and as mentioned before, the Great Recession very negatively affected Spanish public investment, to the point that the index fell to a minimum of less than 400 in 2014.

Regarding the public investment effort, there are three results, somewhat in tune with the evolution previously mentioned, that should be highlighted: first, its continuous ups and downs, reflecting a high volatility; second, the huge increase recorded in the 1980s; third, the even stronger decline underwent from 2008 to 2014.

As for the composition of public investment, there are also two important facts that should be stressed: on the one hand, the huge (albeit declining) share of public investment devoted to infrastructure, and, on the other, the low but increasing share devoted to ICT.

The results for (net) public capital roughly mimic those of public investment. The main difference is that, as expected, public capital has been growing constantly over time (from an index of 100 in 1964 to one of more than 750 in 2008); the only exception to this positive evolution took place in the last few years, in which the index declined to around 720 in 2014. A very similar evolution was registered by the ratios "public investment/GDP" and "public investment/population".

To sum up, the following points should be stressed:

1. Public investment in Spain has been very volatile and pro-cyclical over time. It has experienced large increase periods during boom times and huge fall periods during recessions.

2. Public capital has been increasing fairly constantly (but not always at the same rate) over time, with the only exception being developments during the most acute phase of the financial crisis.

3. Investment in infrastructures always represents the main component of public investment, but the most expansive item has been investment in ICT. This is also true regarding public capital.

Considering all of this, it seems that the agenda for public investment in Spain in the future should have three main goals:

1. To reduce the level of volatility, for which the development of long-run investment strategies would be an important instrument.

2. To adopt a more anti-cyclical stance. As part of the aforementioned strategies, public investment should be considered as an anti-cyclical policy tool, in particular to smooth future drops in the business cycle.

3. To increase the share devoted to ICT. Without forgetting the importance of physical infrastructure, it is clear that improving access to ICT infrastructure should become a priority for policy makers, since ICT may act as a remarkable enabler of economic development. In other words, the growing trend in this type of public spending should be consolidated and, if possible, expanded in the coming years.

Although there is no doubt that this is a hard agenda to accomplish, it should obviously be pursued. The fate of public investment and public capital in Spain (and, for that matter, of economic growth) is, to a great extent, in the hands of policy makers, as it ever has been.

References

Abiad, A., D. Furceri and P. Topalova (2015) "The Macroeconomic Effects of Public Investment: Evidence from Advanced Countries", *IMF Working Paper* 15(95), https://doi.org/10.5089/9781475578874.001

Aschauer, D. A. (1989) "Is Public Expenditure Productive?", *Journal of Monetary Economics* 23(2): 177–200, https://doi.org/10.1016/0304-3932(89)90047-0

de Jong, J., M. Ferdinandusse, J. Funda and I. Vetlov (2017) "The Effect of Public Investment in Europe: A Model-Based Assessment", *ECB Working Paper* 2021, https://www.ecb.europa.eu/pub/pdf/scpwps/ecbwp2021.en.pdf

OECD (2016) *OECD Economic Outlook*. Paris: OECD Publishing.

Perez, J. J. and I. Sotera (2017) "Developments in Public Investment during the Crisis and the Recovery", *Bank of Spain, Economic Bulletin* 4: 1–11, https://www.bde.es/f/webbde/SES/Secciones/Publicaciones/InformesBoletinesRevistas/NotasEconomicas/T4/files/bene1704-nec10e.pdf

PART II

—

CHALLENGES

6. In Search of a Strategy for Public Investment in Research and Innovation

Daniela Palma,[1] Alberto Silvani[2]
and Alessandra Maria Stilo[3]

Introduction and Main Points at Issue

The role of research and innovation (R&I) as key drivers of economic growth has been gaining increasing importance and has now become an object of renewed concern in the European policy agenda. The intensity of research and development (R&D) expenditure on GDP in the European Union (EU) has grown over the past decade, but at decreasing rates, and it is still well below that recorded for Japan and the United States (US). Globally, however, the growth of R&D expenditure has been driven by massive investments in newly industrialized Asian countries, especially by China, whose share of world R&D expenditure has increased from 5% in 2000 to 21% in 2015 (European Commission 2018b). In line with this trend, China has recently outperformed the EU R&D investment in terms of both total amount and GDP percentage, and further growth is expected to continue, according to the current Five Year Plan (Figure 1).

However, the sluggish growth of R&D investment in the EU is also the result of large differences across the Member States. This calls not only for a closer assessment of major patterns of R&D expenditure at the country level but also for special attention to the role played by public funding with respect to the more-than-ever complex evolution of technological innovation and the need for the productive structure to be supported to continuously capture the potential of new technologies. It is, in fact, not by chance that such a perspective now appears at the core of the strategic guidelines devised by the next Research and Innovation Framework Programme Horizon Europe (European Commission 2018a). A major emphasis of the Programme has been put on the need to build new and stronger synergies between the public- and private-side stakeholders in

---

1   Agenzia nazionale per le nuove tecnologie, l'energia e lo sviluppo economico sostenibile — ENEA.

2   CRANEC — Centro di Ricerche in Analisi Economica e Sviluppo Economico Internazionale, Università Cattolica del Sacro Cuore, Milano; Consiglio Nazionale delle Ricerche — CNR.

3   Consiglio Nazionale delle Ricerche — CNR; Università degli Studi di Urbino, Carlo Bo

    https://doi.org/10.11647/OBP.0222.06

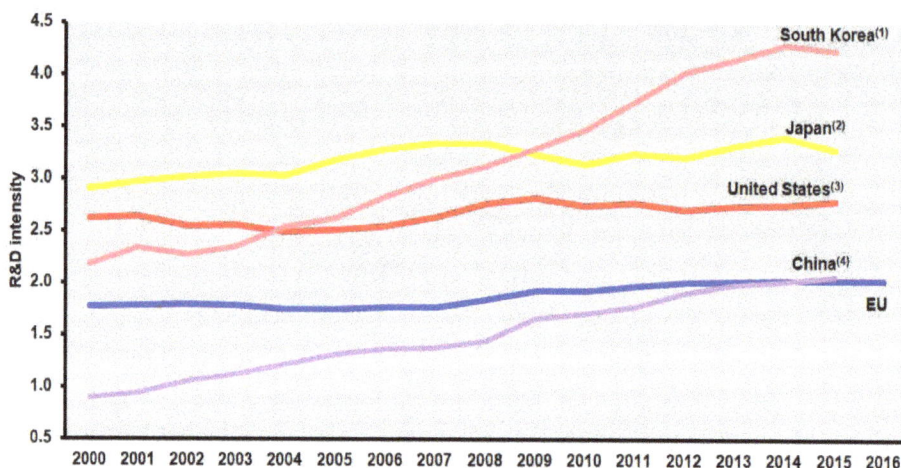

Fig. 1 Evolution of R&D intensity, 2000–2016

Notes: (1) KR: There is a break in series between 2007 and the previous years. (2) JP: There is a break in series between 2008 and the previous years and between 2013 and the previous years. (3) US: (i) R&D expenditure does not include most or all capital expenditure; (ii) There is a break in series between 2003 and the previous years (4) CN: There is a break in series between 2009 and the previous years. *Source*: DG Research and Innovation — Unit for the Analysis and Monitoring of National Research and Innovation Policies – Science, Research and Innovation performance of the EU 2018. *Source of data*: Eurostat, OECD.

order to overcome the main barriers that still hold back industrial scale-up processes and competitiveness of the EU economy. Nonetheless, this should constitute only part of an advanced stage of the EU approach to research and innovation policies.

Looking at all of the EU strategies to support and boost research and innovation, we also have to consider direct and indirect funds used to create new research infrastructures or support existing ones (European Commission 2019a). These include scientific equipment and instruments, scientific data archives, communication networks, computing systems and any other research and innovation structure open to external users. With the actions on infrastructure, the EU aims to not only reduce fragmentation of the research and innovation ecosystem and avoid duplication of effort but also enhance public-private cooperation, by making industries more aware of opportunities to improve their products and by facilitating programs of co-development of advanced technologies. Bearing in mind that the infrastructure strategy is quite relevant, we nevertheless consider this funding as a part of the total EU R&D expenditure and will do so for this chapter.

Although it is clear that the EU as a whole still lags behind the US and major Asian countries in terms of R&D intensity and that in recent years the gap has widened further with regard to business R&D expenditure, the emergence of deeper divides across the Member States (notably between major northern and southern countries as well as between the western and eastern areas) may very well be the result of existing country-specific structural divergences that have developed on different grounds. This requires a better understanding of differences in country patterns of R&D expenditure, with a more detailed look at the evolution of the various main sources of R&D funding and their relationship to major structural factors shaping the characteristics of national research and innovation ecosystems. The objective is to put into perspective the need for R&D investment across the Member States, trying to assess to what extent the role of public R&D funding is consistent with the development of national research and innovation ecosystems and in which terms the lack of sufficient R&D investment could be adequately refrained in the EU policy framework.

6.1. The EU in Depth

The EU vocation for public investment in R&D has been largely confirmed over the past decade, and only a slight decrease in public R&D intensity (on GDP) has emerged after 2012 (Figure 2). This contraction was smaller than that in the US and Japan, and the EU still holds the highest share of global public R&D investment (European Commission 2018b). As a matter of fact, an increase of total public R&D expenditure in the EU took place every year between 2007 and 2015, while a similar dynamic occurred in a more limited period between 2012 and 2015 with regard to the total of national government budgets for R&D (European Commission 2018b). This last trend is only partially reflected in the variations of national government budgets for R&D as a share of total general expenditure. The share of public budget allocated to R&D, which increased until the beginning of the international crisis up to nearly 1.5% and

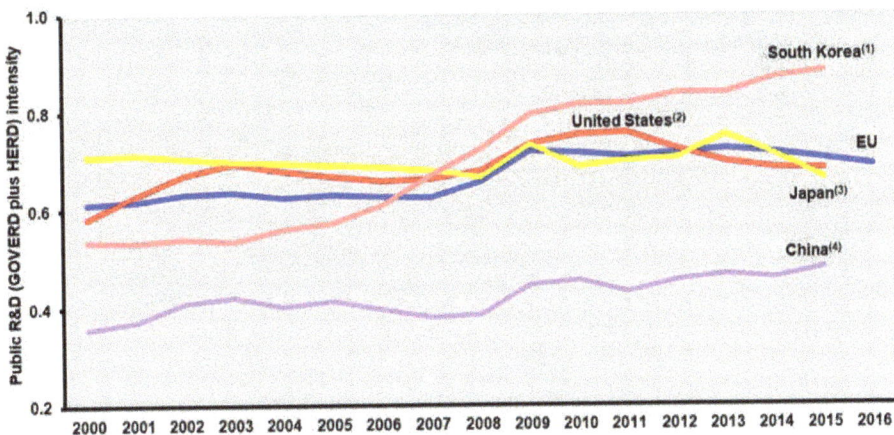

Fig. 2 Evolution of public R&D intensity, 2000–2016

Notes: (1) KR: There is a break series between 2007 and the previous years. (2) US: (i) Public R&D expenditure does not include most or all capital expenditure; (ii) There is a break in series between 2003 and the previous years. (3) JP: There is a break in series between 2008 and the previous years and between 2013 and the previous years (4) CN: There is a break in series between 2009 and the previous years. *Source*: DG Research and Innovation — Unit for the Analysis and Monitoring of National Research and Innovation Policies — Science, Research and Innovation performance of the EU 2018. *Source of data*: Eurostat, OECD.

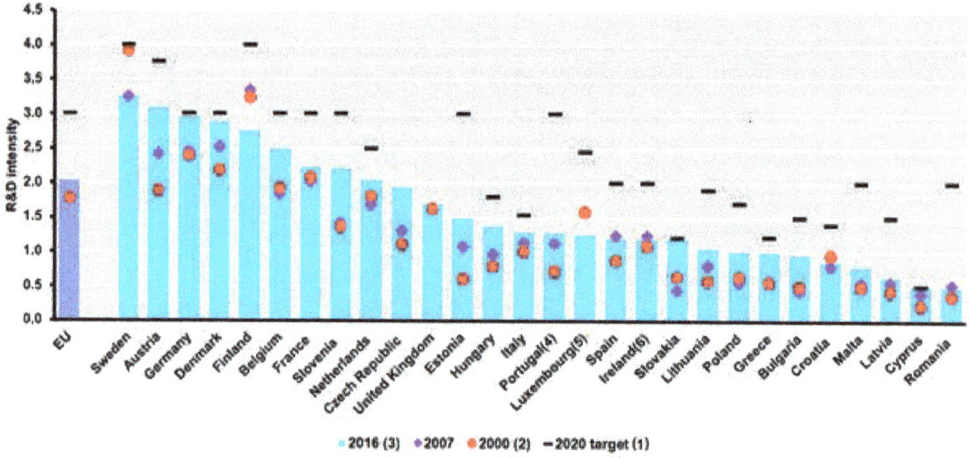

Fig. 3 R&D intensity, 2000, 2007, 2016 and 2020 target

Notes: (1) CZ, UK: R&D intensity targets are not available. (2) EL, SE: 2001, HR: 2002, MT: 2004. (3) BG, CZ, EE, FR, LV, LT, HU, PL, RO, SI, SK: 2015 (4) PT: The R&D intensity target is between 2.7% and 3.3% (3.0 % was assumed). (5) LU: The R&D intensity target is between 2.3% and 2.6% (2.45% was assumed). (6) IE: The R&D intensity target is 2.5% of GPN, which is estimated to be equivalent to 2.0% of GDP. For DK, EL, FR, LU, HU, NL, PT, RO, SI, SE, UK: breaks in series occur between 2000 and 2016. *Source*: DG Research and Innovation — Unit for the Analysis and Monitoring of National Research and Innovation Policies — Science, Research and Innovation performance of the EU 2018. *Source of data*: Eurostat, Member States.

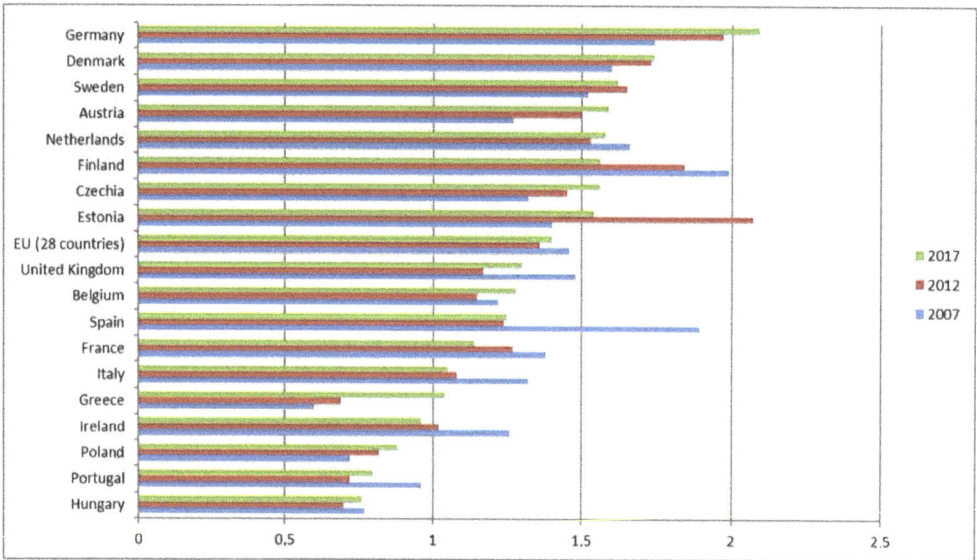

Fig. 4 Share of government budget appropriations or outlays on R&D — percentage of total general government expenditure

Source of data: Eurostat. Figure created by the authors.

declined between 2010 and 2012 up to 1.36%, shows a very slight increase after 2012, staying between 1.37% and 1.39% with an adjustment to 1.4% only in 2017. By and large, it is interesting to note that over the past decade (2007–2017) the EU's total of national government budgets for R&D has increased by 16.5% and that the share of public budget allocated to R&D in 2017 is only -5% lower than the peak percentage of 1.48% in 2009.

The present dynamics of public R&D investment in the EU is the result of large divergences among the Member States in the pattern of change of the share of public budget allocated to R&D. A first divide with respect to the EU global trend can be observed between countries that increased their investment in R&D as a share of public budget and those that went in the opposite direction. But deeper insights into the behaviour of public R&D budgets in the EU can be gained by looking at the differences among the Member States with regard to the share of total R&D expenditure on GDP (GERD/GDP) (Figure 3), especially within the EU15 aggregate. Increasing shares of the public budget allocated to R&D are observed for most of the northern EU15 countries, characterized by the highest shares of total R&D expenditure on GDP (Figure 4), including Germany, Austria, Sweden, Denmark and Belgium; another two countries, Finland and the Netherlands, still rank well above the EU average in 2017 but show a contraction of the R&D share of the public budget. On the other side, EU15 Member States with the lowest share of total R&D expenditure on GDP, notably the southern countries (Greece, Italy, Portugal and Spain) and Ireland, show sharp contractions of the share of public budget allocated to R&D during the central years of the international crisis, with only partial adjustments to higher levels at the end of the period (2016–2017) in the case of Portugal and Greece. Compared to the other EU15 countries, and with the exception of Belgium and France, these countries still have the lowest shares of the public budget allocated to R&D, well below the EU average. This is clearly a point of concern as, among the core Member States, and unlike Belgium and France, southern European countries and Ireland still have the lowest shares of R&D intensity. A different case is that of the United Kingdom, where the R&D intensity on GDP is well above that of southern countries but slightly below the EU average and where the share of public budget allocated to R&D declined sharply over the past decade (although with some upward adjustments between 2013 and 2017). The dynamics of public R&D investment as a share of government spending is somewhat more erratic in the case of the Eastern EU countries; with the exception of Estonia and the Czech Republic, the use of public budgets to finance R&D expenditure is much more limited here than in the EU15 countries.

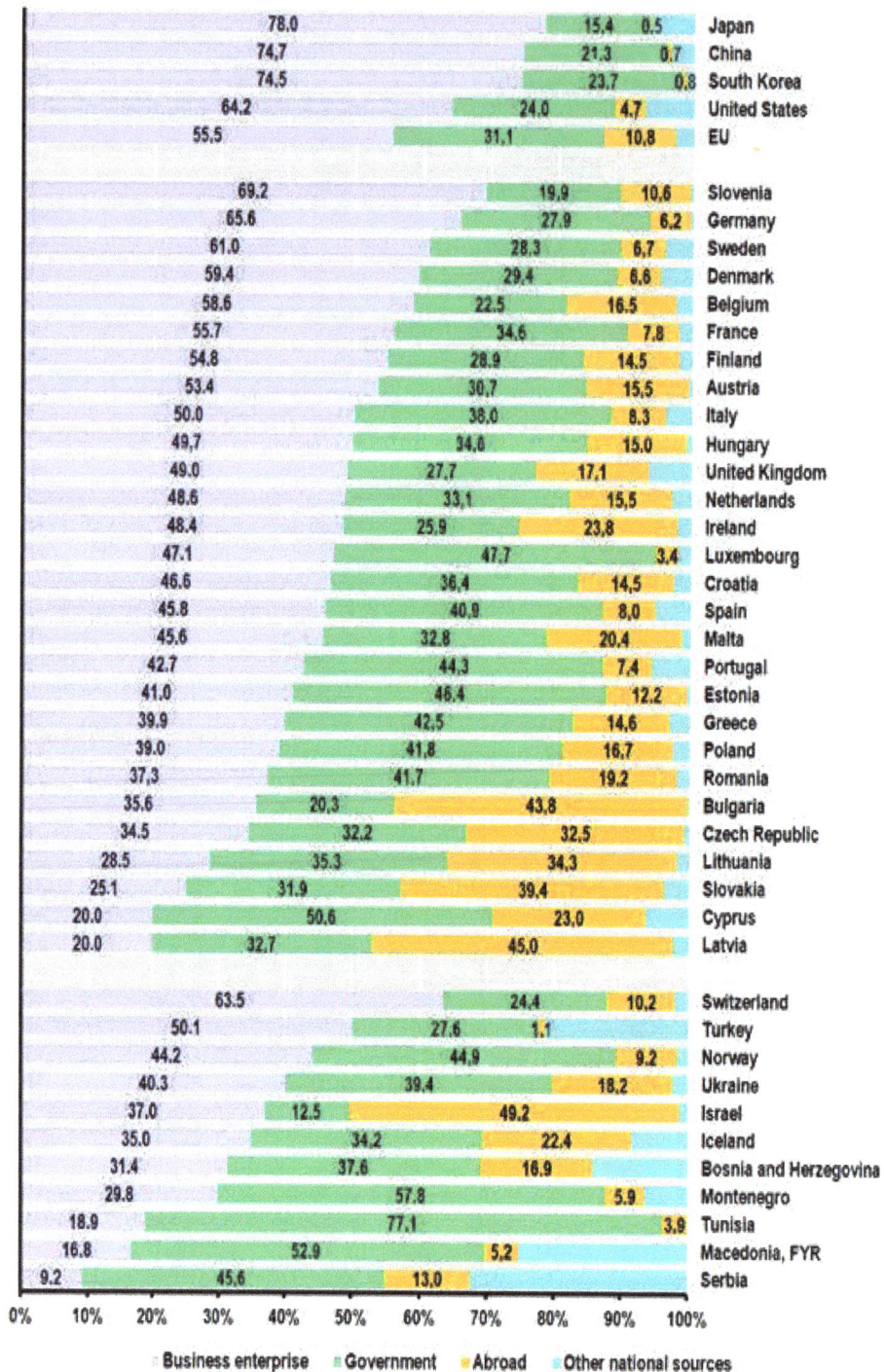

	Business enterprise	Government	Abroad	Other national sources	
78.0		15.4	0.5		Japan
74.7		21.3	0.7		China
74.5		23.7	0.8		South Korea
64.2		24.0	4.7		United States
55.5		31.1	10.8		EU
69.2		19.9	10.6		Slovenia
65.6		27.9	6.2		Germany
61.0		28.3	6.7		Sweden
59.4		29.4	6.6		Denmark
58.6		22.5	16.5		Belgium
55.7		34.6	7.8		France
54.8		28.9	14.5		Finland
53.4		30.7	15.5		Austria
50.0		38.0	8.3		Italy
49.7		34.8	15.0		Hungary
49.0		27.7	17.1		United Kingdom
48.6		33.1	15.5		Netherlands
48.4		25.9	23.8		Ireland
47.1		47.7	3.4		Luxembourg
46.6		36.4	14.5		Croatia
45.8		40.9	8.0		Spain
45.6		32.8	20.4		Malta
42.7		44.3	7.4		Portugal
41.0		46.4	12.2		Estonia
39.9		42.5	14.6		Greece
39.0		41.8	16.7		Poland
37.3		41.7	19.2		Romania
35.6	20.3	43.8			Bulgaria
34.5	32.2	32.5			Czech Republic
28.5	35.3	34.3			Lithuania
25.1	31.9	39.4			Slovakia
20.0	50.6	23.0			Cyprus
20.0	32.7	45.0			Latvia
63.5		24.4	10.2		Switzerland
50.1		27.6	1.1		Turkey
44.2		44.9	9.2		Norway
40.3		39.4	18.2		Ukraine
37.0	12.5	49.2			Israel
35.0	34.2	22.4			Iceland
31.4	37.6	16.9			Bosnia and Herzegovina
29.8	57.8	5.9			Montenegro
18.9	77.1	3.9			Tunisia
16.8	52.9	5.2			Macedonia, FYR
9.2	45.6	13.0			Serbia

Fig. 5 GERD financed by sector (%), 2015

Notes: Sweden, Israel: 2013; France: 2014; Greece, Austria, Iceland, Serbia: 2016; United States: R&D expenditure does not include most, or all capital expenditure; Israel: Defence (all or mostly) is not included. *Source*: DG Research and Innovation — Unit for the Analysis and Monitoring of National Research and Innovation Policies — Science, Research and Innovation performance of the EU 2018. *Source of data*: Eurostat, OECD, UNESCO.

6.2. Public Investment

Looking at the extent to which R&D public funding contributes to the whole of R&D expenditure, another remarkable fact is that the share of total R&D (GERD) financed by government in the EU has declined all the time, although, at 31.1% it is still higher than comparable shares of the US, China, Japan and South Korea (Figure 5), while the share of government financed GERD on GDP is still below that of the US. This trend is reflected in all Member States, but large differences can be observed across countries. In the EU15 Member States, the share of R&D public funding is generally higher in southern countries (Italy, Greece, Portugal, Spain), mainly as a result of less research carried out by the business sector. This is true only in part for the eastern Member States; they show an even smaller share of total research expenditure financed by the business sector, but, as the result of the much higher incidence (largely well above the EU average) that contribution from abroad has on the smaller total R&D expenditure of these countries. At the same time, it should be observed that the decline of the share of GERD financed by government is also the effect of the fall of direct government contributions to business research, which have dropped sharply in all countries since the beginning of the financial crisis (OECD 2018). Instead, the decrease of public funding of R&D involved public research only to a more limited extent, both as a share of GDP and in terms of total government expenditure (OECD 2018). This latter trend is mostly in line with the dynamics already observed for the EU share of the public budget allocated to R&D and is well reflected in the higher education (HERD) and government (GOVERD) components of public R&D expenditure on GDP (Figure 6).

Thus, given the remarkable divergences among the Member States recorded for all public R&D spending, this suggests a more in-depth analysis of the main patterns of public R&D expenditure emerging at the country level. The attempt is also that of unveiling the possible main direction of public R&D spending (and hence the direction of public R&D investment) while accounting for the whole of the R&D funding structure. The aim is twofold: to overcome important drawbacks that characterize the allocation of R&D funds in the public budget with respect to specific socio-economic objectives, and to assess to what extent the need for public R&D investment is consistent with broad R&D country strategies that are supposed to be followed. In fact, given the still substantial lack of information necessary for analyzing the real content of governmental appropriations and the structure of public R&D outlays, crossing data on R&D spending with those on actual R&D expenditure would be of little help in understanding R&D investment strategy by government, especially from the perspective of a comparative analysis between countries. Looking then at the patterns of public R&D expenditure, it is first of all relevant to compare, in terms of GDP and at the EU level, the steep decline of GOVERD expenditures with the upward trend found for both HERD expenditures and BERD (business) expenditures (Figure 6).

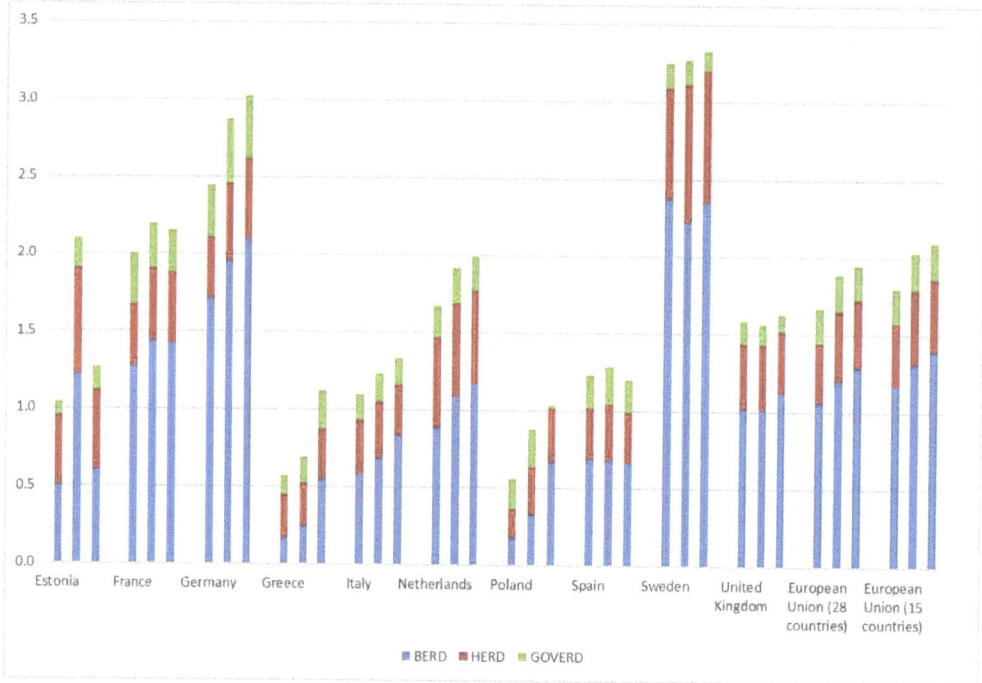

Fig. 6 BERD, HERD and GOVERD % of GDP per country, 2007, 2012, 2017

Source of data: Eurostat. Figure created by the authors.

This appears to indicate the increasing importance of research and innovation as a driver of economic activity, with the consequent need to adequately support the growth of human capital. However, the patterns of R&D expenditure at the country level are generally consistent with the EU trend only for the higher education and the business sectors, while both the dynamics and the intensity of the government expenditure are more country-specific. Furthermore, it should be noted that increasing intensities of R&D expenditure on GDP in the higher education's sector are widely observed with the highest and/or increasing intensities of R&D expenditure in the business sector, although there are some remarkable exceptions in countries where the intensity of R&D expenditure in the business sector is still well below the EU average. Trend reversals to lower intensities of the higher education expenditure are common instead in countries still boasting the lowest business R&D intensities (such as southern countries among the EU15 members) and to countries with the highest business R&D intensities (such as the Netherlands and the UK), although, excepting the UK, the latter still stand well above the EU average of higher education expenditure intensity.

All in all, the growth of R&D in the business sector appears to be an important driver of the total R&D expenditure in the EU as a whole. This is a result of remarkable differences in the R&D business intensities among countries, which were in part reflected in the growth of the higher education expenditure. This is a point of concern especially for Member States with the lowest business R&D intensity, as, in most cases, they have very low growth rates for the higher education expenditure and still show a large gap with respect to the EU average. Moreover, and most importantly, it should be noted that, despite the increase in R&D business expenditure, the EU R&D business intensity still lags well behind that of the US, Japan, Korea and China. However, there does not seem to be enough evidence to conclude that this is a consequence of the decrease of direct government support for business R&D. As has been widely observed (OECD 2018; European Commission 2018b), this decrease has, in fact, been largely compensated for by an increase in indirect support through tax incentives, the growth of which has been much higher in the EU than in the US, Japan, Korea and China, and which are now higher than they have ever been. It has also been pointed out that, among the Member States with the highest business R&D intensities, Germany and Finland did not adopt tax incentives, while more generally it has been observed that the use of tax incentives can hardly turn into expenditure additionality unless it becomes part of a more comprehensive strategy involving direct investment activity by government within a more targeted "mission-oriented" investment view (Mazzucato 2013). Indeed, significant evidence has emerged about additionality effects on R&D business expenditure, pointing out that greater benefits arise for high-tech sectors that already boast a higher R&D orientation (Freitas et al. 2017). As the entire amount of the R&D business expenditure is consistent with the industry specialization (Moncada 2016), this should also call for a closer consideration of the structure of the economy where tax incentives are to be implemented.

Additional R&D financing from abroad has also played an increasing role in all EU countries (European Commission 2018b) and, as mentioned above, has become a key component of total R&D investment, especially in eastern countries. However, when looking at the main public sources of R&D financing as represented by the European Commission Structural Funds and the Horizon 2020 program, we cannot help but notice that they hide major infrastructural divergences among the Member States.

With regard to the Structural Funds, also bearing in mind that in many more developed countries they cover a limited portion of the territory, it is quite clear that the share of funding explicitly allocated to R&I (research and innovation) projects is marginal among eastern countries (Figure 7), with only a few exceptions slightly above the EU average (16%).

Moreover, in these last countries, the extent to which R&I funds contribute to innovation in the business sector is well below the EU average in most cases, while shares well above the average are noticed mostly for countries that also hold the lowest shares of Structural Funds allocated to R&I projects. This could suggest that the initial development lag of these countries was such that funds were first used for the macroeconomic context as a whole, including support for the activity of research centres. The explicit contribution of R&I funds to innovation in the business sector is instead much higher among the EU15 Member states, although a remarkable variability

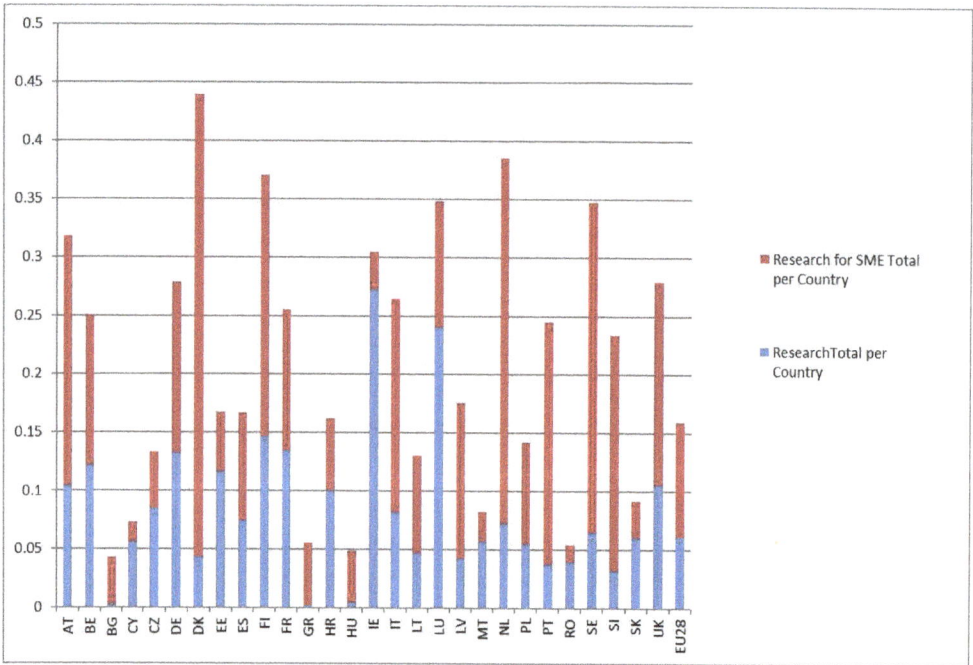

Fig. 7 Structural Funds: share of funding allocated to R&I (devoted to small and medium-sized enterprise (SME) and to research); total per country

Source of data: 2007–2013 database of the cumulative allocations (European Regional Development Fund (ERDF) and Cohesion Fund (CF)) to selected projects and expenditure at NUTS2 (https://ec.europa.eu/regional_policy/sources/docgener/evaluation/pdf/expost2013/wp13_3_db_nuts2_ae.xlsx). Figure created by the authors.

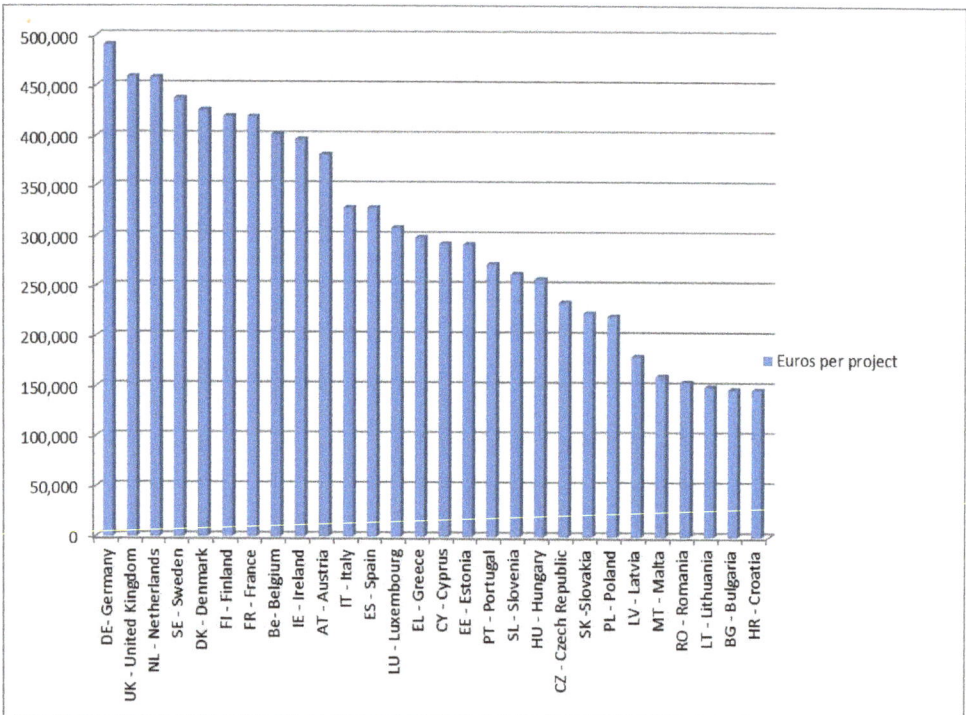

Fig. 8 Horizon 2020: average of European contribution per project and per country

Source of data: Horizon 2020 country profiles, May 2019. Figure created by the authors.

is observed across countries. In particular, the share of research and innovation funds allocated to innovation projects is quite specific for each country and, most importantly, does not show any relationship with the R&D intensity in the business sector.

With regard to the Horizon 2020 program, the latest figures show (Figure 8) that the average EU contribution per project is higher, the higher the countries' total R&D is as a share of GDP, although a further difference emerges between EU15 countries and the eastern Member States. Southern EU15 countries lag behind northern ones, but eastern countries lag almost always (excepting Portugal) behind southern EU15 countries, even when these are countries in which the total R&D expenditure makes up a similar share of GDP.

6.3. Final Remarks and Policy Considerations

The first paragraph of the Joint Statement on "New Economic Growth: The Role of Sciences, Technology, Innovation and Infrastructure" of the G7 of Academies of Science, which met in Rome in 2017, states:

> Science, technology and innovation have long been important drivers of economic growth and human development. Growth relies on the integration of basic and applied research, at both public and private levels, on an international scale. The challenge is to ensure that, even during phases of economic slowdown, science and technology continue to support the objectives of sustainability and improved living standards in all countries. Institutional arrangements are needed to make sure that the potential of science and technology is aligned with the paths and strategies of economic development, social inclusion and environmental sustainability, as argued by the United Nations report "Transforming our world: the 2030 Agenda for Sustainable Development." (G7 Academies of Science 2017)

This implies an increasing investment in infrastructures — both tangible and intangible — that contribute to inclusive development and to progress in science and technology, as mentioned in policy recommendations of the statement.

In this respect, the quantity (intensity of the R&D effort and the number of researchers) and the quality of the research produced, measured by the scientific impact and the ability to transfer it as innovation in the economy and society, determine measurable rankings that place the different scientific and innovative systems and their aggregations on a supranational scale, according to criteria and indicators that we have examined and compared in this chapter. All the most recent comparative analyses based on statistical data and their processing as quoted in the bibliography agree in registering a worldwide growth of these indicators (the effort in R&I), marked, however, by strong differentials between countries. The positioning of individual countries is confirmed, combining a strong economic dynamic with a corresponding commitment in R&D. Within this general framework, different groupings of countries are outlined on the basis of the industrial structure, the importance of the commitment to research by companies, and the ability of the public actor not only to compensate for weaknesses and "market failure" but also to stimulate the propensity to research and innovation with planned and targeted initiatives and not simply contextual policies and interventions.

The existence of differentials between countries in research and innovation performance, and within them between areas and regions, cannot, however, be tackled simply by rebalancing the resources used and/or orienting them towards common initiatives. Likewise, higher efficiency cannot be derived from strategies based on a reduction of public funding or on forcing public/private interaction, without the corresponding guidelines, or delegating the motivation for public funding of companies to the tax incentives and the choice of contents and objectives to a generic "demand-pull force" (Mazzucato 2013, 2019). In fact, it is necessary to assess to what extent the resources dedicated to R&D, and the relative spending modes are able to turn into an effective development lever, starting from the structural characteristics of the entire research and innovation system (Wirkierman et al. 2018). Moving from this last consideration, the present chapter, therefore, aims to underscore the "system infrastructure" nature of the research activity. It does so by highlighting, through the main results of the analyses and the most recent data on the subject, that the investment in research cannot be separated from policies and/or strategies that take into account the strengths and weaknesses of the productive fabric of each country.

In this context, the public actor is committed to playing a key role in orienting processes, both with respect to triple or quadruple helix models and to the construction of a strategy that is able to face the challenges of new technologies as well as of the behaviour of companies at the global level. To this is added, in particular for Europe, the dimension of supranational cooperation and the supporting role exercised by Structural Funds, which, beyond the purpose of overcoming structural imbalances among countries, highlight different propensities with respect to their use in support of research and innovation. Partnership and subsidiarity are, therefore, two particular elements of the strategy in support of research and innovation that must be integrated into the evaluation of the public budget allocation for research spending.

The lines of analysis followed in our work focused in particular on public investment, both direct and in support of companies, including the infrastructural endowment. Some trends have emerged that have already been highlighted by the various institutional organizations, from the OECD to the European Commission. As far as Europe is concerned, there are clear distinctions in the country profiles that, with considerable simplification, can be characterized with respect to two "geographical" directions: from north to south and from west to east, where a strong correlation seems to emerge between a substantial and growing public intervention and the presence of a significant business system with a strong propensity for R&I. By contrast, in less developed countries (which are characterized by a poor effort in R&D in the business sector) it is difficult for the public actor to exercise a leverage function with respect to the role of the companies. This turns to "contextual" infrastructural interventions, both in the technological field and as related to the overall infrastructural country endowment, by means of a "targeted" use of Structural Funds. Also, in this regard, even the examination of technological infrastructures as such and those aimed at research, despite the specificity of individual cases, indicates the presence of country-specific models. It was therefore considered useful, as analogous to what the OECD already does, to examine the vertical relations between public financing to beneficiaries and the executors, i.e. subjects in charge of performing R&D (in most cases public bodies), by analyzing the relationship between direct funding and the role exercised by support through tax incentives. As an example, Germany and Finland, which are high-tech countries, have not implemented tax credit policies that means giving priority to direct financing.

With respect to the use of Structural Funds, the attractiveness of funds "from abroad," or the propensity to participate and win on competitive funds, the differences among countries make it clear that we are not in the presence of a single "winning model" to follow. A careful analysis of the Community Scoreboard (European Commission 2019b) presents the double advantage of a reading over time and a spatial representation, according to the indicators used, of the positioning of individual countries. The report, while confirming the nature and characteristics of this positioning, points out that there are specific features of the countries that the indicators are hardly able to represent and that could offer the possibility of targeted interventions to be calibrated with respect to the desired objectives without requiring substantial resources. However, it seems clear that the confirmation of a polarization of "cases of excellence" does not help the realignment process called for by the cooperation, particularly with respect to the ability of weaker countries to use research results. This effect appears to be even more negative the more one considers the advance of newly industrialized countries and the potential reduction of interactions at the international level linked to new protectionist trade policies.

In the European context there is an attempt to tackle the above-mentioned polarization and the related growth of disparities between countries with, essentially, two instruments: (1) strengthening the infrastructural endowment, according to a logic of subsidiarity that uses different means such as Structural Funds and more generally other EU policies, and (2) promoting at the same time scientific excellence, cooperation and innovative capacity with the framework program instrument. In this regard, the choices made in Horizon Europe, both on method and merit of the "missions," and in general the policy to promote innovation and to build up and use technological and research infrastructures, even with limited resources, seem to provide a response to the role of guidance and support of the public actor coordinated at a supranational level. It remains to be seen how this translates into concrete contextual actions, in a correct balance between direct intervention and fiscal incentives and in not confining research to a "subsidiary" and "ancillary" role with respect to the more explicit industrial and commercial policies.

Our analysis has made use of a harmonized system of data that, born in the OECD context almost sixty years ago, has developed and established itself as the dominant data system, and has given rise to "supporting tools" both in the form of the production of manuals and through the promotion of committees to settle and elaborate proposals. This is a precious reality that has directed not only the collection phase, but also the use of data by analysts, scholars and decision-makers. However, on the whole, analysis of the data underlines the need to overcome some deficiencies that make difficult a better use of available information. In fact, it is difficult to interpret the strategy that guides investment processes, also considering the logic of the so-called "black box" of research that links decisions to results and their use, through implementation. This is due to the inherent limits of the GBARD (Government Budget Allocation for R&D) set-up and its classification (OECD 2015) and to the difficulty of establishing a link with the decision-making processes exercised by the beneficiaries of the resources. Also, the ex-post reading on the expenses does not help with respect to additionality, directionality and, above all, determination of the mix of resources needed to guide choices. We respond today to a growing demand for measurability of the impact of public R&D investment (in particular to facilitate the choices and the optimal allocation of resources) in a way that is not fully coordinated and without a fully equipped "toolbox" at our disposal.

It follows that better knowledge tools are required, starting from a structured evaluation of the policies, the related information, and the knowledge baggage that enables the establishment of relationships between the different interventions and the promotion of an impact assessment that is not related to merely a single intervention. The experience gained concretely and in several exercises at the European level within the Framework Program, although not unique and always successful, constitutes an undoubted point of reference from which to start.

Given this framework, the implementation of a new course of public investment research policies should, therefore, envisage a renewed orientation of the strategies consistent with the new course of missions/objectives formulated at the European level and, at the same time, point to a coordination with policies aimed at increasing the innovative potential of the economic system, in relation to the characteristics of the productive specialization of each country.

References

Bodas Freitas, I., F. Castellacci, R. Fontana, F. Malerba and A. Vezzulli (2017) "Sectors and the Additionality Effects of R&D Tax Credits: A Cross Country Microeconomic Analysis", Research Policy 46: 57–72, https://doi.org/10.1016/j.respol.2016.10.002

European Commission (2018a) "Horizon Europe Impact Assessment — Staff Working Document, June 2018", https://ec.europa.eu/info/publications/horizon-europe-impact-assessment-staff-working-document_en

European Commission (2018b), "Science, Research and Innovation Performance of the EU 2018. Strengthening the Foundations for Europe's Future", https://ec.europa.eu/info/sites/info/files/srip-report-full_2018_en.pdf

European Commission (2019a) "Technology Infrastructures — Commission Staff Working Document", https://ec.europa.eu/transparency/regdoc/rep/10102/2019/EN/SWD-2019-158-F1-EN-MAIN-PART-1.PDF

European Commission (2019b) "European Innovation Scoreboard 2019", https://ec.europa.eu/growth/industry/policy/innovation/scoreboards_en

G7 Academies of Science (2017) "New Economic Growth: The Role of Science, Technology, Innovation and Infrastructure", https://royalsociety.org/~/media/about-us/international/g-science-statements/2017-may-3-new-economic-growth.pdf?la=en-GB

Mazzucato, M. (2013) *The Entrepreneurial State: Debunking Public vs. Private Sector Myths*. London: Anthem Publishing.

Mazzucato, M. (2019) "Governing Missions in the European Union", https://ec.europa.eu/info/sites/info/files/research_and_innovation/contact/documents/ec_rtd_mazzucato-report-issue2_072019.pdf

Moncada Paternò Castello, P. (2016) "Corporate R&D Intensity Decomposition: Theoretical, Empirical and Policy Issues", *IPTS Working Papers on Corporate R&D and Innovation* 2.

OECD (2015) *Frascati Manual 2015: Guidelines for Collecting and Reporting Data on Research and Experimental Development*. Paris: OECD Publishing, https://doi.org/10.1787/9789264239012-en

OECD (2018) *OECD Science, Innovation and Technology Outlook 2018. Adapting to Technological and Societal Disruption*. Paris: OECD Publishing, https://doi.org/10.1787/sti_in_outlook-2018-en

United Nations (2015) "Transforming our World: The 2030 Agenda for Sustainable Development", https://sustainabledevelopment.un.org/content/documents/21252030%20Agenda%20for%20Sustainable%20Development%20web.pdf

Wirkierman, A., T. Ciarli, M. Savona (2018) "Varieties of European National Innovation Systems", *ISI-Growth Working Paper* 13, http://www.isigrowth.eu/wp-content/uploads/2018/05/working_paper_2018_13.pdf

7. Social Investment and Infrastructure

Anton Hemerijck,[1] Mariana Mazzucato[2]
and Edoardo Reviglio[3]

Introduction: The Welfare Lesson from the Great Recession

Ten years after the first economic crisis of twenty-first century capitalism, Europe seems to have passed the nadir of the Great Recession. Time to count our blessings: a rerun of the Great Depression has been avoided and recovery, albeit timid, is under way, while unemployment and poverty are coming down. The jury is still out on whether economic and job growth will return to pre-crisis levels. Unemployment remains high in the European Union (EU), especially in the economies heavily scarred by the European debt crisis, such as Greece and Spain. The political aftershocks of the Great Recession — ranging from a rather hard Brexit, the rise of populism in Western Europe, the spread of illiberal nationalism in Eastern Europe, and escalating trade tensions between China and the United States (US) — forecast the deceleration of the world economy, and the challenges of a costly transformation into a greener world economy now confront the European Union project, anchored on a premise of peace, prosperity and democracy, underpinned by an existential predicament.

In the final quarter of the twentieth century, the friction between welfare states' social and economic priorities has often been described as irreconcilable. The American economist Arthur Okun coined the "big trade-off" between equality and efficiency, proclaiming that, to the extent that welfare spending is used as a political instrument to reduce inequality, this harms economic growth because of the market distortions that come with comprehensive social protection. However, as Figure 1 reveals, this predicament no longer holds. Many welfare states in Continental and Northern Europe have proven capable of reconciling high levels of employment with comparatively low inequality (see the upper-right side of Figure 1).

1   European University Institute, Florence.
2   Institute for Innovation & Public Purpose — University College London.
3   Cassa Depositi e Prestiti — CDP; Università Luiss Guido Carli, Rome; International University College, Turin.

https://doi.org/10.11647/OBP.0222.07

Even though social spending levels have been consolidated over the past two decades, practically all European welfare regimes have been recalibrating the basic policy mixes upon which they were built after 1945 in a multi-dimensional fashion, most importantly to address new social risks (Hemerijck 2013). Before the 2008 Global Financial Crisis struck, across the more mature welfare state of Europe social investment reform was swiftly becoming the fil rouge in welfare reform. In the face of intensified demographic ageing and disruptive technological change, future economic growth will rely heavily on high levels and employment and improvements in productivity. Today there is ample proof that social investments in child-care, long-term care, education and training, active labour market policy, lifelong learning and active ageing, paid parental leave, family services and benefits, in a complementary fashion, significantly contribute to employment, productivity, demographic balance, even through improved fertility, and tax revenue, and help reduce long-term reliance on compensatory social protection policies, at lower levels of poverty. Although the Great Recession interrupted the social investment turn in many countries, social investment reform today is even more imperative than before to make up for a lost decade. Unsurprisingly, Nordic countries with independent currencies, inclusive safety nets and a strong social service tradition, have been best able to protect social investment progress. Euro area countries, under the Fiscal Compact, have, by and large, taken a back seat on social investment.

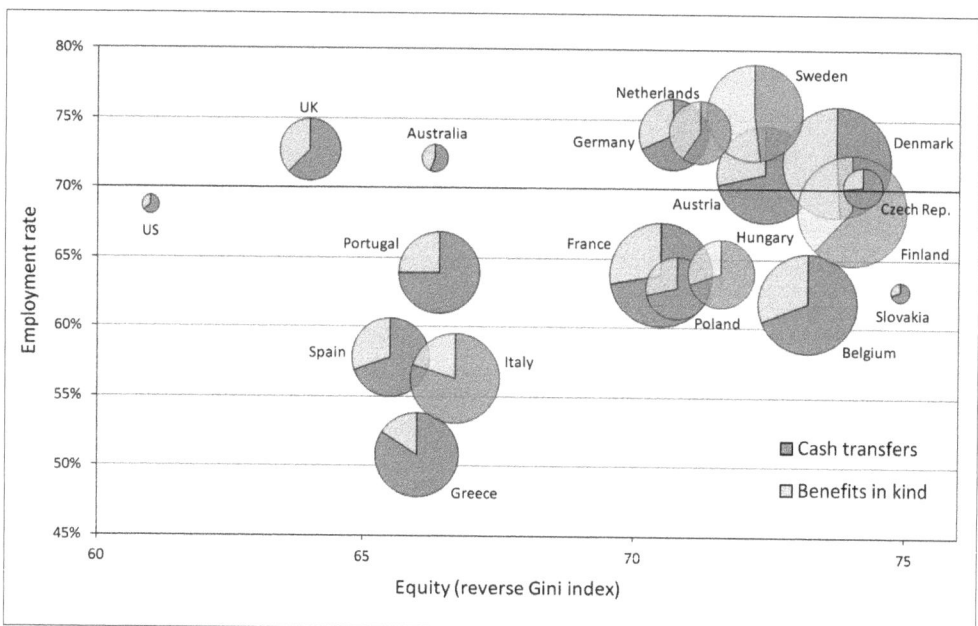

Fig. 1 Employment rate, equality and welfare spending in selected OECD countries (averages 2010-2015). *Note*: Only OECD countries with at least 5 million inhabitants are shown; missing data for Canada. The black line marks the Lisbon employment target of 70%. The size of the pie-chart markers indicates the total welfare spending.

Source: Hemerijck and Ronchi (2020).

For almost two decades, EU institutions have professed their support for social investment welfare provision, from the idea of "social policy as a productive factor" in the 1997 Amsterdam Treaty, through Social Affairs Commissioner Laszlo Andor's "social investment package" in 2013, to the principles laid down in the 2017 European Pillar of Social Rights. However, in practice, the social investment impetus has been put on ice with the onslaught of the Great Recession. There is no justification for this continued volatile and contradictory policy orientation. Today, the evidence on social investment returns is stronger than ever before. Moreover, structurally low interest rates present us with a post-crisis opportunity not to be wasted. Not least, European publics expect pro-EU political forces to put their money where their mouth is in terms of enabling citizens to live dignified, secure lives. It is time for EU-institutions to abandon austerity and make a real commitment to social investment and its supporting infrastructure.

7.1. The Social Investment Life-Course Multiplier Effect

As the Great Recession was triggered by a financial crisis, just like the Great Depression, rather than a stagflation real-economy crisis (as in the 1970s and 1980s), it offered up a test-case for the Keynesian-Beveridgean welfare state. This welfare state is based on compulsory social insurance, able to act as an automatic stabilizer in times of recession, cushioning crises through anti-cyclical consumption smoothing. By and large, automatic stabilization social security, largely absent in the 1930s, provided the largest stimulus in most countries while protecting household income after 2008.

The number (quantity) and productivity (quality) of current and future employees and taxpayers are central to the long-term financial sustainability of the welfare state. Maximizing employment, employability and productivity helps to sustain the "carrying capacity" of the modern welfare state. To do this, states need to effectively coordinate the following three policy objectives: (1) raising and maintaining the employment "stock" (human capital, skills, health of population); (2) facilitating "flows" between various labour market and (gendered) life-course transitions; and (3) using "buffers" for the mitigation of social risks (unemployment, sickness) through income protection and economic stabilization (Hemerijick 2017). Commitments in these areas produce mutually reinforcing positive effects over the life cycle. They generate aggregate economic growth and social well-being at the individual and household levels, and are key to making social investment work.

The growing evidence on how effective social investment reinforces high employment, low poverty, decent growth in fiscal balance, has inspired Anton Hemerijck to conjecture the operation of a social investment "life-course multiplier", whereby cumulative social investment returns over the life-course plausibly generate a cycle of well-being, in terms of employment opportunities, gender equity, and a significant mitigation of intergenerational poverty. The virtuous cycle initiates from early investments in children through high quality ECEC (Early Childhood Education and Care), which translate into higher levels of educational attainment, which in turn, together with more tailor-made vocational training, spill over into higher and more productive employment in the medium term (Brilli 2014; Heckman 2006; Cumba and Heckman 2007). To the extent that employment participation is furthermore supported by effective work-life balance policies, including adequately funded and publicly available childcare, higher levels of (female) employment with potentially lower gender pay and employment gaps can be foreseen (del Boca, Locatelli and Vuri 2005; Korpi, Ferrarini and Englund 2009). On top of protecting households against worklessness and poverty (Härkönen 2014; Cantillon and Vandenbroucke 2014), more opportunities for women and men to combine parenting with paid labour, moreover, is likely to have a dampening effect on the so-called "fertility gap", the difference between the desired number of children (aspirational fertility) and the actual number (Beaujouan and Sobotka 2014; Borgstrom et al. 2016; d'Albis, Greulich and Ponthière 2017) A final knock-on effect is a higher effective retirement age, provided the availability of active ageing and lifelong learning policies, including portable and flexible pensions, for older cohorts (Walker, 2002; Jenkins et al., 2003; Schmid, 2015). Higher and more productive employment implies a larger tax base to sustain welfare commitments and to keep the virtuous cycle of capacitating social justice alive.

For our contribution, what is important to emphasize with respect to social investment reform is that the welfare state has become ever more service-oriented. To the extent that the cash-benefit welfare infrastructure is essentially a well-functioning ATM-machine, the social investment welfare state is one that relies heavily on infrastructure (of day-care centres, schools, hospitals, nursery homes, post-graduate training facilities that require significant investment in both physical and professional prowess), and, most importantly, on state capacity.

7.2. A Golden Social Investment Rule in the Stability and Growth Pact

For almost two decades EU institutions have professed their support for social investment. However, in practice, the social investment impetus has been put on ice with the onslaught of the Great Recession. It is important to remember that the single currency and the Economic and Monetary Union (EMU) were negotiated at a time when the "supply side" revolution in economic theory and the folk-theorem of the big trade-off between equity and efficiency were riding high. The architects of the Maastricht Treaty naively believed a monetary union tied to the Stability and Growth Pact (SGP), would inescapably force Member States to keep their "wasteful" welfare states in check, underwritten by the Maastricht Treaty's infamous "no-bailout" clause, in the belief that all public spending, especially social spending, is wasteful. As such, the rule book of the SGP disqualifies public investments in lifelong education and training in the knowledge economy as wasteful consumptive expenditures.

There is no justification for this ideological short-sightedness anymore. Today, the evidence for social investment returns is stronger than ever before. Moreover, structurally low interest rates present us with a post-crisis opportunity not to be wasted. Not least, European publics expect pro-EU political forces to put their money where their mouth is in terms of enabling citizens to live dignified, secure lives.

We must ratchet up domestic social investment with EMU support by exempting human capital "stock" investments from the rules of the SGP. The post-crisis collapse in interest rates should be used to establish, consolidate and expand social investments that benefit future generations and consolidate fiscal health, especially in the face of adverse demographic trends.

We therefore propose a "Golden Rule" of exempting human capital stock spending from the euro area fiscal rule book for 1.5% of GDP for about one decade, as a flagship initiative of the new European Commission. A viable division of responsibilities between the EU and the Member States is possible without trespassing on treasured national welfare state jealousies. Social security "buffers," the core prerogative of the national welfare state, should remain in the remit of national welfare provision. The "flow" function — which concerns labour market regulation and collective bargaining in synchronization with work-life balance, gender equality and family-friendly employment relations — is best served by mutual learning and monitoring processes of open coordination at national and EU level, engaging national governments with relevant experts and the social partners in sharing good practices.

What we are left with is guaranteeing social investment in lifelong human capital "stock". Here the EU needs to change the fiscal rules in the SGP regarding social investment. Citizens all over the EU are craving support for social investments, and the financial costs are minimal given the short- and long-term profitability of the economic and social returns.

7.3. A New Deal for Social Europe: Boosting Social Infrastructure

Lifelong human capital "stock" includes investment in social infrastructure. In the EU, since 2007 investments, both public and private, have fallen by 20%. In public investments, as much as 75% of the reduction is due to the collapse of the works carried out by local administrations which, in the European average, represent around two thirds of the total public investment (European Commission 2016; Fransen, del Bufalo and Reviglio 2018; EIB 2019). Investment in social infrastructure — infrastructure that pertains to social services — has been especially weakened. This is the case for three sectors that are crucial for the future well-being of European citizens: health, education and housing.[4]

Current investment in social infrastructure in the EU has been estimated at approximately €170 bn per year.[5] The minimum infrastructure investment gap in these sectors is estimated at €100–150 bn, representing a total gap of at least €1.5 tn for the period between 2018 and 2030 (Fransen, del Bufalo and Reviglio 2018).

Social infrastructures are important because they shape the nature of our society. High-quality large-scale investments in social infrastructure are especially important for the EU given demographic projections, radical structural changes in the labour market and innovation. The question is, however, how to find financing to close such an enormous gap at a time of high public debt in many regions with a long-term perspective for only moderate economic growth rates?

This challenge is at the heart of former European Commission President Romano Prodi's call for a New Deal for Social Europe and contained in the recently presented Report of the High-Level Task Force on Investing in Social Infrastructure in Europe, promoted by the European Long-Term Investors Association (ELTI) and the European Commission (Fransen, del Bufalo and Reviglio 2018).

Europe's future demographics pose daunting challenges for the coming decades. Europe today already has one of the lowest proportions in the world of working population to non-working population (children and pensioners). In 2060, one in three European citizens will be over sixty-five (of whom one in three will be more than eighty years old), while only 57% of the population will be of working age (fifteen to sixty-four).

This aging of the population will have significant effects, particularly on the cost of health care and pension systems. In addition, substantial investments will need to be made in prenatal, scholastic and university structures. All this will need to happen at the same time as demand for affordable housing for new families, students and young workers continues to grow.

Incentives for procreation and well-targeted immigration policies should become an integral part of the new European social and economic agenda. If the European demography is not revived, the risk of a progressive decline of the European civilization

---

4   "Fiscal consolidation during the crisis has, in fact, strongly reduced fiscal space for public investments in some regions. For economic infrastructure (transport, energy and telecoms) which is mostly done at the central level, and for that done by the corporate sector and by local utilities (which is mostly outside the perimeter of the public sector) the reduction has been less pronounced. Some EU countries, where investments in small and medium-sized public works in social infrastructure are made at sub-national level, have seen a dramatic decrease in spending on social infrastructure. Because sub-national governments carry out two-thirds of total public-sector investments on average in the EU [...] and these investments are of a small and medium size, we have a major challenge here that is different from general infrastructure investments" (European Commission 2016, p. 101).

5   According to estimates of the Prodi Report (Fransen, del Bufalo and Reviglio 2018), current p.a. spending in Education and Life Learning is estimated at €65 bn, and the annual investment gap at €15 bn; for Health and Long-term care current p.a. spending is estimated at €75 bn, and the annual investment gap at €70 bn; and current p.a. spending in Affordable Housing is estimated at €28 bn, and the annual investment gap at €57 bn.

becomes dramatically real. The speed of globalization requires us to act rapidly and to be ambitious.

Among the High-Level Task Force's recommendations are many addressed to the European Union and the Commission, including: stepping up the use of innovative financial products; providing more assistance in project development at the local level; implementing regulatory improvements; European Semester reporting; suggestions for the next Multiannual Financial Framework; proposals to move towards upward convergence; and a call to establish a far-reaching European public-private fund for social infrastructure. It should be noted that although the High-Level Task Force promotes a European approach, it is careful to respect the principle of subsidiarity.

This call for action seeks the greatest social investment ever undertaken in Europe. We must not, however, be afraid of this initiative. In a time of political disaffection and distrust, an ambitious, broad and effective effort will send a strong message to European citizens that their institutions and governments want to bring people and society back to the centre of the European project.

7.4. How to Invest in Social Infrastructure to Fill the Gap? The Creation of a European Fund for Social Infrastructure

The Prodi Report proposes innovative solutions to finance health, education and social housing at a sustainable cost for European public finances. Social infrastructure is mostly funded through public budgets, since they barely produce cash flows on their own. Most of the time, direct contracts are financed by long-term loans. Thanks to quantitative easing, the spreads between Member States have been reduced significantly. But this will not last forever, and local authorities' debt offers little room for manoeuvre (Prodi and Reviglio 2019).

Two issues therefore arise. The first concerns the possibility of investments that do not weigh on public debt. The second is to ensure that the weakest countries and those most in need of social infrastructure can finance it at a lower cost.

Suppose a municipality or region needs to invest in social infrastructure but has no fiscal space. It can decide to implement it through innovative forms of institutional public-private-community-not profit partnerships (Foster and Iaione 2016, 2019). If the construction risk is transferred to the private individual it will not weigh on public debt (Fransen, del Bufalo and Reviglio 2018; EPEC 2016). The local administration will pay for the work through an "availability fee" which will affect expenditures year after year, but not its debt. Costs can be kept down by a national or European grant, public guarantees or tax incentives. Fiscal space can be provided through a "special clause for social investments". Contributions in kind can be made using local public heritage assets (land or buildings, for example). An institutional "technical assistance" system can ensure that risks and profits are well distributed between the public and the private sectors. This solution, known as "blending", helps contain debt and, at the same time, may represent an incentive to reduce waste in current expenditures. First- and second-generation PPP in the UK and elsewhere have not been always very successful. But this does not mean that new, more advanced and innovative schemes may be structured today. More of these "urban regeneration initiatives" should be supported. Time is of the essence. Aging society and support to the younger generation must become a priority in EU policy agenda. If we don't act bravely, Europe is destined for an inexorable decline.

This means, as we shall argue in the last part of this chapter, building mutualistic partnerships. There are many publics in 'the public.' In the public value framework, contestation of actual value production and evaluation systems is a critical success factor. Involving civil society organizations in framing public policy goals (missions) is a central part of the co-creation process. Producing public value requires collaboration and co-creation; public value cannot be created from the top down. Missions present an opportunity to put citizen participation at the heart of social innovation policy.

Some EU countries are desperately in need of infrastructure and growth, but are penalized by their credit rating. The creation of a European Fund for Social Infrastructure would address this.[6] It would issue European Social Bonds to all Member States. The bonds would have a high rating and mitigate the risks associated with certain projects. This would largely solve the problem of sovereign spreads. The Fund would have a technical assistance network (the European Investment Bank (EIB) and State Investment Banks (SIBs) may be the best candidates for this endeavour) to assist administrations in building "European" quality economic and financial plans. Long-term investors, infrastructure Funds and SIBs would contribute to its capital through shares and investing in a liquid market of European Social Bonds issued by the Fund.[7] This would help meet the investors' demand for infrastructural long-term finance instruments. In 1993, then-European Commission President Jacques Delors introduced Eurobonds. There are two main differences between these and the Euro Social Bonds proposed in the Prodi Report. First, the Fund does not require a guarantee from Member States. It manages uncertainty by "tranching" securities according to their riskiness. Second, the Fund would limit itself to social infrastructure and specialize in sectors with specific characteristics. The markets, along with the EIB and the SIBs, would remain in charge of economic infrastructure.

---

6   The High-Level Task Force (HLTF) produced a paper with a proposal to set up a New European Fund for Social Infrastructure as part of a potential EU Social Infrastructure Agenda within the Juncker Plan. The paper has been discussed by internal and external experts and found consensus both on technical and political ground. However, it was decided not to include the paper in the *Report* (Fransen, del Bufalo and Reviglio 2018), but rather mention the work done with the hope that it may be re-discussed within the new Commission.

7   Social infrastructure investments, as a sub-class of infrastructure investment, have some distinctive features: small average size of capital expenditure (capex); high level of operating expenses related to capex; great opportunities for portfolio diversification; bundling of projects; low volatility of returns; low correlation to other assets; potential attractiveness for large long-term investors (see EDHEC-Risk Institute 2012).

7.5. Firms or Markets in Infrastructure Financing

This section argues that it would make economic sense to analyses the possible establishment of a large European public-private fund for financing social infrastructure (Fransen, del Bufalo and Reviglio 2018; Prodi and Reviglio 2019). From an economic perspective a large fund is like a firm and as such, could have a long-term stabilizing role within the European financial market for infrastructure financing. We will make the point using a well-known debate in economic theory that started with Ronald Coase's paper on "The Nature of the Firm" (Coase 1937).

Equity for project financing at the global level is worth over $350 bn (Inderst 2017). There is a small market today which, according to most experts, will experience great growth rates in the coming decades. It is difficult to predict when and how fast. Usually, when the financial industry is moving with such strong determination, as it has been doing in recent years, then it may become a game changer. Policy makers and regulators are pressed to move fast to create the right conditions for expanding these markets. It is difficult to predict how the process will unfold (Bassanini and Reviglio 2011; Bassanini 2012; Ehlers 2014; Bassanini and Reviglio 2015; Arezki et al. 2016).

We will try to understand the main determinants of this paradigm shift. When we talk about public-private initiatives, we mean a variety of schemes. We may envisage a project finance market composed of single projects, which have a life of their own. A highway or an offshore wind plant may rely mostly on the cash flows it produces. A project finance initiative, which involves many parties for a very long time (up to fifty years), consists of a "bundle or web of external contracts". The necessary involvement of such a wide range of parties in infrastructure projects — construction companies, operators, government authorities, private investors, insurers and those citizens most directly affected — makes designing an efficient set of contracts a complex but essential task. The nature of contingencies and the proper sharing of risks among the different agents are pivotal. The quality of institutions and the rule of law are often determining factors in providing finance for infrastructure, even when a project by itself appears to be financially viable.

Special purpose vehicles (SPV) engage external firms to plan, construct and manage the infrastructure. If the projects are smaller — as in most social infrastructure sectors — the contracts are standardized and numerous projects bundled together to increase the size of the financial instruments issued for private investors. Such arrangements are doomed to face the typical complexities of the "principal-agent theory of contracts".

The point we wish to make is that firms may be preferred to markets in building and financing infrastructure. In economic theory, this is a question, which goes back to the Coase's paper on "The Nature of the Firm" (1937), in which he tries to explain why some activities are directed by market forces and others by firms. The answer, at the time, was that firms are a response to the high cost of using markets. It is often cheaper to direct tasks by fiat than to negotiate and enforce separate contracts for every transaction. This is easier and cheaper within the firm itself. For example, I switch an employee from one function to another without having to go through negotiations or the setting up of new contracts. For many business arrangements, it is difficult to set down all that is required of each party in all circumstances. Therefore, a formal contract is by necessity "incomplete" and sustained largely on trust. Coase defined a firm as "a nexus of contracts". Most of these contracts, we have argued, are internal to the firm; this means that the firm has more power to change them if needed and it also means that they have lower transaction costs than external contracts. This is a competitive advantage of firms versus markets. Moreover, the firm usually has a large balance sheet, so it may get better financing conditions, as well as more risk-absorbing capacity. The firm is also made up of a long-term community. Employees and their skills tend to remain within the firm, increasing the long-term base for human potential. Finally, a firm has lower general costs because of its scale.

So, while we concentrate on a new "asset class" emerging, we should not forget the role of firms (including funds) in infrastructure building (including social infrastructure). Good examples are the European Investment Bank (EIB), The European Bank for Development and Reconstruction (EBRD), the Council of Europe Development Bank (CEB) and the large European national promotional banks (Bassanini and Reviglio 2012, 2015; Garonna and Reviglio 2015). What makes these institutions such successful cases? The answer is the typical features of a well-run firm, such as: highly skilled personnel and management who share a common mission and have long-term internal contracts with the bank; a large and well-capitalised balance sheet which ensures low funding costs, strong capacities to manage risks and operations in different sovereign risk environments; the capacity to reduce the cost of its co-financing by offering pricing and duration which are lower and longer than commercial banks, thus promoting the "crowding-in" of private/institutional money and, by doing so, the European process of economic and social convergence.

7.6. The Role of State Investment Banks (SIBs) in Financing Social Infrastructure in the European Union

State Investment Banks (SIBs) in Europe include the European Investment Bank (EIB) and the Council of Europe Development Banks (CEB).[8] They are designed to provide medium- and long-term capital for productive investment. They have historically played, among others, an important role in funding social infrastructure (Macfarlane and Mazzucato 2018; Luna-Martinez and Vicente 2012).

The role of SIBs has grown during the crisis and will probably remain crucial for years. They have introduced a new philosophy in the European financial system.

---

8   National State Investment Banks (SIBs) in the EU are also known as National Promotional Banks and Institutions (NPBIs).

They have created new financial instruments and new guarantee schemes; provided significant additional resources to support the economy during the Great Recession, by financing infrastructure and small- and medium-sized businesses, either through the banking system or directly; and set up new European and domestic long-term equity funds to invest in infrastructure projects and improve company capitalization.

More generally, they continue to play an important role in financing the real economy (primarily in terms of long-term, patient, capital investment), by using their professional banking and investment skills and risk absorption capacity, and by acting as brokers of developmental/transformational financing.

Moreover, they have expanded their role thanks to their credibility as intermediaries in financial flows. There are several reasons for this: they have a long history (track record); they behave in a predictable, non-volatile way; they remain untainted by financial crisis abuses; they are known to structure transactions carefully; they have in-depth local knowledge; they benefit from preferred creditor status; they have political weight; and they have provided returns that are consistent with the risk (and the market) concerned (Bassanini, Pennisi and Reviglio 2015).

Traditionally their role in the financial system is to intervene to fill market failures, to be complementary to the market (and not in competition with it) being careful not to "crowd-out" private capital. Today, as we shall argue, these missions need deep re-thinking. We shall try to explain how and why we need this "radical" conceptual transition.

7.7. The Concept of "Public Value" and the Role of Social Action

Public value is value that is created collectively for a public purpose (Mazzucato and Ryan-Collins 2019; Macfarlane and Mazzucato 2018; Mazzucato and Penna 2016). This requires an understanding of how public institutions, such as mission-oriented public banks, can engage citizens in defining purpose (participatory structures), nurture organizational capabilities and capacity to shape new opportunities (organizational competencies); dynamically assess the value created (dynamic evaluation); and ensure that societal value is distributed equitably (inclusive growth). Purpose-driven capitalism requires more than just words and gestures of goodwill. It requires purpose to be put at the centre of how companies, public investment banks and governments are run and how they interact with civil society. This is especially true for social innovation which has a very tight relationship between the traditional mission of promotional banks and participatory democracy. Social infrastructure, in fact, shapes the nature of our society and as such needs direct participation from citizens.

We consider "public value mapping" and "public value failure" as counterpoints to market failure theory, as a means of justifying government intervention and public policy.

Public value results from the collective imagination, investments and pressure from social movements. To produce effective social movements, knowledge and capabilities are required in the planning, production, management and interactions among the different interest groups and citizens.

The conventional view is that public goods are required to fill the gap created by a lack of investment by the private sector. This is another example of the state playing the market-fixing role. However, public value goes beyond public goods. Rather than asking what gap or failure public goods are filling and fixing, we should ask what are the outcomes that society desires, and how can we make these happen? To do this, it is useful to begin with an understanding of markets as outcomes of the interactions between different actors in the economy.

The concept of public value enables us to overcome the dubious dichotomy between market and state. The market-failure justification also implies that pure private market goods can exist independently of public action. However, as illustrated by the seminal work of Karl Polanyi, *The Great Transformation*, there are very few examples of such phenomena. Most markets were forced into existence by collective action and policy. Many government actions enable markets to function or create and shape markets through investment, demand generation through procurement, legal codes, antitrust policies, university scientists and physical infrastructure. Markets are co-created by actors from all sectors, but economic theory does not view public actors as creators and shapers. This new role for governments as co-creators of markets would make it possible to shift not only the rate but also the direction of economic growth through collective action. Thus, the concept of public value is fundamental for guiding public action in shaping markets and co-creating the direction of economic growth. Public investment banks can have a crucial role in this change of paradigm.

7.8. How Social Investment and Social Infrastructure is Part of Public Value

The search for value should not be limited to soul-searching inside the private sector. Public institutions must also carefully consider their role in creating public value. The most ambitious public organizations did more than just fix market failures. They had ambition, purpose and a mission that extended beyond day-to-day politics.

We argue that public value should be understood as a way of measuring progress towards the achievement of broad and widely accepted societal goals that are agreed on by participatory processes. Creating a social space where citizenship rethinking public sector delivery and social infrastructure reshape the very nature of community. Participatory democracy in common value creating contributes to reshape capitalism.

To get real about value we need to concentrate on purpose throughout governance and production, recognize that economic value is created collectively, and build more symbiotic partnerships among public institutions, private institutions and civil society. This is not about levelling the playing field but tilting it towards the direction of sustainable and inclusive growth. The concept of public value must be nested within a theory and practice of creating value within the public sector. From a policy perspective, it is essential to answer and operationalize the four following challenges:

1. What value is created: a purpose-driven approach engaged with civil society;

2. How to create it: capabilities within the public sector and dynamic partnerships;

3. How to assist it: dynamic metrics beyond cost benefit analysis;

4. How to share its benefits: risks and rewards for inclusive growth.

7.9. The Need for Mission-Oriented State Investment Banks

Finance is not neutral; the type of finance available can affect both the investments made and the type of activity that occurs (O'Sullivan 2004; Mazzucato 2013). The types of financial institutions and markets that exist have a material impact on activity in the real economy.

Financing social infrastructure requires not just any type of finance, but long-term patient strategic finance. Short-termism and risk-aversion means that the private sector will often not invest in higher-risk areas until future returns become more certain. Because the governance arrangements of SIBs typically do not create pressure to deliver short-term returns, they can provide patient financing over a longer time horizon, prioritize wider social and environmental objectives, and take a different approach to risk and reward.

Although certain sectors might be more suited for sector-specific strategies, there is a growing consensus that SIBs that are "mission-oriented", with investment activities guided by specific missions focused on overcoming key societal challenges, tend to be more effective than those which are focused on more neutral economic objectives, such as promoting "growth" or "competitiveness", sometimes referred to as "grand challenges". These include environmental threats, such as climate change, and demographic, health and well-being concerns, as well as the difficulties of generating sustainable and inclusive growth (Macfarlane and Mazzucato 2017). "Mission-oriented" policy responds to these grand challenges by identifying and articulating concrete problems that can galvanize production, distribution and consumption patterns across various sectors. In doing so, it recognizes that:

- economic growth has not only a rate but also a direction;

- innovation requires investments and risk taking by both private and public actors;

- the state has a role in not only fixing markets but also in co-creating and shaping them;

- successful innovation policy combines the need to set directions from above with the ability to enable bottom-up experimentation and learning; and

- missions may require consensus building in civil society.

A mission-based approach can help to ensure that SIBs do not end up merely supporting a static list of sectors — a strategy that often gets criticized for its risk of "picking winners". Rather, mission-oriented policies focus the vertical element not on sectors but on societal challenges, that require different sectors to invest and innovate. This involves picking the problems and helping any organization (across the public sector, private sector, third sector and across all manufacturing and services) that are willing to engage with the investments and activities that such challenges require. In other words, they require picking the "willing" not picking the "winners".

There is therefore an opportunity to tailor the mandates of Europe's SIBs towards supporting a mission-oriented agenda. To fulfil a mission-oriented mandate, SIBs must have a wide range of instruments at its disposal, including both debt and equity, suited to different areas of the risk landscape. For example, equity investments may be suitable for radical innovation, while debt instruments, such as long-term loans, may be better for lower-risk activities. This will enable SIBs to invest across the innovation chain from the pre-R&D phase all the way through to providing long-term patient capital for established firms. In addition to lending operations, many SIBs offer advisory services such as strategic planning, capacity building, and training programs that help to create viable projects and catalyze investments that otherwise would not happen (Macfarlane and Mazzucato 2017).

A key difference between mission-oriented NPBIs and private financial institutions is the breadth of expertise and capacities contained within staff. In many cases this includes not only financial expertise but significant in-house engineering and scientific knowledge about the sectors the bank is active in and the nature of the investments being made. This enables investment decisions to be based on a wider set of criteria rather than relying on market signals alone, meaning that they are better placed to appraise social and environmental considerations (Macfarlane and Mazzucato 2017).

Acting as lead investor necessarily means absorbing a high degree of uncertainty and accepting failures when they happen. In making investments SIBs can use their balance sheet to structure investments across a risk-return spectrum so that lower risk investments help to cover higher risk ones. For this to work, it is important that SIBs are able to capture some of the reward (the "upside") that is made possible by their risk-taking and investment in order to cover the inevitable losses. This can be done by employing mechanisms such as retaining equity in the innovative companies it supports, or co-owning intellectual property with innovative firms it invests in (Macfarlane and Mazzucato 2018).

SIBs and other public financial institutions are often criticised on the basis of "picking winners", "crowding-out" or funding large incumbent companies. While there are instances where criticism may be merited, part of the reason for this lies in the absence of monitoring and evaluation frameworks which adequately capture the dynamic spillovers generated by the mission-oriented investments made by these institutions. As a result, it is important to develop appropriate monitoring and evaluation frameworks which do not focus on market failures but which instead assess the extent to which they have been successful at catalyzing activity that otherwise would not have happened (Macfarlane and Mazzucato 2018)

Finally, in order to be successful, it is important that mission-oriented SIBs work closely with other actors in the wider financial, business and innovation ecosystems. In some cases, it may be most appropriate to invest directly in firms and infrastructure aligned with the missions of the SIB, while in other cases it may be more appropriate to co-invest with other actors (Macfarlane and Mazzucato 2018). Structured properly, investments should seek to "crowd-in" private investment by giving private sector actors the confidence they need to invest (Macfarlane and Mazzucato 2018).

7.10. Closing Remarks

In this chapter, we make three proposals.

First, at a time where an entire generation still views the EU as the austerity headmaster, social investment provides an opportunity for the EU to revive its political capital. Reviving the EU with an assertive "social investment pact" (not package) would confront head on the political vacuum between right-populist welfare chauvinism and the ongoing calls for overnight fiscal consolidation that has emerged at the heart of the European project in the crisis aftermath. In this context, the EU is faced with two options: First, business as usual. EU Member States may choose to muddle-through with the ideology of the long-term myth of unproductive social spending, instead of adapting to new realities. In this scenario, the EU will risk not only bearing the expensive economic costs of blindness, but this would also precipitate a political backlash in undermining the resilience of the European project. A more constructive option would be for the EU to ratchet up domestic social investment with EMU rules that allow for exempting human capital "stock" investments from the Stability and Growth Pact (SGP). Concretely, this would take the form of a "Golden Rule" exempting human capital "stock" spending from the euro area fiscal rule book for 1.5% of GDP for about decade, as a flagship initiative of the new Commission. Given the absence of a stabilization budget for the euro area, investing in the economic and social resilience of national welfare states is imperative. As the economist Jean Pisani-Ferry (2019) convincingly argued in a recent article: "When Facts Change, Change the Pact". The time for social investment to be accounted at its just value is now. Today's favourable low interest rate environment should be put to use to establish, consolidate and expand social investments that benefit future generations and consolidate fiscal health in the face of adverse demography.

Second, good social services need good social infrastructure. A major boost is needed in long-term social infrastructure investment. Such needs will have to consider future changes in European social models. Social infrastructure investment is very like economic infrastructure investment in many respects, but there are also distinctive features to consider.

The proportion of social infrastructure that is publicly financed is on average almost completely paid by tax payers' money. How do we ensure that a member country with a particularly penalizing sovereign rating (and fiscal position), but very much in need of infrastructure and growth, can finance itself at "sustainable" rates? We propose the creation of a large European Fund for Social Infrastructures — with public-institutional-SIBs shareholding — which issues European Social Bonds with a high rating capable of distributing the risk downstream — on projects — to give finance to all member countries, overcoming, at least in large part, the problem of sovereign spreads and foster "upward convergence".

The Fund would have a technical assistance network to assist administrations in building "European" quality economic and financial plans. In turn, the European Fund would have a reputation that would attract long-term patient investors. Both in terms of their participation in the fund's capital (through shares) and through investment in European Social Bonds, this would create the match between long-term investors, such as pension funds and life insurance, and infrastructural financial instruments, on which much has been written and discussed, but that has not yet been realized in the dimension that both demand and offer seem to require.

Third, recent decades witnessed a trend whereby private markets retreated from financing the real economy, while, simultaneously, the real economy itself became increasingly financialized. This trend resulted in public finance becoming more important for investments in capital development, technical change and social innovation. Within this context, we believe that a growing role should be played by played by a particular source of public finance: State Investment Banks (SIBs).

The role of "mission-oriented" SIBs in social innovation — and how SIBs can play a more central role by transforming from institutions which simply "fill market failures" to institutions which "shape the market", thereby becoming major providers of sustainable long-term and patient finance for the public good — is one of the great challenges that Europe must now face. We beg policy makers at all levels to take very seriously the present social challenge and to ask themselves, "if not now, when?"

References

d'Albis, H., A, Greulich and G. Ponthière (2017) "Education, Labour, and the Demographic Consequences of Birth Postponement in Europe" *PSE Working Papers*, https://halshs. archives-ouvertes.fr/halshs-01452823

Arezki, R., P. Bolton, S. Peters, F. Samama and S. Joseph (2016) "From Global Savings Glut to Financing Infrastructure: The Advent of Investment Platforms", *IMF Working Paper* 16(18), https://www.imf.org/external/pubs/ft/wp/2016/wp1618.pdf

Bassanini, F. (2012) "Financing Long Term Investment after the Crisis: A View from Europe', in *Sovereign Wealth Funds and Long-Term Investing*, ed. by P. Bolton, F. Samama, J. E. Stiglitz, (New York: Columbia University), pp. 37–44, https://doi.org/10.7312/columbia/9780231158633.001.0001

Bassanini, F. and E. Reviglio (2011) "Financial Stability, Fiscal Consolidation and Long-Term Investment after the Crisis", *OECD Journal: Financial Markets Trends* 1: 37–75, https://doi.org/10.1787/fmt-2011-5kg55qw1vbjl

Bassanini, F. and E. Reviglio (2015) "From the Financial Crisis to the Juncker Plan", in *Investing in Long-Term Europe. Fixed, Re-Launching Fixed, Fixed, Network and Social Infrastructure*, ed. by P. Garonna and E. Reviglio (Rome: LUISS University Press), pp. 59–80.

Bassanini, F., G. Pennisi and R. Reviglio (2015) "Development Banks: From the Financial and Economic Crisis to Sustainable and Inclusive Growth", in *Investing in Long-Term Europe. Re-launching fixed, Network and Social Infrastructure*, ed. by P. Garonna and E. Reviglio (Rome: LUISS University Press), pp. 312–16.

Beaujouan, É. and T. Sobotka (2014) "Two Is Best? The Persistence of a Two-Child Family Ideal in Europe", *Population and Development Review* 40(3): 391–419, https://doi.org/10.1111/j.1728-4457.2014.00691.x

Borgstrom, E., R. Morris, D. Wood, S. Cohn and S. Barclay (2016) "Learning to Care: Medical Students' Reported Value and Evaluation of Palliative Care Teaching Involving Meeting Patients and Reflective Writing", *BMC Medical Education* 16(1): 306, https://doi.org/10.1186/s12909-016-0827-6

Brilli, Y. (2014) "Does Child Care Availability Play a Role in Maternal Employment and Children's Development? Evidence from Italy", *Review of Economics of the Household* 14(1): 27–51, https://doi.org/10.1007/s11150-013-9227-4

Cantillon, B. and F. Vandenbroucke (eds) (2014) *Reconciling Work and Poverty Reduction. How Successful are European Welfare States?* Oxford: Oxford University Press.

Coase, R. H. (1937) "The Nature of the Firm", *Economica* 4(16): 386–405, https://doi.org/10.1111/j.1468-0335.1937.tb00002.x

Cumba, F. and J. Heckman (2007) "The Economics of Human Development. The Technology of Skill Formation", *American Economic Review* 97(2): 31–47, https://doi.org/10.1257/aer.97.2.31

del Boca, D., M. Locatelli and D. Vuri (2005) "Child Care Choices by Working Mothers: The Case of Italy", *Review of Economics of the Household* 3: 453–77, https://doi.org/10.1007/s11150-005-4944-y

Deleidi, M., M. Mazzucato, V. de Lipsis, J. Ryan-Collins and P. Agnolucci (2019) *The Macroeconomic Impact of Government Innovation Policies: A Quantitative Assessment*. UCL Institute for Innovation and Public Purpose, Policy Report working paper series (IIPP WP 2019-06), https://www.ucl.ac.uk/bartlett/public-purpose/wp2019-06

Deleidi, M., F. Iafrate and E. S. Levrero (2019) *Public Investment Fiscal Multipliers: An Empirical Assessment for European Countries*. UCL Institute for Innovation and Public Purpose, Policy Report working paper series (IIPP WP 2019-08), https://www.ucl.ac.uk/bartlett/public-purpose/sites/public-purpose/files/final_working_paper_deleidi_iafrate_levrero_19_aug.pdf

EDHEC-Risk Institute (2012) "Pension Fund Investment in Social Infrastructure. Insights from the 2012 Reform of the Private Finance Initiative in the United Kingdom", https://www.edhec.edu/sites/www.edhec-portail.pprod.net/files/publications/pdf/edhec-publication-pension-fund-investment-in-social-infrastructure-f_1332412681078.pdfjpg

Ehlers, T. (2014) "Understanding the Challenges for Infrastructure Finance", *BIS Working Papers* 454, https://www.bis.org/publ/work454.pdf

EIB (2018) *EIB Investment Report 2018/2019: Retooling Europe's Economy.* Luxembourg: European Investment Bank, https://www.eib.org/attachments/efs/economic_investment_report_2018_en.pdf

EPEC (2016) "A Guide to the Statistical Treatment of PPPs", https://www.eib.org/attachments/thematic/epec_eurostat_statistical_guide_en.pdf

European Commission (2016) "Report on Public Finances in EMU, Institutional Paper 045", https://ec.europa.eu/info/sites/info/files/ip045_en_0.pdf

Foster, S. and C. Iaione (2016) "The City as a Commons", *Yale Law & Policy Review* 34: 281–349, https://digitalcommons.law.yale.edu/cgi/viewcontent.cgi?article=1698&context=ylpr

Foster, S. and C. Iaione (2019) "Ostrom in the City: Design Principles and Practices for the Urban Commons", in *Routledge Handbook of the Study of the Commons*, ed. by D. Cole, B. Hudson and J. Rosenbloom (London: Routledge), pp. 235–55,https://doi.org/10.4324/9781315162782-19

Fransen, L., G. del Bufalo and E. Reviglio (2018) *Boosting Investment in Social Infrastructure in Europe. Report of the HLTF Force on Investing in Social Infrastructure in Europe chaired by Romano Prodi and Christian Sautter.* Luxembourg: Publications Office of the European Union, https://www.fondazioneifel.it/notizie-ed-eventi/item/download/2376_ee5d868e16ae749daced6f41cce3709c

Garonna, P. and E. Reviglio (eds) (2015) *Investing in Long-Term Europe. Fixed, Re-Launching Fixed, Fixed, Network and Social Infrastructure.* Rome: LUISS University Press.

Härkönen, J. (2011) "Children and Dual Worklessness in Europe: A Comparison of Nine Countries", *European Journal of Population* 27(2): 217–41, https://doi.org/10.1007/s10680-011-9232-3

Heckman, J. (2006) "Skill Formation and the Economics of Investing in Disadvantaged Children", *Science* 312(5782): 1900–02, https://doi.org/10.1126/science.1128898

Hemerijck, A. (2013) *Changing Welfare States.* Oxford: Oxford University Press.

Hemerijck, A. (ed.) (2017) *The Uses of Social Investment.* Oxford: Oxford University Press, https://doi.org/10.1093/oso/9780198790488.001.0001

Hemerijck, A. and S. Ronchi (forthcoming, 2020) "European Welfare States' Detour(s) to Social Investment", in *The Oxford International Handbook of Public Administration for Social Policy: Promising Practices and Emerging Challenges*, ed. by J. Boston, E. Ferlie, F. Filgueira, Y. Jing, E. Ongaro and V. Taylor (Oxford: Oxford University Press).

Inderst, G. (2017) "Social Infrastructure Investment: Financing Sources and Investor Perspective", *HLTF SI*, Draft for discussion, June 15.

Jenkins, A., A. Vignoles, A. Wolf, and F. Galindo-Rueda, Fernando (2003) "The Determinants and Labour Market Effects of Lifelong Learning", *Applied Economics* 35(16): 1711–21, https://doi.org/10.1080/0003684032000155445

Kattel, R., M. Mazzucato, J. Ryan-Collins and S. Sharpe (2018) *The Economics of Change: Policy Appraisal for Missions, Market Shaping and Public Purpose.* UCL Institute for Innovation and

Public Purpose, Policy Report working paper series (IIPP WP 2018-06), https://www.ucl.ac.uk/bartlett/public-purpose/wp2018-06

Korpi, W., T. Ferrarini and S. Englund (2009) "Egalitarian Gender Paradise Lost? Re-Examining Gender Inequalities in Different Types of Welfare States", *Swedish Institute for Social Research*, Stockholm University, Paper presented at Equalsor Conference, Berlin 9 May 2009.

Luna-Martinez, J. and L. Vicente (2012) "Global Survey of Development Banks", *World Bank Policy Research Working Paper* 5969, http://documents.worldbank.org/curated/en/313731468154461012/pdf/WPS5969.pdf

Macfarlane, L. and M. Mazzucato (2018) *State Investment Banks and Patient Finance: An International Comparison*. UCL Institute for Innovation and Public Purpose, Policy Report working paper series (IIPP WP 2018-01), https://www.ucl.ac.uk/bartlett/public-purpose/wp2018-01

Mazzucato, M. (2013) "Financing Innovation: Creative Destruction vs Destructive Creation", *Industrial and Corporate Change* 22(4): 851–67, https://doi.org/10.1093/icc/dtt025

Mazzucato, M. and C. Penna (2016) "Beyond Market Failures: The Market Creating and Shaping Roles of State Investment Banks", *Journal of Economic Policy Reform* 19(4): 305–26, https://doi.org/10.1080/17487870.2016.1216416

Mazzucato, M. and R. Kattel (2019) "Getting Serious about Public Value", *IIPP Policy Brief* 07, https://www.ucl.ac.uk/bartlett/public-purpose/sites/public-purpose/files/iipp_policy brief_07_getting_serious_about_value.pdf

Mazzucato, M. and L. Macfarlane (2017) *Patient Strategic Finance: Opportunities for State Investment Banks in the UK*. UCL Institute for Innovation and Public Purpose, Policy Report working paper series (IIPP WP 2017-05), https://www.ucl.ac.uk/bartlett/public-purpose/wp2017-05.

Mazzucato, M. (2013) *The Entrepreneurial State: Debunking Public vs. Private Sector Myths*. London: Anthem Publishing.

Mazzucato, Mariana (2018) *Mission-Oriented Research & Innovation in the European Union: A Problem-Solving Approach to Fuel Innovation-Led Growth*. Luxembourg: Publications Office of the European Union, https://era.gv.at/object/document/3844/attach/mazzucato_report_2018.pdf

Mazzucato, M. (2019) "Governing Missions in the European Union", https://ec.europa.eu/info/sites/info/files/research_and_innovation/contact/documents/ec_rtd_mazzucato-report-issue2_072019.pdf

Mazzucato, M. and J. Ryan-Collins (2019) *Putting Value Creation back into "Public Value": From Market Fixing to Market Shaping*. UCL Institute for Innovation and Public Purpose, Policy Report working paper series (IIPP WP 2019-05), https://www.ucl.ac.uk/bartlett/public-purpose/sites/public-purpose/files/public_value_final_30_may_2019_web_0.pdf

O'Sullivan, M. (2014) "Finance and Innovation", in *The Oxford Handbook of Innovation*, ed. by J. Fagerberg, D. C. Mowery and R. R. Nelson (New York: Oxford University Press), pp. 240–65.

Pisani-Ferry, J. (2019) "When Facts Change, Change the Pact", *Project Syndicate*, April 29, https://www.project-syndicate.org/commentary/europe-stability-pact-reform-investment-by-jean-pisani-ferry-2019-04?barrier=accesspaylog

Polanyi, K. (1944) *The Great Transformation: The Political and Economic Origins of Our Time*. New York: Farrar & Rinehart.

Prodi, R. and E. Reviglio (2019) "A New Fund for Europe. The Creation of a New European Social Bond Would Help EU Member States Meet their Infrastructure Needs without

Exacerbating Public Debt", in *OMFIF Global Public Investor*, ed. by Danae Kyriakopoulou (London: OMFIF Ltd), pp. 132–33.

Schmid, G. (2015) "Sharing Risks of Labour Market Transitions: Towards a System of Employment Insurance", *British Journal of Industrial Relations* 53(1): 70–93, https://doi.org/10.1111/bjir.12041

8. From Trans-European (Ten-T) to Trans-Global (Twn-T) Transport Infrastructure Networks. A Conceptual Framework[1]

Paolo Costa,[2] Hercules Haralambides[3] and Roberto Roson[4]

8.1. The Trans-European Transport Network and its Evolution (1996–2013)

Even before the Trans-European Transport Network (Ten-T) appeared formally in the Maastricht Treaty in 1992, European transnational transport flows have followed a pattern recalling this network.[5]

Ten-T networks (road, rail and inland navigation) have been, and still are, the beneficiary of a vast program of public investment, publicly funded by the European Union and Member States, and partly financed by the private sector. The network has been under planning, designing, improvement and realization ever since its inception in the mid-1990s. A new cycle of planning, designing and implementation of the network, foreseen by the EU guidelines for Ten-T's development,[6] is currently underway, to be completed by 31 December 2023.

The need to transform a patchwork of national networks into a single European one, characterized by common standards and full interoperability, has been recognized since the preparatory work for the Treaty of Rome in 1957 (Bonnefous 1951).

---

1 This chapter is the result of a joint effort by the three authors who share responsibility for it. Paolo Costa provided the framework and drafted sections 8.1., 8.2. and 8.4., Hercules Haralambides and Roberto Roson drafted sections 8.3. and 8.5., respectively.

2 Dipartimento di Economia — Università di Venezia Ca' Foscari.

3 Dalian Maritime University (China); Texas A&M University (USA); Erasmus Universiteit Rotterdam.

4 Dipartimento di Economia — Università di Venezia Ca' Foscari; Departamento de Economía — Universidad Loyola Andalucía Sevilla; Green — Università Bocconi, Milano.

5 Article 129 b), c) and d) of the Maastricht Treaty (European Union 1992) provides for the construction of both transport and energy and telecommunication networks

6 Council Regulation (EU) 1315/2013.

 https://doi.org/10.11647/OBP.0222.08

Notwithstanding this, infrastructure policies aimed at guiding the post-Second World War reconstruction of Europe remained confined within each national box of policy tools, in the name of "keeping national" both the anticyclical role of the Keynesian multiplier (of public investment), and the pursuit of the objectives of economic integration of the then less developed areas (especially Southern Italy and, since the early 1970s, Ireland).

Ten-T reached the heart of European policy, and the "satisfaction of the common European interest" was added to the national criteria that filter all infrastructure development programs which derive their legal basis from the Maastricht Treaty. This has been the result of efforts to reconcile the need to accelerate the construction of the internal market and the EU policy objectives of growth and employment. Simply put, completing the internal market required the elimination of cross-border *missing links* and *bottlenecks*,[7] so as to ensure access to the heart of the market from peripheral regions and to prepare transport networks and systems capable of competing globally. On the other hand, transport infrastructure investments, and their long construction periods, were seen by many Member States (in our view, often wrongly) as an ideal way of fighting unemployment, which, at the beginning of the 1990s, was hitting more than 17 million Europeans, one third of whom were young people. Of course, the positive effects on European competitiveness, in the medium- to long-term, did not escape the attention of any EU government.

The overarching goal was to combine a Keynesian approach to boost aggregate demand with the benefits of a substantial reduction in transport costs. The latter objective, it was correctly expected, would reduce unit costs of production; expand markets for outputs and inputs (including labour) and lead to higher international competitiveness of the single internal market, thus increasing growth capable of creating jobs (Haralambides 2019).[8] These guiding principles permeated the whole development of the Ten-T Network and its implementation, and dictated the definition of its investment priorities in 1996, 2004 and 2013.

The above principles are still central on the eve of the new Ten-T policy revision, enriched, however, by the 2004 and 2013 objectives of environmental and energy sustainability, stressed by the need to combat climate change and contain energy costs. Among others, lowering the *pollution intensity* of transport (greenhouse gases in particular), as well as its *energy intensity*, is thought of as being able to encourage a modal shift towards rail, sea and inland navigation, instead of the dominant "road" and "air" transport modes. All along, the assumption has been that a more

---

7   The questions here are: how is it possible to build a European single market without physically connecting any given point (A) with any given point (B), and how could we do this when the road, rail and inland navigation network presents so many missing links at old country border crossings, not to mention the bottlenecks still affecting many nodes and links in the network?

8   "Networks are the arteries of the single market. They are the lifeblood of competitiveness, and their malfunction is reflected in lost opportunities to create new markets and hence in a level of job creation that falls short of our potential" (European Commission 1993, p. 89).

TENT Corridors	Inland Waterways	Maritime				Multimodal	Rail	Road	Total	TENT Corridors
	total	Med	North	other	total	total	total	total	Total	
Atlantic	34,7	0	0	76,9	76,9	61,3	1319,2	53,8	1545,9	Atlantic
Baltic Adriatic	0	67,3	0	136,8	204,1	50	1876,1	246,5	2376,7	Baltic Adriatic
Mediterranean	10,7	182,8	0	0	182,8	89,3	2449,7	148,1	2880,6	Mediterranean
North Sea Baltic	67,5	0	13,4	58,4	71,8	11,3	2432,3	496,6	3079,5	North Sea Baltic
North Sea Med	1153,5	32	115,5	73,8	189,3	44,7	340	89,3	1816,8	North Sea Med
Orient-East Med	33,9	6,4	0	2,2	34,2	25,9	1708	188	1990	Orient-East Med
Rhine Alpine	27,6	0	8	4,1	18,5	23	570,1	62,9	702,1	Rhine Alpine
Rhine Danube	381,9	0	0	10,8	10,8	15,3	3285,3	81,4	3774,7	Rhine Danube
Scan Med	0	6	0	80,5	86,5	41,1	2036,6	0	2164,2	Scan Med
TOTAL	1709,8	294,5	136,9	443,5	874,9	361,9	16017,3	1366,6	20330,5	TOTAL

Fig. 1 Distribution of EU Ten-T funds by transport mode and core corridor

Source of data: Euro Commission, 2018. Figure created by Paolo Costa.

competitive performance of the "non-road" and "non-sky" modes, made possible by infrastructural and technological modernization and a fairer allocation of external costs through their internalization in transport prices, would favour the "modal split": a modal shift that could lead to a more sustainable satisfaction of transport demand.[9] Finally, the integration of the European economy into the world economy has also been a cited objective but, as we will see below, one of very low impact on policy formulation until now.[10]

The implementation of the Ten-T policy moved on accordingly. The current allocation of European Ten-T funds to different modes along the nine corridors of the core network is represented in Figures 1 and 2: 78.8% of the money goes to rail infrastructure, 8.4% to inland waterways and 6.7% to road infrastructure. Maritime transport, including ports, gets 4.3% of the EU funds, with only 1.45% going to the — currently most promising — Mediterranean ports.[11]

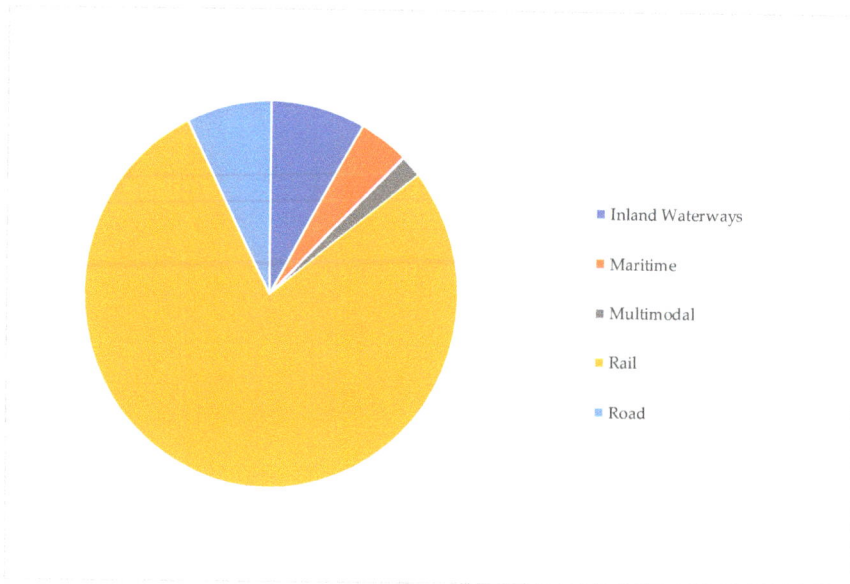

Fig. 2 Distribution of EU Ten-T funds by transport mode

Source of data: Euro Commission, 2018. Figure created by Paolo Costa.

---

9   In turn, the shift from road to rail would lead to greater sustainability in terms of safety, as a key to a zero-casualty transport strategy.

10   The "opening" of the Ten-T network to the world was suggested in the Final Report written by Expert Group no. 4, coordinated by Paolo Costa, working at the revision of the Methodology for Ten-T planning dedicated to the "Ten-T Extension outside the EU" (European Commission 2010).

11   This is occurring while rail transport performance in the EU is still unsatisfactory in terms of volume transported and modal share. On average, road transport accounts for 75% of the market, while rail has actually declined slightly since 2011 (European Court of Auditors 2017).

From 1994 to 2013 the *geography* of the Ten-T Network has been evolving, so as to address the progressive eastward enlargement of the Union, as well as the changing settlement patterns brought about by the long-term economic and social developments in Europe. Some nodes and links of the network were thus becoming technically or geographically obsolete, some less useful and others highly in-demand. There has been little consideration of the demands for change in the geography of the Ten-T networks, and in their modal structure, coming from both inside *and* outside Europe, due to new connectivity requirements deriving from the increasing integration of Europe into the global economy.

To be more precise, there has been no lack of attention given to the neighbouring countries bordering the European Union, both to countries which are candidates for EU enlargement and to those belonging to the "ring of friends". All of them have been the subject of the *neighbourhood policy* launched in 2004[12] mainly with the objective of avoiding the emergence of new dividing lines, new Berlin walls, between the enlarged EU and its neighbours.

What was underestimated was the fact that international transport flows were and are changing in volume,[13] and geographic patterns are changing with profound consequences particularly as regards, now, to the increasing importance of southern European ports as the gateways to the continent of Asian cargoes.

Equally underestimated is the disruptive impact of new transport technologies and their "digital twin" on infrastructure networks. The authors of this chapter believe that the major issue to take into consideration in designing the 2023 Ten-T revision will probably be the geographical and technological disruptions of the existing infrastructure network.

This consideration will have to be tackled, on top of dramatic disruptions coming from other sources, such as: *e-commerce* (leading to more freight transport and increasing the share of relatively carbon-intensive modes); *increasing vehicle automation* (pushing up demand for road freight and shifting freight from rail and inland waterways onto roads); *manufacturing re-shoring and 3D printing* (with a significant decrease in internationally traded goods that greatly reduces sea and air transport volumes); *high capacity vehicles (HCV)* (carrying bigger loads than regular trucks, limiting emissions and congestion, reducing overall costs, increasing safety, but causing a reverse modal shift from rail to road); and *decarbonizing technologies for*

---

12 Five main transport axes linking the EU with its neighbours were identified by a High Level Group chaired by Loyola De Palacio and formalized in the "Guidelines for Transport in Europe and neighbouring regions (COM/2007/32)". The interests and commitment of the neighbouring countries were then assessed by the communication "Progress of exploratory talks regarding cooperation in the field of transport with the neighbouring countries COM(2008)". The Ministerial Conference — *The Future of Trans-European Transport Networks: Bringing Europe Closer to its Neighbours* — held in Naples on October 2009 paved the way to the transport neighbourhood policy still in operation.

13 Freight volumes will continue to grow strongly, with global freight demand projected to triple between 2015 and 2050 (ITF (2019)).

heavy-duty long-haulage — electric roads, hydrogen, batteries — (potentially capable of altering the relative convenience of different transport modes).[14]

8.2. Demand for New Connectivity: Europe's Economic, Social and Political Integration in a Global Context

The 2013 revision of Ten-T defined a "two layer" set of networks: the so-called *core network*, a set of only nine (core) corridors linking the major urban nodes among them and to major ports, airports and rail-road terminals and the *comprehensive network*, pervasively connecting all major European urban centres. The core network has been set to become *efficient, safe, green and smart* by the year 2030, while the completion of the comprehensive network is foreseen for 2050. The core network is also expected to cater for the growing relations between the EU economic space — assumed to remain the largest in the world for at least a few more decades — and the rest of the world. In this scenario, competition within the internal market will continue to be at the root of EU core business, under the understanding that growth in one Member State is inextricably linked to the growth in any other Member State.

In 2008 China acceded to the World Trade Organization (WTO) and in just over ten years at the time of writing (2019) China's external trade has accounted for 50% of global trade. At the same time, multilateral trade negotiations opened up — to their benefit — the economies of many emerging markets, led by BRICS.

According to the OECD's International Transport Forum, by 2030 the world trade is foreseen to have increased by a factor of 3.4 and this growth will come mostly from emerging economies and global markets (ITF 2019). In such a scenario, Europe's dependence on trade will intensify, putting ports and airports under great pressure. Adjusting European ports and airports to the new level of activity becomes thus an absolute and immediate priority, particularly in view of the long gestation periods of large infrastructure investments. This priority was not neglected in the technical process of the 2013 revision of the Ten-T Network, and found its way through *de facto*, in the definition of the nine "core corridors", all of which starting or finishing at a port city, or including major ports in their layout.

But the implementation strategy designed by each core corridor coordinator unfortunately did not reflect the importance of this priority: missing links and bottlenecks in the internal network seem still to be more relevant than creating effective gateways and doors to the world. The allocation of EU funds (Figures 1 and 2) reflects this "wrong" choice. We are convinced that it is time to move from "Europe as a single market" to "A single Europe in the global market". The key question is *how*.

Demand for transport, especially for goods, is a function of the size and geography (spatial distribution) of production and consumption. With a given transport technology,

---

14 For a simulation of the combined effects of these potential disruptions on freight transport worldwide, see ITF (2019).

the flows that satisfy a certain transport demand are controlled by the capacity and geography of the networks (links and nodes) along which these flows run.

If the technology, the geography of flows/networks and capacity are given, then transport flows assigned to the network will move from any "origin" to any "destination" along the network, behaving "like water" that always follows the shortest (minimum cost) path. This will occur unless "deviations" — due to indivisibility, cumulative processes or market imperfections — take place, or because missing links or capacity bottlenecks in the network fail to be eliminated.

If a new geography of production and consumption areas produces a pattern of flows that significantly departs from the historical one, this will tend to retroact on the net, demanding investments in transport infrastructures aimed at transforming, à la Alfred Marshall, "existing plants", which have become obsolete, into "adequate ones". Disruptions in the geography of transport therefore tend to generate disruptions in the geography of infrastructures.

A distinctive feature of the world of transport is that its scenarios are characterized by recurrent geographical transitions, where we are confronted with radical changes in the geography of production, income and consumption. This is exactly what is happening now at the global and European scale: a change has already translated into a revolution in the geography of international trade, which is moving along routes that make increasingly evident the obsolescence of historical modal and intermodal networks.

8.2.1. The growing importance of the extra-EU markets

The reason why phenomena that are changing the geography of the world economy are of profound interest to the whole of the European Union is simple. Even if Europe remains the most economically integrated region in the world — much more than the USMCA (ex Nafta) and the East and Southeast Asian regions — it is nonetheless becoming increasingly open to the world, and the current US-China trade war is only slowing down this inevitable process.

From 2002 to 2008 the ratio of extra-EU to intra-EU exports has increased slowly but steadily in almost all European countries (Figure 3). On average, in the whole EU28, the ratio has risen from 0.464 to 0.478. Since 2009, in the midst of the Great Recession, the ratio has begun to grow even more significantly. The EU28 average rose from 0.494 (2009) to 0.612 (2015), an increase of 24%. The projection of the same ratio to 2030 suggests that, by that date, non-EU exports will be worth as much as 65% of intra-EU exports, with a clear difference between the behaviour of the countries of the "new Europe", all still aiming at exploiting the potential of the internal market (ratio of extra-EU to intra-EU exports still less than 30% by 2030), and the countries of the "old Europe" whose extra-EU market will be worth 75% of the intra-EU one.

Until a few years ago, Europe believed it could safely neglect what was happening around it and focused almost exclusively, and in a rather introverted way, on the completion of the internal market. So great was its preoccupation with, for example, such things as market shares and other aspects of competition law, that decisions and rulings of its Directorate-General for Competition *penalized* European companies in their global competitive strife. In effect, these decisions and rulings were instead "music to the ears" of Europe's international competitors.

For years, Europe's "proud" conviction that it was the world's largest trading bloc reinforced its belief that everything could continue to be played "within the Union" or, at most, by just taking into account the only world economic powers relevant at that time: the USA and Japan which, together with the EU, formed the so-called "Triad" (Ohmae 1985) that dominated the world. For example, only twenty years ago, the geography of international trade was dominated by the "transatlantic relationship" between Europe and the United States, and between the latter and Japan; a triangle in which only China and South Korea began to fit.

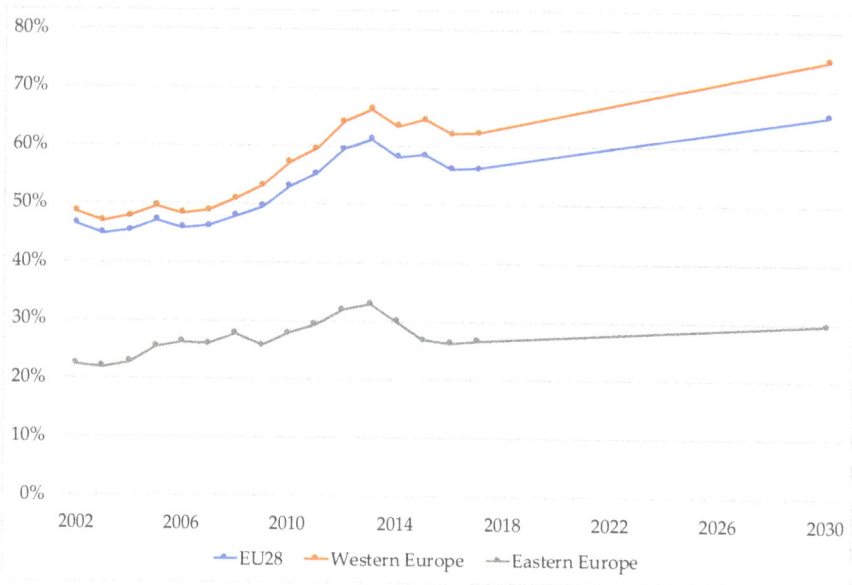

Fig. 3 Ratio of extra-EU and intra-EU exports, 2002–2016, and forecast to 2030

Source of data: Euro Commission, 2018. Figure created by Paolo Costa.

The Great Recession of 2009, which, for *some* European countries, lasted until 2013 or beyond, suddenly made it painfully clear what was happening in the meantime in the rest of the world: a shift of the centre of gravity of the world economy outside the advanced countries of the OECD area, favoured by a formidable reduction in transport costs, as a result of competition and economies of scale in ocean transportation, and by advances in logistics and vertical integration, resulting from the fragmentation of the different phases of industrial production.

In a way, the Great Recession urged Europe to better study phenomena beyond *economics*, which are changing the geography of the world. Among others, the demographic dynamics of the world population.

Today, 60% of the world population lives in Asia (4.5 billion) and 17% in Africa (1.7 billion). Only the remaining 23% live in the rest of the planet (10% in Europe). Between now and 2050, half of the increase in world population (1.3 billion people) will manifest itself in Africa, while another 750 million will be added in Asia. By 2050, 80% of the world's population will be living in Asia and Africa. Europe will be the only part of the world having a lower population in 2050 than in 2017. Obviously, *demographic shifts* such as these are already having their impact on the regional distribution of global income. Today, the Asian bloc represents more than a third of the global GDP, while North America is just under 28% and Europe is at 21.37%. Projections to 2050 reinforce pro-Asia shifts. If to these projections one adds the significant incremental differences in labour productivity, one can easily assume that every long-term scenario will be decisively characterized by a move in global demographic and economic weights towards a lasting Asian centrality.

Following OECD (2011), it seems reasonable to imagine the doubling of world GDP by 2030, driven by a sustained growth in the emerging economies. By the same year, the GDP of North America would increase by only 50% and that of Europe by 40%. On an even longer horizon (2050), and with a world population exceeding 9 billion people, world GDP could grow up to four times that of 2005 (almost ten times for China and India). The combined effect of the low growth of the European population, and the even lower growth of European GDP and disposable income, should however mean that the per capita income of Europe and of the other advanced countries remains — even in 2050 — higher than that of the rest of the world.

It is against this background that the economic geography of the world and, with it, that of its trade will be redrawn.

Accordingly, the demand for freight transport could increase by a factor of 2.5 to 3.5. In the case of emerging economies (non-OECD countries) this factor could be even higher, in the neighbourhood of 4 to 5. Demand for transport, now fulfilled over new, substantially different, transport networks, will inevitably result in heavy demand for new infrastructure which, in view of its long gestation period, should be planned now, so as not to hinder trade and world growth.

In summary, and according to the plausible scenarios above, the two ongoing processes that should convince the EU to shift its focus from an inward-looking viewpoint to the evolution of transport and transport infrastructure in a broader global view are:

1. The emergence and strengthening of Asia's central role in the world economy;

2. The rapid development of the southern and eastern shores of the Mediterranean.

This picture, however, is not without further complications: the centre of gravity of the European economy will shift to the east, within and outside the current borders of the Union, driving a redefinition of the geography of production within Europe.

8.2.2. Asia's central role in the global economy and trade

Emerging Asian economies will become central to the global economy, because they will be no longer just the place of origin of European, American and Japanese imports, but also increasingly crucial destinations of exports from OECD countries.

The Asian focus is particularly important for the European economy and its transport sector, as evidenced by actual maritime flows,[15] which are clearly prevalent in Eurasian relations and, more generally, on a global scale. According to the UNCTAD surveys of containerized ocean traffic between the world's macro-regions since 1996, there is a growing disproportion in traffic flows along the three main global routes.[16] By far, the most important exchange for Europe today is the Europe-Asia-Europe one (23 million TEU traded in 2017) which, although slightly lower than the transpacific flows between Asia and America (26 million TEU), is now three times more important than the transatlantic route (7 million TEU).

In short, trends in regional growth (GDP) and world commerce show that, even if the market of North America will continue to remain the most important extra-European one (as far as Europe is concerned), the affirmation of Asia as a final market, as well as the centre of the world manufacturing production, makes the Europe-Far East relationship the most important interregional relationship for the economy of the European continent.

This is the reason why both researchers and traders are exploring new ways of fuelling this relationship, possibly through routes that had been neglected so far. For instance, the polar route from China to the North Sea via the Bering Strait and the Arctic Ocean: a route that is expected to be open soon all year round, because of the effects of global warming on polar ice. Other cases are the rail route from China to Germany via Russia or ex-Soviet Eurasian republics, the sea route that from China reaches the North Sea circumnavigating Africa, and the maritime one that crosses the Pacific and the Atlantic from China to the North Sea via the Panama Canal. This is also the reason why China has addressed its most important international policy strategy — the Belt and Road Initiative — to the Eurasian region.[17]

All routes that can acquire some meaning on their own, but always without contesting the primacy of the "Royal Road", i.e. the route between Europe and the Far East via Suez. Its superiority lies in its reduced transit times, as well as in its ability to intercept, on its way to the Mediterranean and Northern Europe, cargoes from such

---

15   More precisely those of containerized trades assumed as a traffic numerary.
16   The sum of the traffic flows along these three main global routes, however, is of the same order of magnitude as intra-Asian traffic alone.
17   See below.

countries and territories as Malaysia, Indonesia, Philippines, Thailand, India, the Persian Gulf and East Africa. The organization of shipping traffic along this route, and its best exploitation, is crucial for the European economic growth.

8.2.3. The potential of "MENA (Middle East and North Africa) shores" and the Mediterranean Sea basin

The development of the countries surrounding the Mediterranean Basin (Southern Europe, North Africa and the Near East) will add significant volumes of intra-Mediterranean maritime flows to those connecting Asia and Europe. The modernization and reform of ports in Greece, Italy, France and Spain, will offer the "southern gates" to the Asian cargo. The role of Mediterranean ports in serving the European "heartland", and their increasing market share in Europe-Asia's trades, now challenges the so far unquestionable dominance of the Hamburg-Le Havre range of ports of the European North, with Spain's Valencia expected to overtake Bremerhaven in 2019. A "rebalancing" of European gateways that will call for a corresponding adaptation of the intra-European land transport infrastructure network (rail, road and inland waterways) has to be connected to the next steps of Ten-T planning.

In the long run, however, something will be added by the economic growth of Africa and the Middle East. This phenomenon has unfortunately been recently overshadowed by political turbulence. The political instability in Libya and Syria, and the political and economic instability in Turkey, is stunting the growth of their economies, which were reaching rates not very different from those of the emerging Asian economies. It is reasonable to expect that the growth processes will soon recover in these areas, making these markets of great significance to European development. The most obvious example is Turkey, which, before the recent political and economic-financial crisis, was growing at a Chinese pace and, for European exports, has constituted a market of the same size as China.

8.2.4. The shift of the European economy's centre of gravity to the East

If what is happening beyond Suez and the Mediterranean is affecting the economic geography of Europe on the sea side, on the land side too change no longer passes unnoticed — consider, in particular, the progressive shift of Europe's centre of gravity towards the east. The 2004 enlargement that brought the "new Europe" into the Union started a process of geographical rebalancing of the European economy. And although today sees the "old Europe" still accounting for almost 90% of the EU's gross domestic product, the "new Europe" is experiencing growth rates permanently higher than those of the "old Europe". If one projects these processes at a 2020 and 2030 horizon, one could safely foresee at least a doubling of the share of the "new Europe" in the European gross product, with a proportional growth of the share of the European domestic market, represented by countries and regions located to the east (and south) of the old centre of gravity.

The European centre of gravity is bound to move further to the east in view of the expected economic growth of the neighbouring former Soviet republics (Moldova, Ukraine and Belarus), as well as Russia, despite, also here, the political interferences of the Ukrainian crisis and the consequent Western sanctions on Russia. Finally, one should note that the area of continental Europe that has most successfully overcome the Great Recession (with an unemployment rate in 2017 lower than 3.8%), perhaps with the exception of Greece, is the one that runs, eastward, from Southern Germany to Southeast Europe. These results are also explained by a shift to the east of the European manufacturing industry.

8.2.5. Consequences for the EU transport infrastructure policy

The centrality of Asia, the development of the southern and south-eastern shores of the Mediterranean, and the shift of Europe's manufacturing centre of gravity to the east are all long-term trends whose consequences in terms of road, rail, inland waterway and port infrastructure policy should be obvious.

The adjustment of Europe to these trends should consequently move along three parallel lines: i) maintain efficient access to Europe's historical, productive and consumptive heart; ii) increase the accessibility of regions that were less central yesterday, but are soon bound to increase their economic centrality, possibly becoming an engine of development for the entire continent; iii) link Europe's infrastructural plans to similar developments taking place outside its borders, most notably China's Belt and Road Initiative (BRI).

Even if there is still a lot of ground to cover to bridge a decades-long infrastructural gap[18] between Northwest and Southeast Europe, some of the above processes are already underway, as evidenced by the substantial amount of investments in transport infrastructure made in Central and Eastern European countries. Less coherent is the European transport infrastructure policy, implicit in the construction of Ten-T networks: little attention is paid to adapting the node-ports, acting as global gateways, and the connected internal links.

The relative obsolescence of historical ports, built over the past decades in response to a geography of traffic that no longer exists today and, in turn, the low capacity of many port nodes — together with the inadequacy of the networks connecting them to the internal market — that today would ensure the minimum cost path to freight, is evident. In addition, the state of many port-nodes is today in crisis (technical obsolescence) because of the technical progress that fuels the oligopolistic competition

---

18   Investments in internal transport infrastructures (roads, railways and canals) in Western Europe have been at around 0.8% of GDP since 2000; the same investments, on the other hand, passed in Central and Eastern Europe from 1% of GDP in 2002 to 2% in 2009, a phenomenon that can be explained by the efforts made to reduce the initial infrastructural sub-endowment (ITF 2011).

between shipping companies, using ever larger ships, capable of carrying ever growing mega-cargoes demanding new adequate port and land infrastructure.

Adapting the capacity of the port-node gates to the networks of "minimum cost path" would achieve the double result of reducing both the higher direct transport and logistic costs — paid by market operators — and those indirect negative externalities from pollution, congestion and accidents, that, even if not yet fully appreciated by the market, are nevertheless a burden on the collectivity. For instance, it has been demonstrated (Cappelli, Libardo and Fornasiero 2011) that the transport of a container that goes from China to Germany (Munich) via Rotterdam, instead of Venice, produces at least 78 kg of additional CO_2 per TEU (up to 600 tons of CO_2 for a containership of 8,000 TEU). In enabling, for instance, Venice to handle one million TEUs more per year, from the Far East and on its way to Europe, roughly 125,000 tons less of CO_2 per year would be emitted, in addition to time savings and lower fuel costs. Unfortunately, this evidence has not produced results yet.

The geography of European ports has not changed much. On the contrary, in the face of the changing geography of the origins and destinations of traffic, the historical ports have reacted by trying to achieve economies of scale that could compensate, at least in part, the higher transport costs due to the lengthening of distances by sea and land. The rest of the higher costs due to longer distances were instead passed on to the port users, taking advantage of the considerable market power enjoyed by the historical ports. Distracted or conniving infrastructure policies have so far favoured such inefficiencies to the detriment of traffic receivers. This is why many of them, actually close to the Mediterranean ports, have continued to be served by the North Sea ports, for traffic to and from "beyond Suez", despite at least five more days of navigation and a few hundred more kilometres by land.

This is a situation that the European transport infrastructure policy has been hoping to correct before 2030, the date at which the construction of the Core Trans-European Transport Network and its core corridors, finally taking into proper account the heightened significance of the Mediterranean maritime routes, should be completed. Crucial to this aim is the review of the Union guidelines[19] that the Commission has to carry out by 31 December 2023. In evaluating which "amendments" are needed in order to take care of the "changes in passenger and freight transport flows", as well as the "developments in national transport infrastructure investments", it is advisable to identify ways and means for tackling the geographical and technological obsolescence of all current networks.

Some ideas for addressing "geographical obsolescence" are those discussed above. Some thoughts on tackling "technological obsolescence" are discussed in the next paragraph, dedicated to the *disruption* of the worldwide maritime freight transport network and its infrastructure. On this issue, we believe that the key nodes to be connected should be the global ports, i.e., those connecting seaborne global flows. This

---

19   Council Regulation (EU) 1315/2013.

is because of their role in consolidating/deconsolidating mega-cargoes moving from (to) ports to final destinations (origins) by rail, HCV or, why not, hyperloop.

A further final paragraph is dedicated to the fact that moving from Ten-T to Twn-T, from the "European" to the "Global", demands global agreements. The novelty is the necessary interlocution with foreign counterparts, in dovetailing European and global networks. The Chinese Belt and Road Initiative is possibly the most relevant strategy to be considered in this context.

8.3. Dealing with the Disruption of the Worldwide Maritime Freight Transport Network and its Infrastructure

One major disruption reshaping the whole world of freight transport, both services and the links and nodes of their infrastructure networks, is that regarding global supply chains that comprise at least one ocean leg, i.e., the vast majority of international trade flows (UNCTAD 2017).

Ships, ports, rails, roads, warehouses, etc. are under disruption all over the world, confronted with a clear-cut choice: either to undergo a process of upgrading or to put themselves under the risk of being abandoned, because of technical or geographical obsolescence, and replaced by new, state-of-the-art pieces of infrastructure, or private capital assets.

The *gigantic* process of global "infrastructural change", estimated to amount to trillions of US dollars, is currently taking place without any comprehensive assessment of its efficiency, sustainability or fairness. That is, without any alignment of private and public objectives or, in the case of Europe, only partially achieving the Union's overarching policy objective of economic convergence and greater economic and social cohesion. No one actually knows if citizens and businesses are getting the best value out of infrastructure networks and related investments, existing or under disruptive adjustment, as there is no international cooperation, or at least consistent dialogue, on this matter.

On the contrary, donor countries and organizations such as the European Investment Bank (EIB), the European Bank for Reconstruction and Development (EBRD), the World Bank and International Finance Corporation (WB/IFC), the Asian Infrastructure Investment Bank (AIIB), etc. appear to be *competing on infrastructure*, lending or granting funds to cash-hungry countries in an uncoordinated fashion, without sound, sophisticated, cost-benefit analyses that, when applied, rarely goes beyond a case by case partial and biased exercise. There is an urgent need for assessing the systemic impact of whole transport infrastructure network. Some novel analytical tools and approaches are now available and are reviewed below. The alternative reliance on the mere criterion of the *amount of lending*, the latter being often also the criterion of success of lending policies or promotion of lending officers is not leading to the best use of scarce financial resources.

However, one should not forget that infrastructure investments have long gestation periods until they yield fruit, while many loans need to be repaid in the meantime. In this regard, it should also not be forgotten that world debt is exceeding the GDP of the United States, while China's Non-Performing Loans represent 25% of that country's GDP. A new global economic meltdown cannot therefore be excluded, bearing in mind that the cause of the 2009 crisis was precarious — not to say conniving — lending to aspiring homeowners.

What follows, summarized in Table 1, is a brief description of certain recent trends. Growth in trade (UNCTAD 2018), oligopolistic market structures, and often misplaced business expectations regarding the illusionary benefits of economies of scale (EoS) in shipping, all encourage a seminal, disrupting innovation: the construction of ever larger containerships. This is a development which has already started to manifest significant diseconomies in ports, along the supply chain, and among many disgruntled shippers, particularly in Europe, where shipping industry concentration (alliances) is higher, and the contestability of the market lower than in Asia and North America

Table 1 Innovation-driven disruption of the world maritime freight transport network

Disruptive innovation	Infrastructure disruption	Capital asset disruption	Market structure disruption	Business model disruption
Panamax	Route disruption			
Suezmax	Further route disruption			
Megaships	Port disruption/ obsolescence	Ship fleet disruption	Oligopolistic competition	Ship sharing (alliances)
Megaports/ port systems	Rail infrastructure disruption/ obsolescence			
	Road infrastructure disruption/ obsolescence			
	Inland waterways disruption/ obsolescence			
Mega cargoes	Consolidation/ deconsolidation points	Warehouses, logistic equipment		Ship/port/ Logistic integration
Supply chain digitalization				Ship/port/ Logistic digital integration; platformed services

(for a comprehensive analysis of "gigantism" in container shipping, see Haralambides (2019)). It might be interesting to also mention at this junction that, due to the new Asian centrality in global manufacturing, seaborne trade of manufactures has been carried principally along two main routes: the transpacific one, connecting China to the USA, and the Asia-Europe one. It is mainly along these two routes where repeated rounds of replacement of existing ships with new bigger ones takes place. Those replaced are either scrapped, or deployed as *feeders* to secondary markets and ports (a practice known as *cascading*) many of which have neither the trade volumes nor the technology to receive them.

The progressive substitution of existing ships with larger ones is producing much more profound consequences on port facilities.

Only few of the existing ports can accommodate containerships of the latest generations, and even for those which do, serving such ships is becoming an increasing headache. A further increase in ship size can only be achieved by increasing the beam of the ship beyond the current 60 metres, something that would however render useless the latest generation of ship-to-shore cranes. Complying with carrier requests for the "same" turnaround times, irrespective of ship size, causes significant diseconomies in cargo handling operations. It is not so difficult to understand why: as crane productivity cannot be stretched much beyond 30 moves/hour (it actually declines after a certain *crane density*),[20] the only way to serve a larger ship in the same time (e.g. 48 hours) is by adding more and bigger (in terms of air draft and outreach) cranes. However, increasing crane density reduces crane productivity, nullifying the advantages of having bigger hatches (Haralambides 2019).

Furthermore, big ships impose substantial demands on port capacity, without however paying commensurately for this demand. For instance, where before one could accommodate three Panamax vessels (i.e. three berths) along one kilometre of quay-wall, today, in the same space, one can only host two mega-vessels of the latest generation (about 400 metres long). Berth utilization obviously goes down and so does the utilization of Ship-to-Shore (StS) cranes, since bigger ships mean lower call frequency (Haralambides 2019). All this would be fine, however, as long as carriers were bringing more traffic to the port with their larger vessels. But this doesn't happen either. Call size, it has been proven, is only moderately correlated with vessel size.

Therefore, ports eligible to handle the megaships of today and tomorrow are those rich both in adequate nautical accessibility (deep waters) and large spaces on land and efficient and sustainable connections via rail and road (and inland waterways) to large markets. Since all three conditions can in most cases be modified by adequate investments, the choice of the megaports of tomorrow is a delicate one and can lead to substantial *port disruption*, with two opposite potential risks:

1. Creation of port overcapacity, when too many ports are trying to stay on the contestable global markets and/or

---

20   Crane density is defined as the number of cranes per 300 metres of quay length.

2. Rail, road and inland waterways infrastructure under-utilization when a lack of port capacity acts as a crucial "missing link" in the networks (*rail, road, etc. disruption*).

In conclusion, the coordinated use of all transport infrastructure, to be used along the routes followed by global supply chains, is crucial for "getting the best value for citizens and businesses" from existing or disrupted infrastructure. By definition, here is a delicate "governmental" role at stake at all levels: national, regional (European) and global.

But the economic usefulness of megaships does not depend only on a sufficient level of capacity utilization, something increasingly difficult to attain were it not for carrier cooperation in global shipping alliances, but also on spending most of their time at sea. The capital intensity of these ships obliges them to limit their ports of call at each end to just a few hub ports or load centres such as Shanghai, Singapore, Hong Kong, and currently in Europe, Rotterdam and Hamburg, from where huge surges of containers are consolidated or further forwarded (feedered) with smaller vessels, rail or road, to regional and local ports. Complex hub-and-spoke networks have thus evolved whose logistical fine-tuning and optimization bears directly on consumer pockets.

The consolidation/deconsolidation of mega-cargoes passes through successive steps, dealing with sub-consolidation/deconsolidation phases. Mega-cargoes call for supply chain integration. That is why the choice of megaports will decide which links and nodes of the land multimodal transport infrastructure network will have to be constructed, or further developed, to cope with the new freight consolidation/deconsolidation trends, along each supply chain route (land leg and port node on the departing country; maritime leg, and port node and land leg on the receiving country).

The choice (competitively, when possible) among different routes is somehow in the hands of governments — in the case of Europe, both at European and national levels — because of their final say about infrastructure provision. The choice, however, is also controlled by the potential "private" investor in port infrastructure, as well as by the supply chain user, the latter being mostly the freight forwarder or the logistics service provider, who combine the maritime leg, the ports, and land transport. If, as in the current situation, no regulator "supervises" this process, the only agent not controlling the cost and the quality of the service provided would paradoxically be the final consumer who pays the bill.

It is worth noting that the complexity of the mega-cargo consolidation/deconsolidation process, and the necessity of dealing with sub-consolidated/sub-deconsolidated cargo lots, make the value added generated in this logistics phase greater than that generated by the pure maritime transport service. A new business model is consequently emerging: the one that foresees the vertical integration, under the same firm roof, of the maritime and port services, and/or of the maritime, port and logistics services (integrated physical business model). This integration is eligible for being digitally operated in a suitable platform, run by one of the operators controlling one leg of the supply chain or, preferably, by a specialized, independent third party (digital business model) (Costa et al. 2018).

The overall European transport network disruption taking place because of this "maritime driven" revolution assigns a primary role to those Ten-T nodes characterized as megaports: they become the most important missing links (missing nodes) to deal with, in the amendment of the Ten-T Guidelines of 31 December 2023. But EU megaports are also the missing links across the external EU border: they are connecting the EU with the rest of the world. In terms of Eurasian relations, this means dovetailing them with the Belt and Road Chinese Initiative.

8.4. Dovetailing the EU Ten-T Infrastructure Policy with the Chinese Belt and Road Initiative (BRI)

Until 2013, the evolution of the Ten-T Network was a phenomenon entirely controlled by the European Union.

Extending the Core Ten-T Network outside the EU was until recently only a matter of "closing" the EU infrastructure system, i.e. extending Ten-T to accession candidate countries, as well as to potential ones in the ring of neighbouring friends, in order to enlarge or deepen the internal market: a policy defined in Brussels and, of course, gladly accepted by her counterparts.

"Opening" and connecting the EU infrastructure system to the rest of the world is a totally different story, however. The physical dovetailing of the EU network with external networks is bound to be influenced by preceding policies and strategies, and the dovetailing of the EU Ten-T with the Eurasian land (belt) and maritime (new silk road) networks, supported by the Chinese BRI, is today the most relevant case.

To many, BRI is above all a brilliant manifestation of China's renewed presence on the world stage. The "initiative" constitutes a great diplomatic strategy, many believe, based on a refined exercise of *soft power*, that considers "power *with* others" as more effective than power "*over* others" (Nye 1990).

To quote China's president Xi Jinping (2017),

[...] BRI aims to replace estrangement with exchanges between different civilizations, replace clashes with mutual learning and replace a sense of superiority with coexistence; it aims to boost mutual understanding, mutual respect and mutual trust among different countries. In this light, the BRI is seen as a path towards global peace [...].

And on BRI and the *new economic order*, President Xi continues:

[...] BRI is guided by the principles of consultation and cooperation, aiming at shared benefits. The initiative represents an approach to international cooperation featuring mutual respect, justice, equity and cooperation for win-win outcomes. BRI is committed to multilateralism and an open global economy. As such, BRI will help move economic globalization toward greater openness, inclusiveness and balance [...].

The stated objective of BRI — a one trillion US dollar program — is to achieve greater economic integration and development through better *connectivity*, the latter being the main enabler of trade growth and trade-driven prosperity. Ongoing research by authors of this chapter shows that a 10% improvement in connectivity between countries along the "Maritime Silk Road" would deliver a 3% decrease in Chinese trade costs which would, in turn, boost China's imports and exports by around 6% and 9%, respectively. The latest studies by the World Bank and other international institutions also suggest that BRI cooperation could cut the costs of global trade by 1.1 to 2.2%.

Chinese investments of transport relevance in the EU, not necessarily always under the BRI umbrella, are impressive. Bloomberg calculates them to be in excess of €300 bn in the past ten years. Ports — the gates of Chinese exports to Europe — score prominently among these investments, with the port of Piraeus, Greece, showcasing second place (after Valencia, Spain, also, presently, under Chinese interest) in the Mediterranean; 7th in Europe; and 36th (from 93 in 2010) in the world.

As mentioned above, and according to many observers and researchers on BRI, China has adopted a *refined* version of projecting "soft power", in the sense that it appears to be exercising a type of "multiple bilateralism", building relations, individually, or in groups (e.g. 16+1), with different countries in Europe, Central- South- and Southeast Asia, East and West Africa and even Oceania and Latin America. But, is it really so?

In Europe, feelings are mixed, in spite of President Xi's reassurances during his recent visit to Europe, according to which it is not China's aim to play one country against the other, neither to advance ad hoc and uncoordinated investments, nor to proliferate an understandable initial "vagueness" in geographically defining BRI. On the contrary, at this point in time, China would welcome a joint effort in dovetailing BRI with the Ten-T Network going forward.

EU Member States are not as unequivocal, however, when it comes to Europe's openness to Chinese investments. A new *core-periphery* divide appears to have emerged, with Germany and France pushing for an EU-wide investment *screening mechanism*, while governments in Greece, Portugal and Cyprus are sceptical of such a move, arguing that it would hamper their countries' ability to attract much-needed capital. In parallel, however, it is the EU Member States themselves who, in their anxiety to compete for Chinese funds, or to accredit themselves as marine terminals on the "silk road", or as land facilities along the "belt", visit China on an almost daily basis. This gives Chinese interlocutors enormous room for manoeuvre in their effort to penetrate the European markets.

It is true that the sale of the majority stock of the Piraeus Port Authority A.S. to COSCO, and especially certain activities that took place thereafter, including Greece's vetoing a UN resolution on human rights, has left a somehow bitter aftertaste in Brussels. Moreover, the Union looks also with some concern at the Chinese penetration into the Western Balkans which, after having acquired the port of Piraeus, are concretely applying their *soft power* for the construction of a "Balkan Silk Road" which should ideally connect Beijing to Athens and from there reach Skopje, Tirana, Sarajevo, Belgrade and Budapest.

In spite of, or even thanks to, all the above, and copying similar procedures of the US Senate, a *screening mechanism* was proposed by the European Commission in 2017 and approved by the Parliament in February 2019. The "mechanism" aims to ensure that "critical infrastructure", such as those relating to energy, transport, communications and data storage (but also those that concern "critical technologies", such as artificial intelligence, robotics, semiconductors and nuclear and space technologies) is not predatorily targeted by foreign investors. The "mechanism" is seen as a coordinating tool at the EU level, which does not intend to replace national mechanisms, nor challenge Member States' prerogative to decide on investments. With regard to transport investments in particular, the European Commission has initiated a discussion on Europe-China, within a so-called "EU-China Connectivity Platform".

Confronted with BRI, each country — and the EU too — is faced with a deliberately complex proposal, whereby it is up to each interlocutor, along BRI, to find their place on one or the other of the global logistical routes, within a wide spectrum of alternative options, relatively indifferent from the Chinese point of view. "Choice", naturally, has always an objective, and alternative options ought to be guided by it. Some logistics chains, for instance, are better than others because they guarantee shorter and more efficient paths. Often, however, *sound economics* is sacrificed in the altar of unfolding strategies, or as a result of the will, ability and bargaining power of either party.

The strategic game is evident in the continuous redesign of BRI's land routes, but also in the *maritime silk road*, which, from 2014 to 2017, has made its western landing more uncertain: as far as the Mediterranean Basin is concerned, in 2014 just the ports

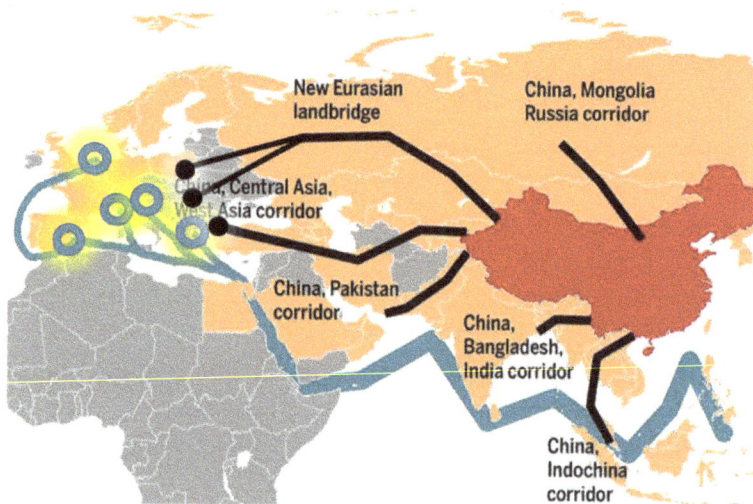

Fig. 4 Potential Ten-T/BRI dovetailing nodes

Source: Paolo Costa, 2019.

of Piraeus and Venice were considered as the possible southern gates to Europe. In 2017, China's interests were also manifested in the Italian ports of Trieste, Genova and Palermo; Spain's Valencia; France's Marseilles; but also in ports outside the Union, such as Suez, Haifa, Istanbul (Kumport), Gibraltar and more (Costa 2017).

Among the many potentially involved nodes, those on the "Belt" (land) are "dictated" by geography while those on the "Road" (sea) are, so far, "suggested" by China (Figure 4).

8.5. Assessing the Systemic Impact of Transport Infrastructure: Some Novel Analytical Tools and Approaches

The key message emerging from the discussion above is the need to elaborate transport and infrastructural policies, considering the broader, systemic impact on the economy, or on the society at large, as well as the compatibility with policies undertaken by other global players. Therefore, when it comes to considering alternative policies in the allocation of public (and private) investment funds, one would like to base the choice on (or at least start with) rational comparisons, based on facts and scientifically accepted theories and models.

Unfortunately, the typical tools such as cost-benefit analysis, multi-criteria analysis, input-output or computable general equilibrium models, etc., all fall short in completely assessing the systemic consequences of (large) infrastructure investments. This is clearly due to two main reasons:

1. The extreme complexity and interplay of the effects;

2. The lack of reliable data.

However, it may be worthwhile to briefly mention here two recent contributions and methodologies, which promise to provide a more useful support for decision-making in this context.

One is illustrated in a recent paper by Treb Allen and Costas Arkolakis (2019). They develop a general equilibrium geographic framework to characterize the welfare effect of transportation infrastructure investments, tackling three distinct but conflating challenges. First, an analytical characterization of the routing problem, where infrastructure investment between any two connected locations decreases the total trade costs between *all* pairs of locations. Second, a general equilibrium geography setup where market inefficiencies arise due to agglomeration and dispersion spillovers. Third, a framework that admits analytical characterizations of traffic congestion. Allen and Arkolakis apply this model to calculate the welfare effects of improving each of the thousands of segments of the US national highway network.

This research work paves the way for the construction of a global transportation general equilibrium model, which could be of fundamental importance for the assessment of transport infrastructure policies, such as those discussed throughout this chapter. For sure, this would be a very challenging venture, in terms of data and computational power, which would require the collaboration of different research centres around the world. However, there are examples of successful consortia of this kind, managing complex data bases and sophisticated global models, like the Global Trade Analysis Project (GTAP), based at Purdue University.

GTAP-based computable general equilibrium models are being used for policy assessment exercises, such as effects of trade agreements, the impact of Brexit, and long-run implications of economic growth on natural resources and climate change. Therefore, we believe that the development of a new generation of global transportation network models is not an impossible dream. These models could provide the scientifically sound assessment of the policies, trends and phenomena considered in this chapter.

Another, albeit very different, approach has been explored by Franz Hubert and his co-authors (Hubert and Ikonnikova (2011); Roson and Hubert (2015); Csercsik, Hubert, Sziklai and Kóczy (2019)). In these works, a methodology is used for analyzing bargaining games on network markets, which are markets where transactions occur by means of distribution and transportation networks. The overall economic surplus obtained in the market is distributed among all network agents on the basis of their bargaining power, which in turn depends on a variety of factors: position of each agent (e.g., a country) in the network, reliability in the cooperation scheme (e.g., geo-political stability), existence of market distortions and availability of outside options. From this perspective, who controls critical links or nodes in the network extracts the highest surplus. An interesting implication is that building/improving new links or nodes may be justified in terms of bargaining power, rather than in terms of narrow social net benefits.

The typical example here is the one of gas pipelines in Europe. It may not be universally known that the total carrying capacity of the existing pipeline network, in Europe, far exceeds its actual utilization. The construction of large new infrastructure such as North Stream or TAP would not be necessary, therefore, at least in terms of economic logic. However, geo-political considerations, for instance, associated with bypassing some critical countries, are rather evident.

The principle carries over to other transportation networks, and may help in explaining some choices which are made, for example the ones taken in designing the BRI initiative.

Trade is based on cooperation, but trade needs transport infrastructure, where cooperation is, consequently, also necessary. If cooperation generates some mutual benefits, the pie of surplus has to be split in some way. This is where cooperative game theory, when applied to transport infrastructure, can shed some light.

Admittedly, research on network cooperative games, as well as the one on global transportation general equilibrium models, is still in its infancy. We can therefore conclude that the radically changing scenario of global trade flows poses new challenges not only in terms of management and policies, but also in terms of the supporting applied economic research and modelling.

8.6. Some Concluding Remarks

Ten-T has been evolving from 1996 to 2013 trying to cope with the enlargement of the European Union and to encourage modal shifts from road and air to rail, inland navigation and short-sea shipping. However, during these notable efforts, little attention has been paid to the global dimension of European connectivity, which now demands a European contribution towards building a Trans-Global network, Twn-T.

Together with addressing a number of technical disruptions affecting transport and its infrastructure, the new wave of Ten-T revision — due by December 2023 — must depart from what has thus far been an introverted view of Europe as a single market (something that has often penalized European competitiveness) to an extroverted orientation of the Union as a key player in a global market.

The growing economic centrality of Asia since China's accession to WTO; China's strong interest in the Mediterranean Basin as the "super-hub" that connects four continents; and the eastward shift of the European economic barycentre: all of these developments indicate possible solutions for addressing the "geographical obsolescence" of the current Ten-T.

In parallel, innovation-driven disruption of the worldwide maritime freight transport network and its infrastructure necessitates the streamlining of port nodes and rail networks around the world, in a way that at the same time addresses efficiently the current "technological obsolescence" of big parts of European infrastructure, predominantly of ports.

But the new Ten-T Network evolving into a Twn-T one will not anymore be the product solely of European decisions: dovetailing Ten-T with China's Belt and Road Initiative will be unavoidable.

Any dovetailing of Ten-T and BRI networks into a possible Twn-T network would profit a lot from the availability of sound methodologies for assessing the systemic consequences of changes in the Twn-T Network due to large infrastructure investments. Such methodologies do exist even if they are in their infancy. The construction of a global transportation general equilibrium model that could, among others, tackle the routing problem is within reach. The same can be said of methodologies used for analyzing bargaining games on network markets where the bargaining power of each agent (e.g., China or the EU) depends on its position in the network and its reliability in a cooperation scheme.

References

Allen, T. and C. Arkolakis (2019) "The Welfare Effects of Transportation Infrastructure Improvements", *NBER Working Papers* 25487, https://pdfs.semanticscholar.org/d934/8018c20437777de93b1f9b2e319380eee21f.pdf?_ga=2.71221142.749029904.1588693600-1587604656.1572340752

Benelux Group (1955) Benelux Memorandum, 18 May, https://www.cvce.eu/obj/the_benelux_memorandum-en-58119e2d-faf6-4faa-9bc1-d1918343bb6e.html

Bonnefous, E. (1951) "Report on the Coordination of European Communications and the Establishment of a European Transport Authority". Report presented on 5 May 1951 by Eduoard Bonnefous to the Consultative Assembly of the Council of Europe on the Establishment of a European Transport Authority, https://www.cvce.eu/en/obj/report_on_the_coordination_of_european_communications_and_the_establishment_of_a_european_transport_authority_5_may_1951-en-33a9f02c-cf8c-4a9a-afd2-0ea533cad2d5.html

Cappelli, A., A. Libardo and E. Fornasiero (2011) "L'impatto del trasporto intercontinentale di merci: Modelli per la misura degli effetti delle scelte", *Primo Piano sul Porto di Venezia* 21: 7–9.

Costa, P. and Maresca, M. (2014) *The European Future of the Italian Port System.* Venice: Marsilio.

Costa, P. (2017) "Puntare su Venezia perché l'Italia sia al centro della Via della Seta", *Limes* 4: 193–96.

Costa, P. (2018) "Il futuro del trasporto merci in Italia tra sue previsioni e sua costruzione", in *Innovazioni tecnologiche e governo della mobilità*, Part 1, ed. by SIPoTra (Società Italiana di Politica dei Trasporti) (Santarcangelo di Romagna: Maggioli Editore), pp. 114–32.

Costa, P., J. J. Montero, R. Roson and L. Casullo (2018) "The Impact of Disruptive Technologies on Infrastructure Networks". Paper delivered to the 11th meeting of the Network of Economic Regulators, OECD, Paris.

Council Regulation (EU) (2013) No. 1315/2013 of 11 December 2013 on Union Guidelines for the Development of the Trans-European Transport Network and Repealing Decision NO. 661/2010/EU, OJ L348/1.

Csercsik, D., F. Hubert, B. R. Sziklai, and L. Á. Kóczy (2019) "Modeling Transfer Profits as Externalities in a Cooperative Game-Theoretic Model of Natural Gas Networks", *Energy Economics* 80: 355–65, https://doi.org/10.1016/j.eneco.2019.01.013

European Commission (1993) *Growth, Competitiveness, Employment: The Challenges and the Ways Forward into the 21th Century. White Paper. Bulletin of the European Communities, Supplement 6/93.* Luxembourg: Office for Official Publications of the European Communities, https://op.europa.eu/en/publication-detail/-/publication/4e6ecfb6-471e-4108-9c7d-90cb1c3096af/language-en

European Commission (2010) *Ten-T Policy Review. Expert Group 4. Methodology for Ten-T Planning. Ten-T Extension outside the EU.* Brussels: European Commission.

European Commission (2018) *Third Work Plan of European Coordinators (9 volumes).* Brussels: European Commission

European Court of Auditors (2017) *2016 EU Audit in Brief. Introducing the 2016 Annual Reports of the European Court of Auditors.* Luxembourg: Publications Office of the European Union, https://www.eca.europa.eu/Lists/ECADocuments/auditinbrief-2016/auditinbrief-2016-EN.pdf

European Union (1992) Treaty on European Union (Maastricht Treaty), 29 July, OJ C 191, https://eur-lex.europa.eu/legal-content/EN/TXT/PDF/?uri=OJ:C:1992:191:FULL&from =EN

Eurostat (2018) "Extra-EU Trade in Goods", Statistics Explained, https://ec.europa.eu/eurostat/ statistics-explained/index.php/Extra-EU_trade_in_goods

Haralambides, H. E. (2019) "Gigantism in Container Shipping, Ports and Global Logistics: A Time-Lapse into the Future", *Maritime Economics & Logistics* 21(1): 1–60, https://doi. org/10.1057/s41278-018-00116-0

Hubert, F. and S. Ikonnikova (2011) "Investment Options and Bargaining Power: The Eurasian Supply Chain for Natural Gas", *The Journal of Industrial Economics* 59(1): 85–116, https://doi. org/10.1111/j.1467-6451.2011.00447.x

ITF (2011) "Trends in Transport Infrastructure 1995–2009, Statistics Brief, July", https://www. itf-oecd.org/sites/default/files/docs/2011-07.pdf

ITF (2019) *ITF Transport Outlook 2019*. Paris: OECD Publishing.

Jinping, Xi (2017) "Work Together to Build the Silk Road Economic Belt and The 21st Century Maritime Silk Road", *Embassy News*, http://na.china-embassy.org/eng/sgxw/t1461872.htm

Nye, J. (1990) "The Misleading Metaphor of Decline", *The Atlantic Monthly* (March), pp. 86–94.

OECD (2011) *International Future Program, Strategic Transport Infrastructure Needs to 2030: Main Findings*. Paris: OECD Publishing, https://www.oecd.org/futures/infrastructureto2030/ 49094448.pdf

Ohmae, K. (1985) *Triade Power: The Coming Shape of Global Competition*. London: Free Press.

Roson, R. and F. Hubert, F. (2015) "Bargaining Power and Value Sharing in Distribution Networks: A Cooperative Game Theory Approach", *Networks and Spatial Economics* 15(1): 71–87, https://doi.org/10.1007/s11067-014-9270-6

UNCTAD (2018) *Review of Maritime Transport*. New York and Geneva: United Nations, https:// unctad.org/en/PublicationsLibrary/rmt2018_en.pdf

9. Ecological Transition

*D'Maris Coffman,[1] Roberto Cardinale,[2] Jing Meng[3]
and Zhifu Mi[4]*

Introduction

Anthropogenic climate change caused by greenhouse gas (GHG) emissions is widely understood to be the greatest existential threat to human societies in the coming centuries. The Intergovernmental Panel on Climate Change (IPCC) was established in 1988 to coordinate a global response to the coming crisis. In 2006, the United Kingdom's "Stern Review" concluded that early action to mitigate climate change would be the most cost-effective and therefore argued for significant expenditure to address the expected geophysical, political and societal changes wrought by global warming (Stern 2006). Over the intervening decade, the 2008 Global Financial Crisis and its sequelae distracted policy makers' attention from the challenges of global environmental change. The IPCC's publication of the Special Report on Global Warming of 1.5 °C (SR15) in October 2018 has helped to galvanize public opinion and has given rise to unprecedented climate activism. SR15 made clear the scientific consensus — to halt global warming it will be necessary to achieve net zero carbon dioxide emissions by 2050. This renewed urgency has, in turn, shifted the Overton window, whereby state actors now recognize a need for immediate action.

According to the IPCC's formulation in SR15, possible responses to climate change fall into three categories: mitigation, adaptation and remediation (IPCC 2018). Mitigation is taken to mean measures to reduce carbon emissions (e.g. through decarbonization of energy and transport systems or through changes in consumption patterns) or to enhance carbon sinks (e.g. afforestation or reforestation); adaptation means measures that ameliorate the effects of climate change on human populations (e.g. ranging from flood control measures to changing land use and even relocation of cities); and

---

1 Corresponding author — Bartlett School of Construction and Project Management — University College London.
2 Bartlett School of Construction and Project Management — University College London.
3 Bartlett School of Construction and Project Management — University College London.
4 Bartlett School of Construction and Project Management — University College London.

https://doi.org/10.11647/OBP.0222.09

remediation means intentional measures to counteract the effects of GHG emissions, including global warming (e.g. through stratospheric aerosol injection, cirrus cloud thinning, or space mirrors) and ocean acidification (e.g. via ocean fertilization). There are inevitable trade-offs between the costs of mitigation and those of adaptation over decadal time horizons. As the 2018 IPCC's 1.5°C SR15 states: "increasing investment in physical and social infrastructure is a key enabling condition to enhance the resilience and the adaptive capacities of societies" (IPCC 2018, p. 19). Likewise, some climate activists are concerned that the prospect of remediation (particularly the tantalizing potential of negative emissions technologies) will discourage adequate investment in mitigation, or at least complacency about the need to meet the net zero targets (Lockley and Coffman 2016).

Nevertheless, with all three responses, large-scale infrastructure investment is required, with varying degrees of involvement by state actors, multilateral organizations, other non-governmental organisations (including religious groups) and, most significantly, private capital markets. In the current climate, multilateral development banks (MDBs) have taken a leading role.

In concert with the publication of the IPCC report in October 2018, the European Investment Bank (EIB) announced in late September 2018 that it would bring all its activities into alignment with the Paris Agreement. Two months later, in December, the MDBs as a whole announced a joint framework for doing so. In the past eleven months (at the time of writing) since the publication of the SR15 report in October 2018, the scientific consensus that global warming *can* be kept to 1.5°C has weakened. There is no meaningful disagreement, however, with the conclusion that it *should* be limited to as close to 1.5°C as possible. As the report makes clear, the economic costs of adaptation rise significantly with each half degree increase, as do challenges of ensuring the inevitable adaptations are in line with other Sustainable Development Goals (SDGs). Concerns that the 1.5°C target will be missed have further catalyzed political movements in Europe such that "climate emergencies" are being declared at national, provincial and local levels. This has in turn galvanized national leaders to press for greater collaboration on decarbonization efforts.

Emmanuel Macron's determination to establish a new European Climate Bank exemplifies this trend. His efforts have prompted discussions about whether or not the European Investment Bank might play that role once the Juncker Plan (formally known as the European Fund for Strategic Investments (EFSI)) finishes. This is less surprising than it may seem to some, because the EIB's purpose is to mitigate market failure. The main criticism of the Juncker Plan by the European Commission's auditors is that a non-trivial percentage of the loans would have been made anyway. To the extent that climate change is the result of market failure (i.e. the inability of the market to internalize fully the negative externalities associated with GHGs), then there is a role for the EIB to play, particularly in helping to finance the rapid decarbonization of energy and transport which could not happen as quickly as demanded by the SR15 Report if left entirely to market forces. Whether or not the SR15's net zero target is met, there will be a critical role for infrastructure investment both in climate change mitigation and in adaptation. Institutional money managers, including those of pension funds, insurance companies, and sovereign wealth funds will undoubtedly play an important role in the low carbon transition. This is a particularly promising development because of the intergenerational risks and rewards associated with climate change mitigation and adaptation; this presents an important opportunity to renew the intergenerational social compact and to ensure intergenerational equity.

9.1. The Importance of Carbon Accounting

Most lay audiences are now familiar with the term "carbon footprint", which is a measure of the carbon dioxide emitted through a given activity, for instance in heating a house or driving a car. In response to the recent *Flygskam* (or "Flight Shame") movement in Europe, more and more air travellers are electing to "offset" the direct carbon emissions associated with their flights by purchasing voluntary carbon offsets (VCOs). Some are declining to fly, instead preferring to take voyages by train and even ship, as Greta Thunberg elected to do recently in her trip to the United States. Using "carbon footprints" to assess carbon emissions has the virtue of being relatively straightforward to do, and there are many carbon calculators available to the public to assess the carbon trade-offs around household meat consumption, energy use, transportation choices, and similar such decisions.

Unfortunately, lay audiences do not necessarily appreciate that "carbon footprints" are not the only way to assess carbon emissions. Carbon footprints focus attention on carbon produced by the *operation* of a particular asset, such as an automobile, powerplant, airplane or ship. They do not account for the carbon emitted during the *construction* of said asset, nor do they consider the carbon emitted during the *decommissioning* of the asset, both of which can often be substantial. Life-cycle assessment models which consider the carbon embedded in all phases of a product or built asset life cycle can lead to different recommendations for green investment (McDowall 2018). For example, hydropower is widely considered to be attractive because rivers are renewable, unlike fossil fuels, and the production of hydropower does not involve direct carbon emissions. However, when the construction and decommissioning phases of a hydropower project are included in the assessment, the project may be appraised differently. The cement used in the construction of hydropower dams is very carbon intensive (Mar 2009), as is the construction supply chain. By a similar token, decommissioning, when it becomes necessary, of a hydropower plant can involve considerable carbon emissions. Equally importantly, forests represent substantial natural carbon sinks. Dams that flood natural forests destroy these carbon sinks. Some hydropower projects may represent a less attractive alternative than superficially more carbon intensive alternatives. Investors need to be aware that embedded carbon is of growing concern to multilaterals, who are actively commissioning research to develop tools to assess these issues.

Some investors may question the value of accounting for embedded carbon because they worry this will lead to double-counting (a methodological error) as surely the carbon emissions produced by cement would be accounted for in that production process. While this is true on a global level, accounting merely for the carbon footprint of an infrastructure asset distorts the political economy of carbon emissions. The IPCC framework anticipates carbon emissions targets and voluntary carbon quotas; if the latter are adopted, it is necessary to consider the global value chain, as many products which are produced in one country (usually a lesser developed one) are consumed in developed countries (Meng et al 2018). Forcing the producer-nation (or assembler-nation) to take responsibility for the embedded carbon in, say, the iPhone of one of the authors, which was assembled in China (out of components made in the US, Mexico and the Philippines) and consumed in the UK would be unjust. Likewise, the embedded carbon in the production of large energy or transport mega-projects can be substantial. Most scholars agree that responsibility for those embedded carbon emissions should be borne by the beneficiaries of the infrastructure mega-project or of the goods or services so consumed. Investors, in any event, need to be aware of these debates. Ideally, infrastructure desks should have analysts who are adept at life-cycle assessment modelling, if not in doing the modelling themselves at least in understanding how these models are used in project appraisal as there are now part of statutory reporting requirements.

9.2. The Emergence of "ESG" ratings

Although there are increasingly statutory requirements to report the environmental and climate impacts of infrastructure projects, these are developing amidst a wider movement to provide a more holistic set of sustainability metrics, taking the Environmental, Social and Corporate Governance (ESG) dimensions together, as a tool for helping to internalize the positive or negative externalities of a given project. Over the second half 2019 and first quarter of 2020, the European Commission moved to procure consultancy services from a wide range of tendering parties on the development of ESG ratings. The European Commission is well aware of its leading role in green procurement in Europe, and the Commission has begun to develop tools for sustainable finance for use by the European Banking Authority. The results of this tendering process should be available in April or May 2020.

There is reason to hope that the European Commission commitment to developing sound ESG ratings can help avoid some of the criticisms that beset the Juncker Plan, while also improving infrastructure planning and promoting a shift towards a "circular" economy (Dreschel et al. 2018; Bowman 2017; Mascotto 2020), where waste is eliminated and resources continually re-used rather than exhausted (Geissdoerfer

2017). Although some critics remain sceptical, there is a growing consensus that attention to the ESG dimension of investments heightens financial performance and protects firm value (Valente and Atkinson 2019).

9.3. Mitigation: Decarbonization of Energy and Transport

There is wide agreement that it would be impossible to meet any plausible net zero target without decarbonization of energy and transport. Energy decarbonization is well underway, with some European countries (including the UK) able to go for weeks at a time without relying on coal (Ogden 2019). Taken together, decarbonization of the European energy and transport sectors is advancing rapidly and is considered achievable at current technological levels and at minimal cost, less than 1% of GDP (Capros et al. 2014).

Decarbonization of transport (also known as "electrification") is more difficult than decarbonization of energy systems, but achievable with aggressive planning efforts. Decarbonization of the food supply is also necessary, but with the exception of the role of maritime transport in the global food supply chain, largely outside the scope of this chapter.

9.3.1. Energy

As noted, decarbonization of energy systems in Europe has been underway for over a decade with impressive results (Tagliapietra 2019). Most observers urge policy makers to integrate deep decarbonization of energy into broader, cross-sector industrial strategies (Avila 2018). One particularly promising area for both policy makers and investors is renewal gas.

Renewable gas may become a leading source in the transition to zero-emission energy production, especially given its importance in promoting circular economy solutions. Its advantages are environmental as well as economic in nature. The environmental advantage is double as its production not only entails zero-emission of CO_2, but also uses inputs deriving from urban, agriculture and industrial waste, contributing to decreasing their polluting effect when disposed through traditional methods. The economic advantage lies in cost savings deriving from the progressive replacement of natural gas imports. It is estimated that in 2015 the EU could produce up to 122 bcm of renewable gas per year and replace a substantial part of natural gas imports, leading to a cost saving of €138 bn annually (Ecofys 2018). However, the cost saving will not only result from the substitution of current import with domestic production, but also from the possibility to use existing infrastructure for storage and transport. Relying on existing gas grids would also make it possible to alleviate the increasing burden on electricity grids, which in the future are likely to face overloads and disruptions due to the growing share of renewables among the sources of electricity generation.

The European Union has been vigorously promoting the transition to renewable gas because of its contribution to achieving the targets of environmental policy, namely to reduce GHG emission to 30% and reach 27% of energy consumption from renewables by 2030. As a result of the incentives granted by EU policies, production of biogas in the EU has reached 18 bcm of methane equivalent in 2015, making Europe the world's greatest producer.

Despite the aforementioned environmental and economic advantages, some questions remain on the long-term economic benefits of full reliance on renewable gas. Questions particularly concern the possibility to achieve energy independence. In fact, it is estimated that a share of renewable gas, or some inputs for its production (e.g. crops), will still need to be imported.

This issue is important in view of the recent progress in the EU energy policy reforms, which envision a full transition to models based on short-term transactions in spot markets. In fact, in an energy-deprived area such as Europe, the full reliance on models based on short-term transactions is likely to increase the bargaining power of non-EU exporters, potentially threatening energy security and price affordability for consumers (Cardinale 2019). The fact that the transition to renewable gas will not guarantee energy independence suggests the need to carefully monitor the collateral changes that accompany the low carbon transition, especially for what concerns commercial relations between exporters and importers and their respective bargaining power. Moreover, it seems necessary to consider adopting a regulatory framework that includes both long- and short-term transaction models.

The relative desirability of various kinds of renewable energy remain an active research area, especially when different types of carbon accounting are used (McDowall et al. 2018). In life cycle assessment tests, wind power compares favourably to solar photovoltaics (PV). Nuclear energy at current technological levels is regarded as most desirable as an intermediate solution to wean the global energy system from fossil fuels, but nuclear is rarely considered a long-term solution (Prăvălie et al. 2018).

The ESG approach to deep decarbonization of energy has the additional virtue of encouraging co-mitigation of air pollution. While it is possible, as China has done, to reduce pollution sharply using ultra-low carbon (ULE) emissions standards (Tang et al 2019), decarbonization will also have the positive externality of improving air pollution levels (Meng et al. 2019).

In emerging markets, the calculus of deep decarbonization of energy differs somewhat, because energy security is a pressing concern, as is the need to provide reliable electricity to households and firms, against a backdrop of more extreme weather events, which can cause significant load shedding (Gannon et al. 2018). Hydropower is particularly vulnerable to these events (Ahmed et al. 2019).

In emerging markets, back-up power generation using diesel fuel is widespread, especially by export-oriented manufacturing firms (Ahmed et al. 2019). This is an area that needs further research, but preliminary studies suggest the effects can be of such a significant scale as to have the potential to change recommendations about the optimal energy mix for these countries and in any case strengthen the business case for projects that promote energy resilience in these markets (Farquharson et al. 2018). Investors, including multilaterals like the World Bank, will need to pay more attention to these issues going forward.

9.3.2. Transport

Decarbonization of transport is often taken to be synonymous with electrification, though that is by no means the entire story. First, to a greater extent than energy decarbonization, transport decarbonization will require a socio-technical transition away from family-owned autonomous vehicles towards other means of transport. This will require, in turn, significant planning challenges, which will coincide with the advent of smart cities (Zawieska and Pieriegud 2018).

Significant investment opportunities exist in the electrification space, as many European countries have already begun electrification of mass transport systems, including busses, trams and trains (Glotz-Richter and Koch 2016). Planners are increasingly requiring charging stations for electric cars in parking lots and along city streets (Thiel et al. 2010). Most households have probably already purchased their last new automobile powered solely by unleaded fuel, and most car manufacturers are relying on the growth of electric cars and hybrids to keep them in business. Consumer preferences are changing slowly but steadily in this area (Mazur et al. 2018). Electrification of transport is an active investment area for some specialist firms such as Meridiam, through their Transitions fund.

As with energy, a factor accelerating decarbonization of transport is the positive externalities associated with the reduction of automobile induced pollution, which is a grave public health threat in most countries. Pollution rates and emission rates tend to track each other; although rates of increase have slowed in recent years, tackling both will require global cooperation (Meng et al. 2019). The European approach has thus far primarily been to manage the co-mitigation of air pollution and carbon emissions in the transport sector fuel tax policies in the transport sector (Zimmer and Koch 2017). This represents an opportunity for investors, as positive externalities associated with curbing pollution can be incorporated into business cases.

The extent to which the sharing economy, notably car sharing and bike sharing, contribute to the low carbon transition is also an area of active debate (Mi and Coffman 2019). Car sharing and bike sharing have the potential to reduce both emissions and pollution, but not at all such firms behave in pro-social ways. Both planners and investors can play a role in promoting sustainable practices in this sub-sector.

Air travel is another area where decarbonization is essential, but the debate has rarely advanced beyond demand reduction, such as that encouraged by the Flight Shame movement (Pye et al. 2014). There is political momentum in many European countries (though largely not outside Europe) for taxes on frequent flyers and even the abolition of frequent flyer incentive programmes. This is one area where voluntary carbon offsetting has become particularly popular. Public attitudes to the use of biofuels in commercial aviation appear to be changing, and this could become a significant investable space (Filimonau et al. 2018).

Maritime transport remains another area where deep decarbonization is essential to meeting net zero targets. One short-term option is in the area of logistics, because fast freight is an order of magnitude more carbon-intensive than slower freight (McKinnon et al. 2016). Over the medium term, changes in fuel use (towards electrification or at least the widespread use of LNG) may be possible, but the use of biofuels is unlikely without strong financial incentives by policy makers (Balcomb et al. 2019). Fortunately, successful decarbonization of this sector would yield significant gains across the board, given the importance of maritime freight to most supply chains (Benamara et al. 2019).

9.4. Adaptation: Physical and Social Infrastructure

Adaptation to climate change is a less immediately investable space than climate mitigation, but there are opportunities to consider. Coastal flooding is the most immediate source of concern, as sea level rises are all but inevitable (Vousdoukas et al. 2018). Projects on the scale of the Dutch SEAGATE have already been undertaken in the Thames Estuary in the UK (Lumbroso and Ramsbottom 2018), and similar such projects are underway elsewhere. Not surprisingly, insurance partnerships are considered a particularly promising area (Crick et al. 2018).

Median temperature increases represent another area where adaptation is pressing, particularly as it will produce step-change increases in energy demand in vulnerable areas (Burillo et al. 2019). Retro-fitting of housing and commercial office buildings will be required, especially in countries where building stock turns over infrequently.

Climate change has profound implications for global health, but research in this area is only just gaining momentum as the share of health-related adaptation spending has risen to approximately 15% of total global adaptation spending (Watts et al. 2018).

9.5. Remediation: Negative Emissions Technologies and Climate Engineering

Remediation represents the third investable space and covers an extraordinary range of proposals and techniques. Some of them, such as reforestation and afforestation (especially in response to desertification in emerging markets) are neatly aligned with other Sustainable Development Goals. In 2014, the World Bank established a Pilot Auction Facility for Methane and Climate Mitigation to raise finance for methane capture projects by marketing tradeable put options that represented the GHG reduction potential of such projects. These facilities can be scaled up to raise finance for reforestation and afforestation in developing countries; they can even be envisioned as possible sources of finance for technological carbon dioxide removal (Lockley and Coffman 2018).

In the shorter term, carbon capture and storage/carbon capture and utilization technologies are proving helpful in the facilitation of carbon neutrality in the European iron and steel industry and in the chemical industries (Mandova et al. 2019; Kätelhön et al. 2019). Exciting work is already being done on how to optimize European supply chains for carbon storage, using a cooperative model (d'Amore 2019) and this is an area ripe for policy making (Castillo et al. 2019). At the moment, these industries represent the most realistic investable space for institutional money managers.

Also in the short term, reforestation and afforestation projects are likely to receive direct financing primarily from third sector organizations. In September 2019, the Catholic Church expressed support for climate restoration through both biological and technological means, arguing that this is a divine imperative both to protect the natural world and to mitigate the inequalities associated with climate degradation (Auza 2019).

Over the longer term, solar radiation management, while controversial, is regarded by some to be a cost-effective approach, as it is estimated to cost less than \$2 bn annually (Carrington, 2018). Venture capitalists likewise see scalable technologies for carbon capture as a worthwhile target of speculative investment, especially given the involvement of state actors. Many observers, however, are concerned that the most active investors in this space are the corporate venture capital arms of oil and gas companies, as these firms try to find more sustainable business models (Lu 2019; Faran and Olsson 2018). Although most institutional investors will probably wish to avoid over-allocation to this space in the immediate future, remediation must be a part of horizon scanning.

9.6. Conclusions and Recommendations

The low carbon transition is one of the greatest challenges facing human societies. As such, climate mitigation, adaptation and remediation will all be major sources of investment opportunities, particularly for institutional investors, in the next few decades. For the moment, climate mitigation is the most important area, though adaptation and remediation will become more important over time.

Traditionally, attention has been paid most directly to carbon footprints of energy sources and transportation choices, but gradually embedded carbon is becoming an important part of the calculus. Life cycle assessment models are widely used, and infrastructure investors must be able to make sense of the recommendations they generate. More recently, the European Commission has initiated the development of ESG ratings for use by procurement authorities, the European Banking Authority, the European Investment Bank and other European agencies.

Opportunities for decarbonization of energy and transport in Europe are well-established, and appropriate to institutional investors. Emerging markets present different challenges in the energy sector than those in established markets, but projects that promote energy security and energy resilience are areas where private investors and multilaterals can cooperate. Transport decarbonization is often regarded as synonymous with electrification, but smart cities will play a role in changing consumer demand away from autonomous vehicles. The sharing economy can also play a role, subject to close monitoring by regulators. Reductions of carbon emissions and of pollution are highly correlated in both the transport and energy sectors, and are especially important in Central and Eastern Europe.

Adaptations to climate change will generally focus on flood control and accommodations to median temperature increases. This will pose challenges for both physical and social infrastructure. Remediation is comparably an emerging area, but one that will eventually be the focus of considerable interest, especially if the net zero targets are missed. Finally, this is a rapidly changing area, as the scientific consensus on the possibility of limiting Global Warming to 1.5 °C is eroding. Should 2°C or even 3°C scenarios become more likely, then adaptation and remediation strategies will become more urgent areas for investment.

References

Ahmed, I., M. Baddeley, D. D. Coffman, M. Oseni and G. Sianjese (2019) "The Cost of Power Outages to Zambia's Manufacturing Sector", *IGC Working Paper* F-41408-ZMB-1, https://www.theigc.org/wp-content/uploads/2019/09/Ahmed-et-al-2019-final-paper-1.pdf

Ávila, J. P. C., P. L. Llamas and T. G. San Román (2018) "A Review of Cross-Sector Decarbonization Potentials in the European Energy Intensive Industry", *Journal of Cleaner Production* 210: 585–601, https://doi.org/10.1016/j.jclepro.2018.11.036

Auza, B. (2019) "Statement by the Apostolic Nuncio, Permanent Observer of the Holy See to the United Nations. The First Annual Global Climate Restoration Forum", United Nations, New York, 17 September 2019, https://holyseemission.org/contents/statements/5d81339b2bf53.php

Balcombe, P., J. Brierley, C. Lewis, L. Skatvedt, J. Speirs, A. Hawkes and I. Staffell (2019) "How to Decarbonise International Shipping: Options for Fuels, Technologies and Policies", *Energy Conversion and Management* 182: 72–88, https://doi.org/10.1016/j.enconman.2018.12.080

Banister, D., T. Schwanen and J. Anable (2012) "Introduction to the Special Section on Theoretical Perspectives on Climate Change Mitigation in Transport", *Journal of Transport Geography* 24: 467–70, https://doi.org/10.1016/j.jtrangeo.2012.06.004

Benamara, H., J. Hoffmann and F. Youssef (2019) "Maritime Transport: The Sustainability Imperative", in *Sustainable Shipping*, ed. by H. Psaraftis (Cham: Springer), pp. 1–31, https://doi.org/10.1007/978-3-030-04330-8_1

Bowman, M. (2017) "Capitalising on the Juncker Fund: Mobilising Private Climate Finance for Sustainability", *TLI Think!* 79, https://doi.org/10.2139/ssrn.3027529

Burillo, D., M. V. Chester, S. Pincetl, E. D. Fournier and J. Reyna (2019) "Forecasting Peak Electricity Demand for Los Angeles Considering Higher Air Temperatures due to Climate Change", *Applied Energy* 236: 1–9, https://doi.org/10.1016/j.apenergy.2018.11.039

Carrington, D. (2018) "Solar Geoengineering Could Be 'Remarkably Inexpensive' — Report." *The Guardian*, 23 November, https://www.theguardian.com/environment/2018/nov/23/solar-geoengineering-could-be-remarkably-inexpensive-report

Castillo, A. C. and A. Angelis-Dimakis (2019) "Analysis and Recommendations for European Carbon Dioxide Utilization Policies", *Journal of Environmental Management* 247: 439–48, https://doi.org/10.1016/j.jenvman.2019.06.092

Capros, P., L. Paroussos, P. Fragkos, S. Tsani, B. Boitier, F. Wagner, S. Busch, G. Resch, M. Blesl and J. Bollen (2014) "Description of Models and Scenarios Used to Assess European Decarbonization Pathways", *Energy Strategy Reviews* 2 (3–4): 220–30, https://doi.org/10.1016/j.esr.2013.12.008

Cardinale, R. (2019) "The Profitability of Transnational Energy Infrastructure: A Comparative Analysis of the Greenstream and Galsi Gas Pipelines", *Energy Policy* 131: 347–57, https://doi.org/10.1016/j.enpol.2019.03.040

Crick, F., K. Jenkins and S. Surminski (2018) "Strengthening Insurance Partnerships in the Face of Climate Change — Insights from an Agent-Based Model of Flood Insurance in the UK", *Science of the Total Environment* 636: 192–204, https://doi.org/10.1016/j.scitotenv.2018.04.239

d'Amore, F. and F. Bezzo (2019) "Optimal European Cooperative Supply Chains for Carbon Capture, Transport, and Sequestration with Costs Share Policies", *AIChE Journal* p.e16872, https://doi.org/10.1002/aic.16872

Drechsel, P., M. Otoo, K. C. Rao and M. A. Hanjra (2018) "Business Models for a Circular Economy: Linking Waste Management and Sanitation with Agriculture", in *Resource Recovery from Waste*, ed. by M. Otoo and P. Drechsel (London: Routledge), pp. 3–15.

Ecofys (2018) "How Gas Can Help to Achieve the Paris Agreement Target in an Affordable Way". Report prepared for Gas for Climate Consortium, 15 February 2018, http://www.ergar.org/wp-content/uploads/2018/05/Ecofys_Gas_for_Climate_Report_Study_March18.pdf

European Banking Authority (2019) "EBA Pushes for Early Action on Sustainable Finance", 6 December, https://eba.europa.eu/eba-pushes-early-action-sustainable-finance

Farquharson, D., P. Jaramillo and C. Samaras (2018) "Sustainability Implications of Electricity Outages in Sub-Saharan Africa", *Nature Sustainability* 1(10): 589–97, https://doi.org/10.1038/s41893-018-0151-8

Faran, T. S. and L. Olsson (2018) "Geoengineering: Neither Economical, nor Ethical — a risk-Reward Nexus Analysis of Carbon Dioxide Removal", *International Environmental Agreements: Politics, Law and Economics* 18(1): 63–77, https://doi.org/10.1007/s10784-017-9383-8

Filimonau, V., M. Mika and R. Pawlusiński (2018), "Public Attitudes to Biofuel Use in Aviation: Evidence from an Emerging Tourist Market", *Journal of Cleaner Production* 172: 3102–10, https://doi.org/10.1016/j.jclepro.2017.11.101

Gannon, K. E., D. Conway, J. Pardoe, M. Ndiyoi, N. Batisani, E. Odada, D. Olago, A. Opere, S. Kgosietsile, M. Nyambe and J. Omukuti (2018) "Business Experience of Floods and Drought-Related Water and Electricity Supply Disruption in Three Cities in Sub-Saharan Africa during the 2015/2016 El Niño", *Global Sustainability* 1, https://doi.org/10.1017/sus.2018.14

Geissdoerfer, M., P. Savaget, N. M. Bocken and E. J. Hultink (2017) "The Circular Economy — A New Sustainability Paradigm?", *Journal of Cleaner Production* 143: 757–68, https://doi.org/10.1016/j.jclepro.2016.12.048

Glotz-Richter, M. and H. Koch (2016) "Electrification of Public Transport in Cities (Horizon 2020 ELIPTIC Project)", *Transportation Research Procedia* 14: 2614–19, https://doi.org/10.1016/j.trpro.2016.05.416

IPCC (2013) "2013: Summary for Policymakers", in *Climate Change 2013: The Physical Science Basis. Contribution of Working Group I to the Fifth Assessment Report of the Intergovernmental Panel on Climate Change*, ed. by T. F. Stocker et al. (Cambridge, UK: Cambridge University Press), pp. 3–32, https://www.ipcc.ch/site/assets/uploads/2018/03/WG1AR5_SummaryVolume_FINAL.pdf

IPCC (2018) "2018: Summary for Policymakers", in *Global Warming of 1.5°C: An IPCC Special Report on the Impacts of Global Warming of 1.5°C Above Pre-Industrial Levels and Related Global Greenhouse Gas Emission Pathways, in the Context of Strengthening the Global Response to the Threat of Climate Change, Sustainable Development, and Efforts to Eradicate Poverty*, ed. by V. Masson-Delmotte et al. (Geneva: World Meteorological Organization), https://www.ipcc.ch/site/assets/uploads/sites/2/2019/05/SR15_SPM_version_report_LR.pdf

Kätelhön, A., R. Meys, S. Deutz, S. Suh and A. Bardow (2019) "Climate Change Mitigation Potential of Carbon Capture and Utilization in the Chemical Industry", *Proceedings of the National Academy of Sciences* 116(23): 1118–19, https://doi.org/10.1073/pnas.1821029116

Lockley, A. and D. D. Coffman (2016) "Distinguishing Morale Hazard from Moral Hazard in Geoengineering", *Environmental Law Review* 18(3): 194–204, https://doi.org/10.1177/1461452916659830

Lockley, A. and D. D. Coffman (2018) "Carbon Dioxide Removal and Tradeable Put Options at Scale", *Environmental Research Letters* 13(5), https://doi.org/10.1088/1748-9326/aabe96

Lu, H., L. Guo and Y. Zhang (2019) "Oil and Gas Companies' Low-Carbon Emission Transition to Integrated Energy Companies", *Science of the Total Environment* 686: 1202–09, https://doi.org/10.1016/j.scitotenv.2019.06.014

Lumbroso, D. and D. Ramsbottom (2018) "Flood Risk Management in the United Kingdom: Putting Climate Change Adaptation into Practice in the Thames Estuary", in *Resilience: The Science of Adaptation to Climate Change*, ed. by Z. Zommers and K. Alverson (Amsterdam: Elsevier), pp. 79–87, https://doi.org/10.1016/b978-0-12-811891-7.00006-2

Mandova, H., P. Patrizio, S. Leduc, J. Kjärstad, C. Wang, E. Wetterlund, F. Kraxner and W. Gale (2019) "Achieving Carbon-Neutral Iron and Steelmaking in Europe through the Deployment of Bioenergy with Carbon Capture and Storage", *Journal of Cleaner Production* 218: 118–29, https://doi.org/10.1016/j.jclepro.2019.01.247

Mascotto, G., (2020) "ESG Outlook: Five Key Trends Are Driving Momentum in 2020", *American Century Investors — Institutional*, March, https://institutional.americancentury.com/content/institutional/en/insights/topic/esg-sustainable/esg-outlook.html

Mazur, C., G. Offer, M. Contestabile and N. Brandon (2018), "Comparing the Effects of Vehicle Automation, Policy-Making and Changed User Preferences on the Uptake of Electric Cars and Emissions from Transport", *Sustainability* 10(3): 676, https://doi.org/10.3390/su10030676

McDowall, W., B. S. Rodriguez, A. Usubiaga and J. A. Fernández (2018) "Is the Optimal Decarbonization Pathway Influenced by Indirect Emissions? Incorporating Indirect Life-Cycle Carbon Dioxide Emissions into a European TIMES Model", *Journal of Cleaner Production* 170: 260–68, https://doi.org/10.1016/j.jclepro.2017.09.132

McKinnon, A. C. (2016) "Freight Transport Deceleration: Its Possible Contribution to the Decarbonization of Logistics", *Transport Reviews* 36(4): 418–36, https://doi.org/10.1080/01 441647.2015.1137992

Meng, J., Z. Mi, D. Guan, J. Li, S. Tao, Y. Li, K. Feng, J. Liu, Z. Liu, X. Wang, Q. Zhang and S. Davis (2018) "The Rise of South-South Trade and Its Effect on Global CO2 Emissions", *Nature Communications* 9(1): 1871, https://doi.org/10.1038/s41467-018-04337-y

Meng, J., H. Yang, K. Yi, J. Liu, D. Guan, Z. Liu, Z. Mi, D. D. Coffman, X. Wang, Q. Zhong, T. Huang, W. Meng and S. Tao (2019) "The Slowdown in Global Air-Pollutant Emission Growth and Driving Factors", *One Earth* 1(1), 138–48, https://doi.org/10.1016/j.oneear.2019.08.013

Mi, Z., J. Zheng, J. Meng, H. Zhing, X. Li, D. M. Coffman, J. Woltjer, S. Wang and D. Guan (2019) "Carbon Emissions of Cities from a Consumption Perspective", *Applied Energy* 235: 509–18, https://doi.org/10.1016/j.apenergy.2018.10.137

Mar, L. E. (2009) "Carbon Impact of Proposed Hydroelectric Dams in Chilean Patagonia" (Doctoral dissertation, Massachusetts Institute of Technology), https://dspace.mit.edu/handle/1721.1/53068

Mi, Z. and D. D. Coffman (2019) "The Sharing Economy Promotes Sustainable Societies", *Nature Communications* 10(1): 1214, https://doi.org/10.1038/s41467-019-09260-4

Ogden, C. (2019) "UK's Longest Ever Coal-Free Run Comes to an End", *The Environment Journal*, 5 June, https://environmentjournal.online/articles/uks-longest-ever-coal-free-run-comes-to-an-end/

Prăvălie, R. and G. Bandoc (2018) "Nuclear Energy: Between Global Electricity Demand, Worldwide Decarbonization Imperativeness, and Planetary Environmental Implications", *Journal of Environmental Management* 209: 81–92, https://doi.org/10.1016/j.jenvman.2017.12.043

Pye, S., W. Usher and N. Strachan (2014) "The Uncertain but Critical Role of Demand Reduction in Meeting Long-Term Energy Decarbonization Targets", *Energy Policy* 73: 575–86, https://doi.org/10.1016/j.enpol.2014.05.025

Stern, N. (2006) *The Economics of Climate Change: The Stern Review*. London: HM Treasury.

Tagliapietra, S., G. Zachmann, O. Edenhofer, J. M. Glachant, P. Linares and A. Loeschel (2019), "The European Union Energy Transition: Key Priorities for the Next Five Years", *Energy Policy* 132: 950–54, https://doi.org/10.1016/j.enpol.2019.06.060

Tang, L., J. Qu, Z. Mi, X. Bo, X. Chang, L. D. Anadon, S. Wang, X. Xue, S. Li, X. Wang and Z. Zhao (2019) "Substantial Emission Reductions from Chinese Power Plants after the Introduction of Ultra-Low Emissions Standards", *Nat Energy* 4: 929–38 (2019), https://doi.org/10.1038/s41560-019-0468-1

Thiel, C., A. Perujo and A. Mercier (2010) "Cost and CO2 Aspects of Future Vehicle Options in Europe Under New Energy Policy Scenarios", *Energy policy* 38(11): 7142–51, https://doi.org/10.1016/j.enpol.2010.07.034

Valente, A. and D. Atkinson (2019) "Sustainability in Business: How ESG Can Protect and Improve Financial Performance", 40th International Scientific Conference on Economic and Social Development — Buenos Aires, 10–11 May, pp. 234–45, https://www.pearsoncollegelondon.ac.uk/content/dam/region-core/uk/pearson-college/documents/pearson-business-school/case-studies/valente-and-Atkinson-buenosaires2019-final-paper.pdf

Victoria, M., K. Zhu, T. Brown, G. B. Andresen and M. Greiner (2019) "The Role of Storage Technologies throughout the Decarbonization of the Sector-Coupled European Energy

System", *Energy Conversion and Management* 201: 111977, https://doi.org/10.1016/j.enconman.2019.111977

Vousdoukas, M. I., L. Mentaschi, E. Voukouvalas, A. Bianchi, F. Dottori and L. Feyen (2018 "Climatic and Socioeconomic Controls of Future Coastal Flood Risk in Europe", *Nature Climate Change* 8(9): 776–80, https://doi.org/10.1038/s41558-018-0260-4

Watts, N., M. Amann, N. Arnell, S. Ayeb-Karlsson, K. Belesova, H. Berry, T. Bouley, M. Boykoff, P. Byass, W. Cai and D. Campbell-Lendrum (2018) "The 2018 Report of the Lancet Countdown on Health and Climate Change: Shaping the Health of Nations for Centuries to Come", *The Lancet* 392(10163): 2479–514, https://doi.org/10.1016/s0140-6736(18)32594-7

Wei, Y.-M., M. Zhifu, D. D. Coffman and H. Liao (2018) "Assessment of Equity Principles for International Climate Policy: Based on Integrated Assessment Model", *Natural Hazards* 95(1–2): 309–23, https://doi.org/10.1007/s11069-018-3408-7

Zawieska, J. and J. Pieriegud (2018) "Smart City as a Tool for Sustainable Mobility and Transport Decarbonization", *Transport Policy* 63: 39–50, https://doi.org/10.1016/j.tranpol.2017.11.004

Zimmer, A. and N. Koch (2017), "Fuel Consumption Dynamics in Europe: Tax Reform Implications for Air Pollution and Carbon Emissions", *Transportation Research Part A: Policy and Practice* 106: 22–50, https://doi.org/10.1016/j.tra.2017.08.006

10. The Contribution of European Cohesion Policy to Public Investment

Francesco Prota,[1] Gianfranco Viesti[2] and Mauro Bux[3]

Introduction

Cohesion Policy (known also as Regional Policy) is the European Union's main development policy (Viesti and Prota 2008; Viesti 2019). It has evolved over time: from a tool to counterbalance the regional disparities inevitably emerging from the Single Market, and, subsequently, from the Monetary Union, to the investment pillar of the new economic policy coordination (Berkowitz et al. 2015). In the period 2007–2013, as result of the 2008 Global Financial Crisis, Cohesion Policy has been the major source of finance for public investment for many Member States of the European Union, representing up to 57% of government capital investment.

The aim of this chapter is twofold: first, to provide an overview of the expenditures of the European Regional Development Fund (ERDF) and the Cohesion Fund (CF) at national and regional levels over the last decades, and second, to discuss the impact of the investments co-financed through these two funds mainly in terms of physical achievements. We focus on the ERDF and the CF (which represent about 75% of Cohesion Policy funding in the 2014–2020 programming period), since the bulk of their expenditure provides support to public investment.[4]

Our analysis covers three programming periods: 1994–1999, 2000–2006, 2007–2013, though we focus mainly on 2000–2006 and 2007–2013 in order to take into account the Eastern enlargement of the European Union and the effects of 2008 crisis.

---

1   Dipartimento di Economia e Finanza, Università di Bari "Aldo Moro".
2   Dipartimento di Scienze Politiche, Università di Bari "Aldo Moro".
3   Dipartimento di Scienze Economiche, Università del Salento.
4   Regional Policy is delivered through three main funds: the European Regional Development Fund, the European Social Fund (ESF) and the Cohesion Fund. Together with the European Agricultural Fund for Rural Development (EAFRD) and the European Maritime and Fisheries Fund (EMFF), they make up the European Structural and Investment (ESI) Funds. The ERDF provides financial support for the development and structural adjustment of regional economies: public investments, R&D and contributions to private investments; the ESF is the main tool for promoting education, employment and social inclusion in Europe; the Cohesion Fund contributes to environmental and transport investments.

     https://doi.org/10.11647/OBP.0222.10

We use two datasets made available by the European Commission. The first one provides, in a single source, historic long-term regionalised annual EU expenditure data covering four programming periods, but it does not contain thematic information.[5] The second one shows allocations and expenditures from 2000 to 2013 broken down by expenditure categories. Moreover, the study on "Geography of Expenditures", one of the Work Packages of the *ex post* evaluation of Cohesion Policy programmes 2007–2013, has produced a consolidated database covering the regional ERDF and CF investments from 2000 to year 2014 at NUTS2 level (WIIW and ISMERI Europa 2015).[6]

The chapter is structured as follows. Section 10.1. describes the main features of the Cohesion Policy and its evolution across time. Section 10.2. focuses on the total levels of the European Regional Development Fund and Cohesion Fund expenditure in the Member States and looks at the trends observed in the last years. Section 10.3. examines the weight of European investments within the total public expenditure and describes some of the main "tangible" results generated by the implementation of both the ERDF and the CF measures, as far as public physical investments are concerned. Section 10.4. focuses on the regional level and discusses the economic spillovers produced by the Cohesion Policy in favour of the more advanced regions and countries in the EU. Section 10.5. summarizes the main messages of our analysis.

10.1. European Cohesion Policy: An Overview[7]

The evolution of Cohesion Policy has been extensively described in the literature (Viesti and Prota 2008; Molle 2015; Piattoni and Polverari 2016; Viesti 2019). One of the main drivers of this evolution has been the necessity to face the challenges arising from enlargement of the European Union to integrate regions with different levels of development; in particular, those of the countries of Southern Europe in 1981 and 1986 and those of the countries of Central and Eastern Europe in 2004, 2007 and 2013.

The Cohesion Policy emerged in the second half of the 1980s. The Single European Act (1986) added the Title V (Economic and Social Cohesion) to the Treaty of Rome, with the aim of providing a comprehensive reform of the instruments for regional development, namely the Structural Funds (ERDF and ESF). With the Delors package of 1987–1988, €63 bn were allocated to this policy for the period 1989–1993, accounting for a growing share of the total Community budget: from 18%, in 1987, to 29%, in 1993. Moreover, the fundamental principles underpinning Cohesion Policy were set out as follows:

- Concentration: the greater part of Structural Funds resources are concentrated on the poorest regions and countries, namely those having

---

5   The dataset is available in the ESIF Open Data platform (https://cohesiondata.ec.europa.eu/Other/ Historic-EU-payments-regionalised-and-modelled/tc55-7ysv).

6   The dataset is available at https://ec.europa.eu/regional_policy/en/policy/evaluations/ data-for-research/

7   This paragraph is largely based on Viesti (2019).

a GDP per capita lower than 75% of the EU average, at purchasing power parity;

- Programming: multi-annual national programmes aligned on EU objectives and priorities, with the same time span of the EU overall budget;

- Partnership: each programme is developed through a collective process involving authorities at European, regional and local level, social partners and organisations from civil society;

- Additionality: financing from the European Structural Funds may not replace national spending by a member country.

With the Treaty of Maastricht, Structural Funds assumed an even more important role: they became the principal, if not the unique, Community instrument aimed at guaranteeing that the processes of economic growth would benefit all the territories (and thus all the citizens) of the Union. In 1994, with a controversial decision, a new fund, the Cohesion Fund, was set up with the aim of assisting the poorest EU Member States whose gross national income per capita totalled less than 90% of the EU average. Cohesion Fund resources were allocated to infrastructural measures in the field of transport and environment. With the so-called Delors II package, the action of the Structural Funds was further reinforced: €167 bn were allocated for the period 1994–1999 (in the last year, they came to represent 36% of the total Community budget). The main beneficiaries were Spain, Italy and Germany (because of the reunification), followed by Portugal, Greece, France and the United Kingdom.

In 1997, the Commission published the document Agenda 2000 which reconfirmed the centrality of the Cohesion Policy. The European Council of Berlin of 24–25 March 1999 approved the Commission proposals, but with a smaller amount of financing. This was a decision with a very important political meaning in light of the then imminent enlargement of the Union, planned for 2004. The era of broad consensus on Cohesion Policy ended, and for the first time the resources were to be reduced during the programming period: from €32 bn in 2000 to €29 bn in 2006.

In 2004, ten new Member States joined the EU (Cyprus, Estonia, Latvia, Lithuania, Malta, Poland, Czech Republic, Slovakia, Slovenia and Hungary), a major milestone in the Union's development. With the accession of these countries, the regional disparities within the Union become considerably more intense. The resources of the Cohesion Policy represented about three quarters of the disbursements of the Community budget toward the new Member States, and played a fundamental role in accompanying the restructuring processes of those economies.

At that time, the political climate made the discussion on the programming period 2007–2013 particularly long and complex. The budget negotiation was resolved by restricting the size of the budget (despite having to accommodate both the "old" and the "new" Member States to which Romania and Bulgaria would be added in 2007 and Croatia in 2013) and by introducing new compensations for the net-contributing

States. As in the past, resources were earmarked in substantial measure (€177 bn) to the regions with a per capita income lower than 75% of the Community average, now included in a Convergence Objective.[8] The Cohesion Fund had a budget of almost €62 bn. A fundamental aspect of the Cohesion Policy for 2007–2013 was the strong reduction of aid in the EU15. More than half of the €308 bn was allocated to the new Member States.

The construction of the European Cohesion Policy for 2014–2020 was influenced by the publication in 2009 of an authoritative report by an independent Italian expert, Fabrizio Barca (Manzella 2011). The Barca report reiterated the importance of developing integrated intervention programmes built on the basis of the special characteristics of the various regions ("place-based" approach) (Barca 2009). These suggestions were partially put into action. The policy for 2014–2020 in many respects mimics that of the previous period, but it also presents several innovations. Regional allocation criterion changes with respect to the long previous tradition. There is still the category of less developed regions, which correspond as in the past to those with a per capita income in terms of purchasing power below the 75% of the Community average and to which the greatest part of the resources is earmarked. The novelties are represented by the category of "transition" regions (per capita income between 75% and 90%) and by the category of the most developed regions (per capita income above 90%). The Cohesion Fund group now includes the new Member States, Portugal and Greece. The geography of the beneficiaries shifts ever farther towards the East: the new Member States absorb about 55% of the total resources. The significance of these figures is obviously much greater if they are expressed as a percentage of GDP or per inhabitant. Among the old Member States the biggest beneficiary is Italy, followed by Spain; the expenditure diminishes significantly in Germany, while it remains substantially unchanged in Portugal and Greece.

10.2. The Geography of ERDF and CF Expenditures

The first question we aim to answer is: "How much have European countries/regions received under the European Regional Development Fund and the Cohesion Fund?". Table 1 shows the expenditures of the two funds in each Member State from 1994 to 2013, in constant euros; it shows allocations for the period 2014–2020, in current prices, too. It is not possible to add all the periods (current vs. constant euros; expenditures vs. allocations) but the overall picture is still important for understanding the "geography" of the Cohesion Policy. Obviously, in looking at the three programming periods as a whole, it is necessary to keep in mind that the Central and Eastern Europe countries

---

8   All the other European regions were included in a new Regional Competitiveness and Employment Objective, for which €39 bn were allocated. The decision to go beyond the old logic of "zones" in Objective 2 had a very important political significance. Regional Policy was no longer merely a policy to facilitate the growth and convergence of the weak regions, but rather a development policy for the entire European Union.

Table 1 ERDF and CF expenditures by country, 1995–2013 (constant 2015 prices) and ERDF and CF allocations 2014–2020 (current prices), in million euros

Country_ID	Country_name	1994-1999			2000-2006			2007-2013			1994-2013	2007-2013	2014-2020		
		ERDF	CF	Total	ERDF	CF	Total	ERDF	CF	Total	Total	Per capita (euro)	ERDF	CF	Total
AT	Austria	545	-	545	1,051	-	1,051	661	-	661	2,258	75	536	-	536
BE	Belgium	1,174	-	1,174	984	-	984	1,003	-	1,003	3,161	88	953	-	953
BG	Bulgaria	-	-	-	-	805	805	3,209	2,339	5,547	6,352	787	3,568	2,278	5,846
CY	Cyprus	-	-	-	32	62	95	286	204	490	585	567	300	295	595
CZ	Czech Republic	-	-	-	1,130	1,383	2,514	13,604	8,855	22,460	24,973	2,117	11,941	6,144	18,085
DE	Germany	12,436	-	12,436	17,500	-	17,500	16,418	-	16,418	46,353	198	10,774	-	10,774
DK	Denmark	172	-	172	163	-	163	261	-	261	596	45	207	-	207
EE	Estonia	-	-	-	268	480	748	1,906	1,180	3,085	3,833	2,339	1,861	1,062	2,923
EL	Greece	12,813	4,522	17,336	17,403	2,772	20,176	13,100	3,987	17,087	54,598	1,591	8,609	3,266	11,875
ES	Spain	26,375	12,828	39,204	32,308	13,186	45,494	22,921	3,630	26,550	111,248	566	20,861	-	20,861
FI	Finland	592	-	592	1,069	-	1,069	1,001	-	1,001	2,663	182	792	-	792
FR	France	7,447	-	7,447	9,436	-	9,436	8,247	-	8,247	25,130	123	8,426	-	8,426
HR	Croatia	-	-	-	-	-	-	355	288	642	642	156	4,321	2,510	6,831
HU	Hungary	-	-	-	1,431	1,553	2,984	12,689	8,853	21,542	24,526	2,203	10,785	6,025	16,810
IE	Ireland	3,716	2,084	5,800	6,203	644	6,847	385	-	385	13,031	74	411	-	411
IT	Italy	16,093	-	16,093	21,181	-	21,181	20,554	-	20,554	57,829	340	21,661	-	21,661
LT	Lithuania	-	-	-	674	941	1,615	3,526	2,361	5,887	7,503	2,096	3,501	2,049	5,550
LU	Luxembourg	32	-	32	52	-	52	26	-	26	110	43	20	-	20
LV	Latvia	-	-	-	441	779	1,220	2,466	1,577	4,044	5,263	2,091	2,401	1,349	3,750
MT	Malta	-	-	-	54	25	79	427	282	708	787	1,487	384	218	602
NL	Netherlands	849	-	849	1,134	-	1,134	850	-	850	2,833	50	510	-	510
PL	Poland	-	-	0	5,727	6,028	11,755	35,639	22,933	58,572	70,327	1,542	40,214	23,205	63,419
PT	Portugal	13,270	4,555	17,825	15,307	3,440	18,747	11,778	3,135	14,912	51,484	1,449	10,777	2,862	13,639
RO	Romania	-	-	-	-	5,887	5,887	8,779	6,306	15,084	20,972	773	10,726	6,935	17,661
SE	Sweden	505	-	505	1,003	-	1,003	957	-	957	2,465	95	935	-	935
SI	Slovenia	-	-	-	158	289	447	1,981	1,446	3,427	3,874	1,658	1,417	914	2,331
SK	Slovakia	-	-	-	692	881	1,572	6,139	3,994	10,133	11,705	1,862	7,144	4,168	11,312
UK	United Kingdom	7,371	-	7,371	9,498	-	9,498	5,575	-	5,575	22,444	84	5,830	-	5,830

Source of data: European Commission (https://cohesiondata.ec.europa.eu/Other/Historic-EU-payments-regionalised-and-modelled/tc55-7ysv; https://cohesiondata.ec.europa.eu/dataset/ESIF-Regional-Policy-budget-by-country-2014-2020/fift-a67j).

have become members only in 2004 and, therefore, have started to benefit from the Cohesion Policy later than the old Member States.[9] Moreover, initially, the Cohesion Fund covered Greece, Spain, Portugal and Ireland. Later the group incorporated all the new Member States together with Greece and Portugal, while Ireland and Spain — due to the growth of their GDP per capita — became no longer eligible (although the latter retained the right to receive aids in accordance with the transition rules).

Looking at the period 1994–2013, the Iberian countries clearly emerge as the main beneficiaries: ERDF and CF provided €111 bn to Spain and €51 bn to Portugal. However, notwithstanding its later accession, Poland is the second beneficiary country with €70 bn (2004–2013), ahead of Italy (€58 bn), Greece (€55 bn) and Germany (€46 bn). Another group of countries, including both old (France and United Kingdom) and new (Czech Republic, Hungary, Romania) Member States, received more than €20 bn in the whole period. The Cohesion Policy is definitely of minor importance for a group of Centre-North European countries such as Austria, Belgium, Netherlands, Denmark and Sweden.

It is clear that the expansion of the EU to include the post-socialist CEE countries changed the "geography" of the Cohesion Policy, drawing substantial investment away from Southern Europe: funds for Ireland drastically declined, and Spain, after peaking in 2007–2013 with more than €45 bn, declines subsequently; other Member States, especially the larger ones, kept the same amount of funding, with a decline in 2007–2013 only for the UK. The role of new Member States became crucial: expenditures in Slovakia became larger than in France; in Poland they became almost three times those in Italy.

The eastward shift is even more clear if one looks at allocations for 2014–2020, with the amounts declining in Germany, Greece and Spain, and being confirmed in their magnitude (except for Hungary) in the new Member States. In 2020 Poland will be the country that has received, overall, the most ERDF and CF expenditures, overcoming Spain. In brief, what is evident is that the centre of gravity in Structural Funds allocation has shifted from the Southern regions to the Eastern regions of Europe.

However, absolute figures must be matched by per capita amounts. Table 1 shows the ERDF and CF expenditures per capita for the period of 2007–2013. The three Baltic countries, Hungary and the Czech Republic received more than €2,000 per person; the figure is around €1,500 for Greece and Portugal, as well as for Poland, Slovakia, Slovenia; it goes down to €750 for Bulgaria and Romania, and to €550 for Spain, €350 for Italy, less than €200 for Germany and Finland, around €100 for France and the UK. It is clear how varied the impact of the Cohesion Policy is in the different Member States.

---

9   Indeed, the Central and Eastern Europe countries benefited also from the EU's pre-accession structural support.

10.3. The Impact of Cohesion Policy on Public Investment

Cohesion Policy plays a key role in financing public investment in Europe. According to the European Commission, its allocations in 2014–2016 are expected to represent 14% of total public investment in the EU. However, its weight is very different across Member States. In some European countries, Cohesion Policy plays a key role; in others, it is significant, even if to a lesser extent; in others, it is negligible. This difference is due to three factors: (i) the size of cohesion expenditures per country compared to the magnitude of the different European economies, (ii) the geography of the crisis that hit Europe, (iii) the use of European Structural and Investment (ESI) expenditures in different typologies of regions.

WIIW and ISMERI Europa (2015) show the proportion of actual Cohesion Policy expenditures to total government capital expenditures (the sum of fixed investments and capital transfers) for the 2007–2013 programming period: this figure is larger than 50% in some small Central and Eastern European countries (including Hungary), larger than 40% in Poland, larger than 30% in most of the other Central and Eastern European countries. In Hungary 94% of railways and 54% of road investment have been financed by the EU Cohesion Policy. In the EU15, the figure is higher in Portugal and Greece, much lower in most Member States (7% for Spain, 4.4 % for Italy and 2.5 % for Germany). However, WIIW and ISMERI Europa (2015) estimate that Cohesion Policy expenditures may have reached 20% of total capital expenditures in Convergence regions in Spain, 15% in Italy and 10% in Germany.

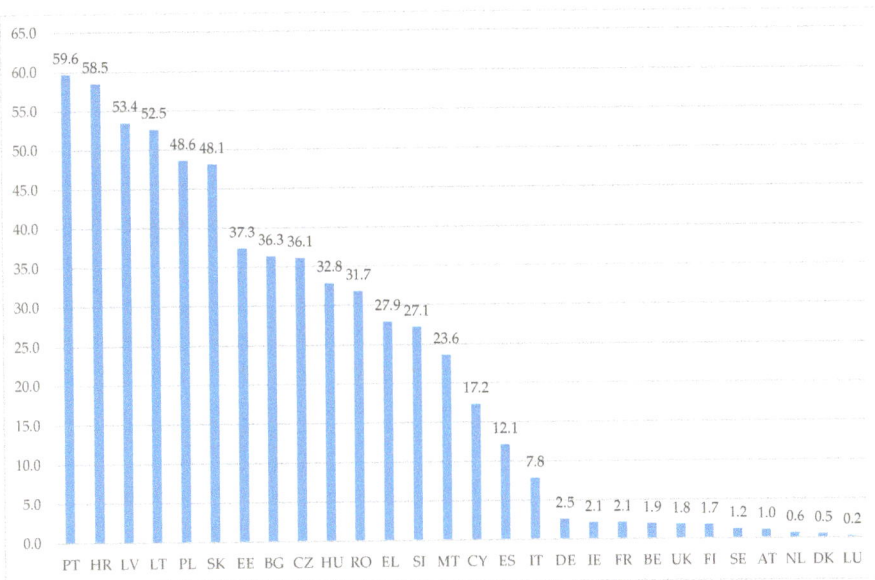

Fig. 1 ERDF and Cohesion Fund allocations, 2015–2017 (percentage of general government capital expenditure)

Source of data: Open data platform, Eurostat — Government statistics. Figure created by authors.

Figure 1 updates and confirms the figures for 2015–2017, using allocations data. The role of ERDF and the Cohesion Fund seems even higher in some countries, namely Portugal (a country in which the burden of servicing the debt is relevant) and Poland. It is reasonable to state that most countries would not have had the financial capacity to carry out such investments otherwise.

Indeed, it is well known that in a number of Member States public investments are still below the pre-crisis period level (Prota 2016); these persistent low levels of public investment (as a share of the GDP) are a cause for concern, because of their possible effect on socio-economic disparities between Member States and regions in the EU. In many countries, therefore, EU funding played a major counter-cyclical role in preventing an even larger reduction in public investment, as confirmed by the increase in EU co-financing rates for Cohesion Policy in the period 2007–2013.[10] The EU co-financing rate was raised to different extents in 16 Member States in which the effects of the crisis of 2008 were most severe and the reduction in public investment expenditure (part of budget consolidation measures) was substantial: in Greece the EU co-financing rate went up to 100%.[11] Obviously, the final effect of the increase in EU co-financing rates, aimed at reducing the amount of national funding, was to cut the overall amount of funding going into Cohesion Policy programmes.

The relative allocation of funding across expenditure items is not identical in all countries and regions. The EU funding is particularly crucial in some key investment areas (Table 2). For 2007–2013 a detailed breakdown of expenditures in eighty-six items is available (WIIW and ISMERI Europa 2015). By aggregating the eight-six intervention priorities to twelve broad policy areas, it emerges that the largest policy area (mainly capital transfers), with about €52 bn, is R&D, innovation and enterprise support. Roads accounts for €39 bn, including €18 bn in motorways in the Trans-European Networks (Ten-T); railways for €15.9 bn (including €12 bn in Ten-T corridors); other transport (urban, multimodal, airports and ports) for €7.6 bn. Environment investment totalled €33.7 bn: main areas of expenditures are water (€16 bn) together with waste, risk prevention and promotion of clean urban transport. Other crucial investment priorities are ICT, energy, tourism and culture, urban and rural regeneration, education, health and social infrastructures.

The study "Geography of Expenditures" (WIIW and ISMERI Europa 2015) has produced a consolidated database covering the regional ERDF and CF investments from 2000 to 2013. Using this database, Table 3 shows the breakdown of the overall cumulative expenditure by selected countries in the six policy areas more relevant

---

10 The verification of additionality for the 2007–2013 programming period shows that the average annual "structural" spending was on average some 1% lower than initially estimated (European Commission 2017). There are however significant differences across Member States. For example, the actual structural spending for 2007–2013 was 35% lower than the ex-ante baseline in Greece. The variation is over 25% in Italy and between 10 and 20% in Hungary, Lithuania and Portugal.

11 Substantial increases also occurred in Italy (from 48% to 65%), from 50% to 72% in the less developed regions, and in Portugal (from 63% to 74%).

Table 2 Expenditures of ERDF and CF by priorities, 2007–2013 (constant 2015 euros)

Priority	2007-2013
R&D, innovation and enterprise support	52.4
ICT	8.5
Railways	15.9
Roads	39.0
Other transports	7.6
Energy	7.9
Environment	33.7
Tourism and culture	9.3
Urban and rural regeneration	8.2
Education infrastructures	8.4
Health infrastructures	4.6
Social infrastructures	2.7

Source of data: European Commission (https://cohesiondata.ec.europa.eu/)

for public investment, covering more than half of total ERDF and CF expenditures: transport, environment, urban and rural regeneration, social infrastructures, IT infrastructures and services, and energy.[12]

Table 3 ERDF and Cohesion Fund cumulative 2000–2013 expenditures by selected countries and policy area, in billion euros (constant 2015 prices)

	Transport infrastructure	Environment and natural resources	Urban and rural regeneration	Social infrastructure	IT infrastructure and services	Energy	Total
Spain	24.0	16.3	7.6	2.4	1.5	0.2	52.1
Poland	26.8	8.0	1.3	2.9	2.4	1.7	43.3
Greece	14.9	4.1	2.2	2.5	2.3	1.1	27.1
Portugal	7.0	4.6	2.5	4.8	1.1	0.6	20.6
Italy	7.6	3.3	3.8	1.4	1.8	1.3	19.2
Hungary	7.3	4.4	0.9	2.6	0.6	0.5	16.3
Czech Republic	7.0	3.7	0.9	1.0	0.5	1.0	14.1
Germany	6.4	3.0	2.5	0.5	0.5	0.6	13.5
France	1.5	2.1	2.1	0.5	0.7	0.6	7.5
Slovakia	2.9	1.5	0.3	1.1	0.6	0.1	6.7
UE-15	65.0	34.0	23.2	12.4	9.0	4.9	148.5
UE-12	49.7	22.0	4.1	9.6	4.8	4.3	94.6

Source of data: European Commission (https://cohesiondata.ec.europa.eu/Other/ Historic-EU-payments-regionalised-and-modelled/tc55-7ysv)

Transport infrastructures are clearly the most important policy area, with more than €100 bn in 2000–2013. This expenditure category is extremely relevant in Spain and

---

12   The different disaggregation in policy areas shown in the Tables 2 and 3 is due to the different classification adopted in the studies from which the data have been collected.

Poland (around €25 bn) and in general in Central and Eastern European countries. This is particularly important since, as shown by Di Comite et al. (2018), investment in transport infrastructure financed by the Cohesion Policy is changing the accessibility of EU regions. In particular, many regions in Eastern Europe have significantly benefitted from improved accessibility as a result of the Cohesion Policy financing transport infrastructure investments. This has favoured intra-European trade and the organization of manufacturing value chains in Central Europe. As shown by Stöllinger (2016), manufacturing activity in the EU is increasingly concentrated in a Central European manufacturing core, implying divergent paths of structural change across Member States. In the rest of the EU regions accessibility has also increased, though less significantly (see Figure 22 in Di Comite et al. 2018). However, in Portugal and Spain ERDF and CF investments were crucial for the improvement, since the mid-1990s, of the road and railway network; the same has happened in Greece (consider the motorway from Igoumenitsa to Athens).

Investment for environment and natural resources, the second policy area in order of importance, totalled €56 bn, followed by urban and rural regeneration (€27 bn), social infrastructures, IT infrastructures and energy. However, priorities for expenditures are different among countries. In EU12, transport and environment are extremely relevant, also as a consequence of the Cohesion Funds rules. On the contrary, in EU15, territorial regeneration and social infrastructures are relatively more important. Some national patterns also emerge: in Spain expenditures for the environment and urban regeneration are particularly high; in Portugal social infrastructures play a key role. Comparing 2000–2006 with 2007–2013 confirms the importance of transport, while public investments in the energy sector increase.

What are the results of the Cohesion Policy as far as public physical investments are concerned? Table 4 shows the main achievements.[13] For 2000–2006, it is useful to consider also the Structural Pre-Accession Instrument (ISPA) fund, alongside the ERDF and CF.

In 2000–2006 more than 14,000 km of new roads were built, plus almost 800 km related to Trans-European Network projects. Additionally, almost 65,000 km of reconstructed road were financed. As regards railways, more than 1,500 km of new railways were constructed, as well as almost 1,000 km of TEN-related railways, and more than 5,800 km of railways were reconstructed. Railway projects were mainly concentrated in the areas of Andalusia and Galicia (Spain), Lisbon and Vale do Tejo (Portugal), Mazowieckie (Poland), Mecklenburg-Vorpommern (Germany) and Puglia (Italy). These regions all experienced forms of improvements directly resulting from the policies at hand, in particular with reference to pre-existing critical aspects such as poor quality of road/rail network, congestion, bottlenecks, missing or poor

---

13 The statistics herein rather underestimate the actual outputs in terms of new or renovated infrastructure, due to some features of the reporting mechanism that asked Member States to keep track of the progress to the EU Commission. However, this data is the most reliable since it comes from official publications and documents of the EU.

Table 4 Main achievements of the Cohesion Policy co-financed public investments (2000–2006; 2006–2013)

	2000-2006 ERDF, CF and ISPA co-financed public investments	2007-2013 ERDF and CF co-financed public investments
Km of new roads (no.)	14,030	4,900
Km of new TEN roads (no.)	785	2,400
Km of reconstructed roads (no.)	64,897	28,600
Km of new railway (no.)	1,522	1,050
Km of TEN railway (no.)	980	2,600
Km of reconstructed railway (no.)	5,857	3,900
Additional population served by water projects (thousand)	14,101	5,900
Additional population served by waste water projects (thousand)	20,447	6,900
New capacity of solid waste treatment created (m3/day)	231,649	-
Annual reduction of energy consumption (GWh)	-	1,440
Annual reduction of reenhouse gas emissions (kilo tonnes of CO2)	-	830
Additional capacity of renewable energy production (megawatts)	-	3,900

Source of data: European Commission (https://ec.europa.eu/regional_policy/it/policy/evaluations/ ec/2000-2006; https://ec.europa.eu/regional_policy/it/policy/evaluations/ec/2007-2013)

intermodal links, ports/airports' lack of capacity (Directorate-General for Regional and Urban Policy and Steer Davies Gleave 2010).

The environmental investments mainly referred to the facilities and distribution network needed to provide clean drinking water to households, the plant and pipelines required for the collection and treatment of wastewater and the facilities needed to collect, recycle and manage solid waste (Applica 2012). In these fields the EU invested in more than 165,000 projects; they were quite effective, given that more than 14 million additional people were served. In addition, more than 6,000 projects on wastewater were financed, which resulted in more than 20 million new people being served.[14] Finally, almost 3,000 solid waste treatment projects were also financed, mainly located in Germany, Spain, France and Italy, resulting in a considerable improvement of total capacity of more than 230,000 m^3/day (ADE 2009). Importantly, from 2000 to 2009, the shares of landfilled waste dropped from 51% to 32% in the EU15 and from 96% to 85% in the EU12. At the same time, the share of recycled waste rose from 31% to 44% in the EU15 and from 2% to 12% in the EU12, with peaks in Slovenia (35%), Estonia (25%) and Poland (20%).

In 2007–2013 both the ERDF and the CF, as already mentioned, focused greatly on transport expenditures. A considerable share was utilized for the constructions of

---

14   The Portuguese region of Norte started with around 40% of population served by wastewater treatment plants in 2000, and ended up with more than 55% in 2006. Also in the Italian region of Lazio, a considerable improvement occurred, as the percentage of population served by secondary and tertiary treatment rose from around 22% in 1999 to around 30% in 2006. On average, the share of population connected to wastewater treatment rose in the period 2000–2009 from 85 to 88 in the EU15 (although with significant lower percentages for countries like Ireland, Greece and Portugal) and from 46 to 55 in the EU12.

new roads or the upgrading of existing ones. For example, in Poland and Romania this share is higher than 60%, and in none of the Member States is it less than 40%. In terms of actual achievements, this resulted in more than 4,800 km of new roads, of which over 70% were built in the EU12, with a substantial amount in Poland. Almost 28,000 km of existing roads were upgraded (70% in theEU10).[15]

More than 1,000 km of new railways were built, almost exclusively in EU15 Member States. The upgrade of existing railways covered almost 4,000 km, of which 60% were in EU15 countries, and the rest in EU12 countries. Trans-European Networks increased by more than 2,400 km of new roads (mainly in the EU12) and by more than 2,600 km of railways (mainly in the EU15). Once again, Poland was one of the countries that benefitted the most from this policy: the completion of the A1 motorway connecting Torun to Strykow, which represented a strategic link between the port of Gdansk, central Poland and the Czech border, is a good example.[16]

Almost 6 million additional people were served by new water projects (more than 60% in the four countries of Southern Europe). Almost 7 million additional people were served by wastewater projects (70% in Southern Europe). It is estimated that an annual reduction of energy consumption of almost 1,440 GWh and an annual reduction of greenhouse gas emission of around 830 kilotonnes of CO_2 in public and residential buildings can be directly attributed to energy efficiency investments co-financed by ESI funds. Urban development and social infrastructure investments were diffused all over Europe. Examples of these projects are: the modernization of schools and colleges in Portugal (benefitting over 300 thousand youngsters); upgrading of training facilities in Spain, Poland, the Czech Republic and Lithuania; improvements in the healthcare system in Hungary; and construction and upgrading of schools in Poland (benefitting almost 2 million people).[17]

As for the programming period 2014–2020, the online European Commission portal provides some information on the most important public investments financed via the ERDF and CF.[18] There are several "major projects" of transport, mainly in CEE countries. The largest is the rehabilitation of the railway line HU Border-Brasov, in Romania (more than €1.3 bn); while the works on the railway line No. 7 Warszawa Wschodnia Osobowa-Dorohusk, in Poland, amount to more than €750 mn. The first non-Eastern country to benefit from large EU financial means for transport investment is Greece, with the completion of the Metro Thessaloniki Main Line and the acquisition of trains for its use. All of these projects have the objective of *promoting sustainable transport and removing bottlenecks*. Major projects are underway also for the environment, such as

---

15 One example is the Bulgarian Trakia motorway project, linking the southeastern cities of Stara Zagora and Karnobat: finalized in 2013, it completed the route from Sofia to the Black Sea port of Burgas.

16 See the reports available at https://ec.europa.eu/regional_policy/en/policy/evaluations/ec/2007-2013/#6

17 See the reports available at https://ec.europa.eu/regional_policy/en/policy/evaluations/ec/2007-2013/#10

18 See the dataset available at https://cohesiondata.ec.europa.eu/2014-2020/ESIF-2014-2020-ERDF-CF-Major-Projects/sjs4-8wgj/data

the protection and rehabilitation of the coastal zone in Romania (€600 mn). Finally, other major projects are in the field of urban transport, such as the construction of the second metro line in Warsaw (€450 mn), the extension of the metro in Sofia (€370 mn), and the Metropolitan line of the Circumetnea railway in Sicily (€360 mn).

10.4. Regional Convergence and Spillovers

The European Cohesion Policy benefits all European regions in order to improve their competitiveness, with a strong focus on less developed areas. The effectiveness of the Cohesion Policy and its impact on growth has been widely analyzed in the literature (for instance, see the surveys by Fratesi 2016, and Pieńkowski and Berkowitz 2016). While the results of the papers using regional growth regressions are largely inconclusive regarding the impact of the Cohesion Policy on growth, the studies adopting a counterfactual impact evaluations technique show a clear positive impact of the Cohesion Policy on growth and other economic indicators (Pellegrini et al. 2013; Giua 2017; Becker et al. 2018).[19]

Figure 2 shows the European regions receiving most of the expenditure of the two funds between 1994 and 2013.[20] Andalusia (Spain), Norte (Portugal), Campania (Italy), Mazowieckie (Poland) and Sicilia (Italy) are by far the main beneficiaries. Looking at the first thirty-five regions with higher expenditures, we find eight regions in Spain, seven in Poland, four in Greece, Portugal and Italy, three in Germany and two in Hungary. As already stressed, Eastern enlargement was crucial: investment in the region of Warsaw (Mazowieckie) in 2004–2013 is as large as investment between 1994 and 2013 in some large Southern European regions such as Campania and Sicilia (Italy), larger than in the region of Athens (Attiki). Several European regions including the capital city are large beneficiaries: together with Warsaw, Athens, Dublin, Lisbon, Madrid and Berlin in EU15, Budapest, Tallinn, Prague and Bucharest in EU12. In some regions, investments financed by ERDF and CF are quite large: twenty Central and Eastern European regions received more than €2 bn in 2004–2013. In Andalusia, between 2000 and 2013 investment in transport amounted to €5.1 bn and in urban and rural regeneration to €3.3 bn. In Portugal €2.1 bn were invested in social infrastructures in the Norte region, and €1.2 bn in the Centro. Investments in transport were larger than €2 bn in fifteen European regions: €5 bn in Spain and Poland, €2 bn in Greece, and €1 bn in Portugal, Italy and Latvia.

In large European countries with substantial economic internal divides (such as Germany, Italy and Spain) territorial concentration is important: in Germany the role of the Cohesion Policy increased, after reunification, in Eastern Landers; in Italy

---

19 Doubts over the conclusions that are frequently inferred from the results obtained from growth regressions have been formulated by Rodrik (2012).

20 Totals must be read with caution because the figures for the different programming periods are in current euros.

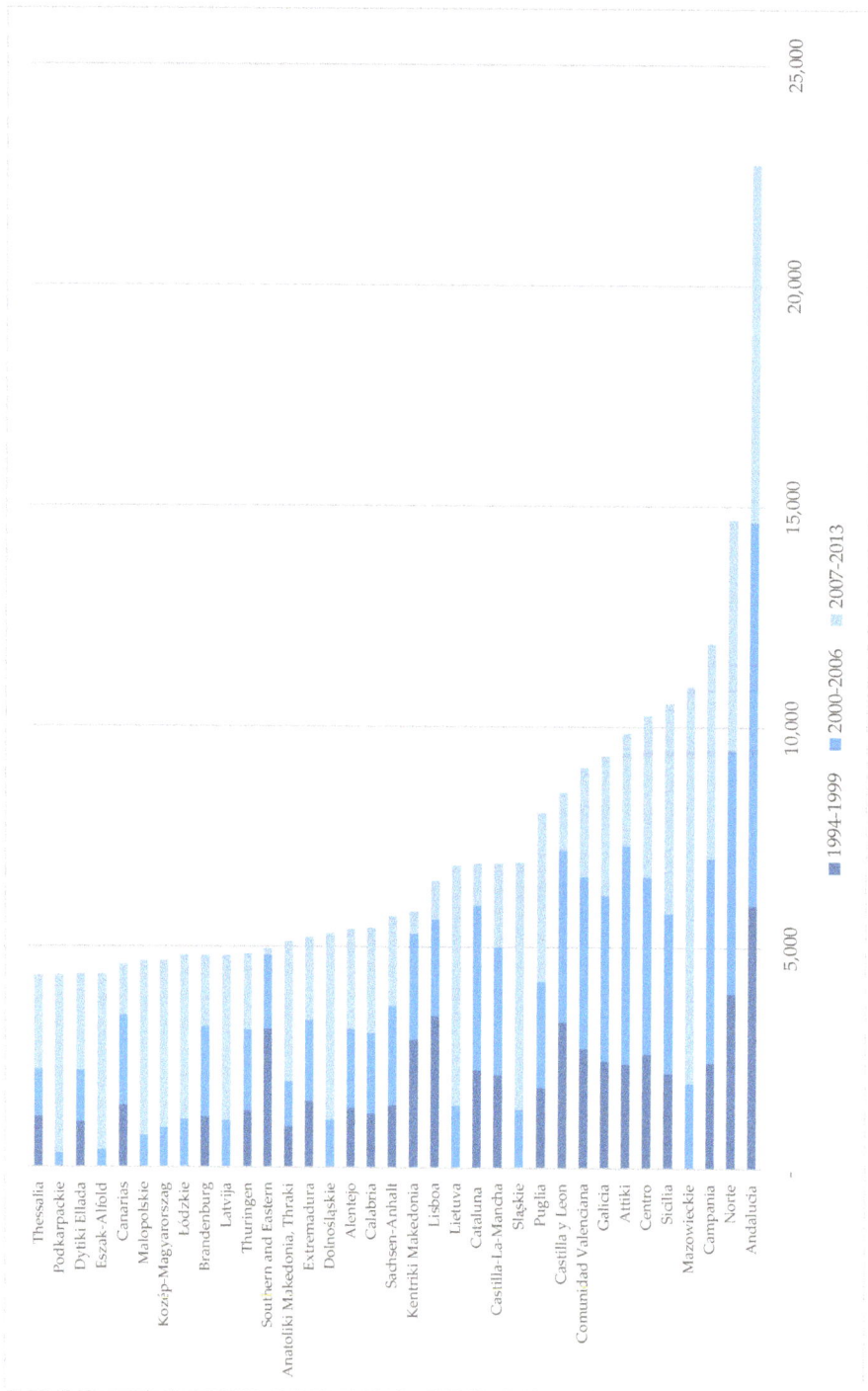

Fig. 2 Historic EU payments by NUTS-2 region and programming period (current euro prices)

Source of data: European Commission (https://cohesiondata.ec.europa.eu/stories/s/Historio-EU-payment-data-by-region-NUTS-2-/47md-x4nq). Figure created by authors.

internal divides remained as such since the beginning of the Cohesion Policy; in Spain, regions in the northeast of the country, together with Madrid, improved their GDP per capita substantially compared to the EU average, exiting the rank of less developed regions and therefore seeing a strong decline of cohesion expenditures. Territorial concentration is also significant in countries such as Portugal, Greece and the United Kingdom. As far as Central and Eastern European Member States are concerned, the Cohesion Policy started covering the whole country; however, due to both their strong growth and the increase of internal divides, some important regions moved, and are moving, away from the group of less developed regions to intermediate or developed ones, with a decrease of cohesion expenditures: this is the case with all the regions containing capital cities.

10.5. Summary and Conclusions

In this final section, we want to briefly summarize the main findings of our analysis.

- The Cohesion policy is the European Union's main investment policy, covering one third of EU budget. All regions and Member States are affected, but its action is substantially stronger in less developed ones.

- Until the big Eastern enlargement, main beneficiaries were in Southern Europe. Since 2004, most of the funds have been allocated in Central and Eastern European regions and countries that now receive substantially larger amounts.

- ERDF and CF expenditures finance around one sixth of European public investment. Their role increased in the last decade. In more recent years they finance 40% or more of total public capital expenditures in most Central and Eastern European countries, but their role is also significant in some Southern European countries, namely Greece and Portugal. They were able to mitigate the steep decline of public investment in the Member States that were hit by the 2008 Global Financial Crisis.

- ERDF and CF expenditures are particularly important for transport infrastructures, both roads and rails, especially in Central and Eastern European countries. The investments in transport infrastructure financed by the Cohesion Policy are changing the accessibility of EU regions. In particular, many regions in Eastern Europe have significantly benefitted from improved accessibility as a result of the Cohesion Policy's financing of transport infrastructure investments. Major investments are under way with the Cohesion Policy for 2014–2020.

- Environmental investments are important as well, even in Southern Europe; ERDF and CF also contribute to social (education, health, social services) and economic (IT, energy) infrastructures.

- The expenditures for the Cohesion Policy produce significant economic spillovers in favour of more advanced regions and countries in the EU.

- Implications of this analysis could be the following. If the low levels of public investment persist for a prolonged period, this will lead to a deterioration of public capital and negatively affect longer-term output. Many economists and research institutions advocate public investment spending to boost both internal demand and the potential output of the EU economy. It is, therefore, fundamental to pursue policies to encourage the growth-enhancing, long-term investments. There is little doubt that more public investment in the EU's infrastructure is needed, especially in less developed regions and Member States.

- The Cohesion Policy has played and is still playing a major role in this framework. Its role within EU policies should be preserved and enhanced. In particular, it is important that the Cohesion Policy for 2021–2027 is funded with an adequate budget, for both Southern and Eastern less developed regions.

- The EU fiscal framework appears unable to foster public investment, even as a counter-cyclical fiscal stabilization tool. The issue of the incorporation of an appropriate "Golden Rule" in the EU fiscal framework — that is, the provision to exclude selected public investment from the budget deficit requirements — should be at the forefront of discussion about the EU's future. A hypothesis could be to exclude investment co-financed by the Cohesion Policy from the Stability and Growth Pact deficit requirement.

References

ADE (2009) "Ex-Post Evaluation of Cohesion Policy Programmes 2000–2006 Co-Financed by the European Fund for Regional Development (Objectives 1 and 2) — Work Package 5b: Environment and Climate Change", https://ec.europa.eu/regional_policy/sources/docgener/evaluation/pdf/expost2006/wp5b_final_report_1.pdf

Applica (2012) "Ex Post Evaluation of the Cohesion Fund (Including Former ISPA) in the 2000–2006 Period — Work Package E", https://ec.europa.eu/regional_policy/sources/docgener/evaluation/pdf/expost2006/wpe_synth_rep.pdf

Barca, F. (2009) *An Agenda for the Reformed Cohesion Policy: A Place-Based Approach to Meeting European Union Challenges and Expectations: Independent Report Prepared at the Request of Commissioner for Regional Policy.* Brussels: European Commission, https://ec.europa.eu/regional_policy/archive/policy/future/pdf/report_barca_v0306.pdf

Becker, S. O., P. H. Egger and M. von Ehrlich (2018) "Effects of EU Regional Policy: 1989–2013", *Regional Science and Urban Economics* 69: 143–52, https://doi.org/10.1016/j.regsciurbeco.2017.12.001

Berkowitz, P., E. Von Breska, J. Pieńkowski and A. Catalina Rubianes (2015) *The Impact of the Economic and Financial Crisis on the Reform of Cohesion Policy 2008–2013*, Regional Working Paper 03/2015. Brussels: European Commission, https://ec.europa.eu/regional_policy/sources/docgener/work/2015_03_impact_crisis.pdf

Di Comite, F., P. Lecca, P. Monfort, D. Persyn and V. Piculescu (2018) "The Impact of Cohesion Policy 2007–2015 in EU Regions: Simulations with the RHOMOLO Interregional Dynamic General Equilibrium Model", *JRC Working Papers on Territorial Modelling and Analysis* 03/2018, https://ec.europa.eu/jrc/sites/jrcsh/files/jrc114044.pdf

Directorate-General for Regional and Urban Policy (European Commission), Steer Davies Gleave (2010) "Ex Post Evaluation of Cohesion Policy Programmes 2000–2006 Co-Financed by the European Fund for Regional Development (Objectives 1 & 2) — Work Package 5a: Transport, Final Report", https://ec.europa.eu/regional_policy/sources/docgener/evaluation/expost2006/wp5a_en.htm

European Commission (2017), "Communication from the Commission. Ex-Post Verification of Additionality 2007–2013", COM(2017) 138 final, Brussels, https://www.europarl.europa.eu/RegData/docs_autres_institutions/commission_europeenne/com/2017/0138/COM_COM(2017)0138_EN.pdf

Fratesi, U. (2016) "Impact Assessment of EU Cohesion Policy: Theoretical and Empirical Issues", in *Handbook on Cohesion Policy in the EU*, ed. by S. Piattoni and L. Polverari (Cheltenham: Edward Elgar), pp. 443–60, https://doi.org/10.4337/9781784715670.00045

Giua, M. (2017) "Spatial Discontinuity for the Impact Assessment of the EU Regional Policy: The Case of Italian Objective 1 Regions", *Journal of Regional Science* 57: 109–31, https://doi.org/10.1111/jors.12300

Immarino, S., A. Rodriguez-Pose and M. Storper (2017) *Why Regional Development Matters for Europe's Economic Future*, Working Paper 07/2017. Brussels: European Commission, https://ec.europa.eu/regional_policy/sources/docgener/work/201707_regional_development_matters.pdf

Manzella, G. P. (2011) *Una politica influente. Vicende, dinamiche e prospettive dell'intervento regionale europeo*. Bologna: Il Mulino.

Molle, W. (2015) *Cohesion and Growth, the Theory and Practice of European Policy Making*. Abingdon: Routledge, https://doi.org/10.4324/9781315727332

Naldini, A., A. Daraio, G. Vella, E. Wolleb and R. Römisch (2018) "Research for REGI Committee — Externalities of Cohesion Policy", European Parliament, Policy Department for Structural and Cohesion Policies, Brussels, https://www.europarl.europa.eu/RegData/etudes/STUD/2018/617491/IPOL_STU(2018)617491_EN.pdf

Panetta, F. (2019) "Lo sviluppo del Mezzogiorno: una priorità nazionale", Intervento del Direttore Generale della Banca d'Italia, Foggia, 21.9.2019, https://www.bancaditalia.it/pubblicazioni/interventi-direttorio/int-dir-2019/Panetta_21_settembre_2019_Foggia.pdf

Pellegrini, G., F. Terribile, O. Tarola, T. Muccigrosso and F. Busillo (2013) "Measuring the Effects of European Regional Policy on Economic Growth: A Regression Discontinuity Approach", *Papers in Regional Science* 92: 217–33, https://doi.org/10.1111/j.1435-5957.2012.00459.x

Piattoni, S. and L. Polverari (eds.) (2016) *Handbook on Cohesion Policy in the EU*. Cheltenham: Edward Elgar, https://doi.org/10.4337/9781784715670

Pieńkowski, J. and P. Berkowitz (2016) "Econometric Assessments of Cohesion Policy Growth Effects: How to Make Them More Relevant for Policymakers?", in *EU Cohesion Policy:*

Reassessing Performance and Direction (*Regions and Cities*), ed. by J. Bachtler, P. Berkowitz, S. Hardy and T. Muravska (Abingdon: Routledge), pp. 55–68.

Prota, F. (2016) "L'effetto dell'austerity sulle politiche di sviluppo nei Paesi dell'Unione europea", in *Le politiche di coesione in Europa tra austerità e nuove sfide*, ed. by M. Carabba, R. Padovani and L. Polverari (Rome: Quaderni SVIMEZ), pp. 57–70, http://lnx.svimez.info/svimez/wp-content/uploads/quaderni_pdf/quaderno_47.pdf

Rodrik, D. (2012) "Why We Learn Nothing from Regressing Economic Growth on Policies", *Seoul Journal of Economics* 25: 137–51.

Stöllinger, R. (2016) "Structural Change and Global Value Chains in the EU", *Empirica* 43(4): 801–29, https://doi.org/10.1007/s10663-016-9349-z

Viesti, G. (2019) "The European Regional Development Policies", in *The History of the European Union: Constructing Utopia*, ed. by G. Amato, E. Moavero-Milanesi, G. Pasquino and L. Reichlin (Oxford: Hart Publishing), pp. 385–97.

Viesti, G. and F. Prota (2008) *Le nuove politiche regionali dell'Unione Europea*. Bologna: Il Mulino.

WIIW and ISMERI Europa (2015) "Ex Post Evaluation of Cohesion Policy Programmes 2007–2013, Focusing on the European Regional Development Fund (ERDF) and the Cohesion Fund (CF) — Work Package 13, Geography of Expenditures', http://ec.europa.eu/regional_policy/pl/policy/evaluations/ec/2007-2013/

List of Illustrations

Introduction

Chapter 1

Chapter 2

Chapter 3

Chapter 4

Chapter 5

Chapter 6

Chapter 7

Chapter 8

Chapter 10

List of Tables

Chapter 1

Chapter 2

Chapter 3

Chapter 4

Chapter 5

Chapter 8

Chapter 10

About the publishing team

Alessandra Tosi was the managing editor for this book.

Adèle Kreager performed the copy-editing, proofreading and indexing.

Anna Gatti designed the cover using InDesign. The cover was produced in InDesign using Fontin (titles) and Calibri (text body) fonts.

Luca Baffa typeset the book in InDesign. The text font is Tex Gyre Pagella; the heading font is Californian FB. Luca created all of the editions — paperback, hardback, EPUB, MOBI, PDF, HTML, and XML — the conversion is performed with open source software freely available on our GitHub page (https://github.com/OpenBookPublishers).

This book need not end here…

Share

All our books — including the one you have just read — are free to access online so that students, researchers and members of the public who can't afford a printed edition will have access to the same ideas. This title will be accessed online by hundreds of readers each month across the globe: why not share the link so that someone you know is one of them?

This book and additional content is available at:

https://doi.org/10.11647/OBP.0222

Customise

Personalise your copy of this book or design new books using OBP and third-party material. Take chapters or whole books from our published list and make a special edition, a new anthology or an illuminating coursepack. Each customised edition will be produced as a paperback and a downloadable PDF.

Find out more at:

https://www.openbookpublishers.com/section/59/1

You may also be interested in:

The DARPA Model for Transformative Technologies
Perspectives on the U.S. Defense Advanced Research Projects Agency
by William Boone Bonvillian, Richard Van Atta and Patrick Windham (eds.)

https://doi.org/10.11647/OBP.0184

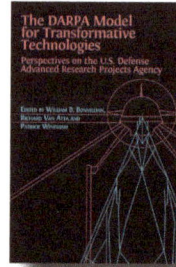

Infrastructure Investment in Indonesia
A Focus on Ports
by Colin Duffield, Felix Kin Peng Hui, Sally Wilson (eds.)

https://doi.org/10.11647/OBP.0189

The Infrastructure Finance Challenge
by Ingo Walter (ed.)

https://doi.org/10.11647/OBP.0106

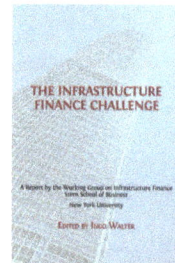

www.ingramcontent.com/pod-product-compliance
Lightning Source LLC
Chambersburg PA
CBHW050039220326
41599CB00041B/7213